Key Issues for Teaching Assistants

Teaching assistants are increasingly relied upon to provide for children who experience difficulties in learning. *Key Issues for Teaching Assistants* is an essential companion for any teaching assistant who wants to understand more about inclusion and diversity in today's classrooms.

While focusing particularly on the diverse roles of teaching assistants in supporting inclusive education, this book will be invaluable for all of those involved in the development of inclusive learning and teaching.

This highly accessible resource explores the values and the possible contradictions in policies and beliefs, enabling teaching assistants to develop a deeper understanding of the fundamental principles of inclusive education. Contributions from leading experts in the field consider common classroom issues such as:

- inclusion and special needs
- dealing with hard-to-reach parents
- tackling bullying and supporting those bullied
- boys, girls and the different ways they achieve
- being the class 'TA' not 'PA'.

Each chapter contains an overview of topical debates, current research and initiatives, emphasizing inclusive approaches and the importance of understanding the perspectives of children, regardless of difference. Useful questions for reflection and a helpful list of suggested further reading material are also provided. Teaching assistants, whether in practice, or as part of their study, will find this book an indispensable resource.

Gill Richards has worked in schools, further education colleges and higher education with learners identified as having special educational needs. She is the Director of Professional Development at Nottingham Trent University.

Felicity Armstrong is Course Leader for the MA in Inclusive Education at the Institute of Education, London.

Key Issues for
Teaching Assistants

Working in diverse and inclusive classrooms

Edited by
Gill Richards and
Felicity Armstrong

Routledge
Taylor & Francis Group

LONDON AND NEW YORK

First published 2008
by Routledge
2 Park Square, Milton Park, Abingdon, Oxon OX14 4RN

Simultaneously published in the USA and Canada
by Routledge
270 Madison Ave, New York, NY 10016

Routledge is an imprint of the Taylor & Francis Group, an informa business

Typeset in Garamond by
Florence Production Ltd, Stoodleigh, Devon
Printed and bound in Great Britain by
TJ International Ltd, Padstow, Cornwall

British Library Cataloguing in Publication Data
A catalogue record for this book is available from the British Library

Library of Congress Cataloging in Publication Data
Key issues for teaching assistants: working in diverse and inclusive
classrooms/[edited by] Gill Richards and Felicity Armstrong.
    p. cm.
    Includes bibliographical references and index.
1. Teachers' assistants.   2. Inclusive education.   3. Special education.
I. Richards, Gill.   II. Armstrong, Felicity.
LB2844.1.A8K49 2008
371.14'124 – dc22   2007018249

ISBN10: 0–415–43424–6 (hbk)
ISBN10: 0–415–43425–4 (pbk)
ISBN10: 0–203–93348–6 (ebk)

ISBN13: 978–0–415–43424–9 (hbk)
ISBN13: 978–0–415–43425–6 (pbk)
ISBN13: 978–0–203–93348–0 (ebk)

Contents

List of contributors		vii
Acknowledgements		x
Introduction		1
GILL RICHARDS AND FELICITY ARMSTRONG		
1	Inclusive education	7
	FELICITY ARMSTRONG	
2	Listening to learners: whose voice counts?	19
	GILL RICHARDS	
3	Supporting Traveller children	28
	KEN MARKS AND MARGARET WOOD	
4	Not in my image: ethnic diversity in the classroom	40
	RAPHAEL RICHARDS	
5	The influence of gender on achievement	51
	STEVE BARTLETT AND DIANA BURTON	
6	The inclusion assistant: young people with high-level support needs in mainstream schools, colleges and universities: developing good practice	62
	MICHELINE MASON	
7	'I'm a TA not a PA!': teaching assistants working with teachers	73
	VICKI ANDERSON AND MAGGIE FINNEY	

8 Inclusive relationships: insights from teaching
   assistants on how schools can reach parents   84
   MICHELE MOORE

9 A new role for special schools?   96
   GILL RICHARDS

10 Inclusion, extension and enrichment: personalized
   gifted and talented provision   108
   MARTYN WORRALL AND JOANNE STEELE

11 How schools create challenging behaviours   120
   JOE WHITTAKER AND NAVIN KIKABHAI

12 Bullying in schools – or bullying schools?   131
   NEIL DUNCAN

13 Disabled children, inclusion and the law in England
   and Wales   142
   DAVID RUEBAIN

14 Social justice, human rights and inclusive education   152
   LEN BARTON

   Index   159

Contributors

Vikki Anderson has taught in schools, further education colleges and in higher education. She currently works as a Learning Support Adviser at the University of Birmingham and delivers continuing professional development. She has published research into behaviour management and listening and responding to the voice of the learner.

Felicity Armstrong is a Reader in Inclusive Education at the Institute of Education, University of London where she is the course leader for the MA in Inclusive Education. She is on the editorial boards of the *International Journal of Inclusive Education* and *Disability and Society*.

Steve Bartlett is Professor of Education Studies at the University of Wolverhampton. He has co-authored books on Education Studies and practitioner research for teachers. He has published a number of research articles on teacher appraisal, teacher professionalism, practitioner research projects and the evolution of education studies as a discipline.

Len Barton is Emeritus Professor of Inclusive Education at the Institute of Education, University of London where he teaches on the MA in Inclusive Education. He is the founder editor of the international journal *Disability and Society*. He is committed to both teaching and the supervision of research degrees in areas related to inclusive education.

Diana Burton is Professor of Education and Dean of the Faculty of Education, Community and Leisure at Liverpool John Moores University. She has co-authored books on Education Studies and practitioner research for teachers. She has published a number of chapters and papers on aspects of learning and teaching, teacher professionalism and the development of education studies.

Neil Duncan has worked in a variety of settings for children identified as having behavioural difficulties. His current work is in teaching and research at the University of Wolverhampton, particularly in the areas of schooling, pupil culture and behaviour. Recently, Neil has been collaborating with colleagues in Australia and the USA on developing new approaches to the study of bullying behaviour.

Maggie Finney has worked as an Educational Psychologist for a city service for many years. She is also a Lecturer in Special Needs and Inclusion at the University of Wolverhampton, where she has been responsible for the design and teaching of a Foundation Degree in Learning Support and a Post-graduate Diploma in Inclusion and Special Needs.

Navin Kikabhai is currently Co-ordinator of Bolton Data for Inclusion at the University of Bolton. He has worked within the compulsory and post-compulsory sectors, teaching maths, inclusive education and teacher education. His research interests include excluded young people, emancipatory research, social networks and examining exclusionary processes in higher education.

Ken Marks is a Research Associate in the Department of Educational Studies at the University of Sheffield. He has a particular interest in work which supports the learning of Traveller pupils, including the use of ICT to bridge the gap between mobile families and their schools.

Micheline Mason has personal experience of growing up as a disabled person and being a parent of a disabled child. From 1990 to 2006 she was the Director of the Alliance for Inclusive Education, where she, with colleagues, carried out DfES research and developed Disability Equality Training. She is now a self-employed trainer and consultant, who also writes books, articles and poetry.

Michele Moore is a Senior Lecturer in Education at the University of Sheffield and Director of the programme of courses *Working With Communities*. She has been involved in projects concerning inclusion, childhood and disability issues for many years, publishing widely in these fields and is Deputy Editor for the international journal *Disability and Society*. She is the co-editor, with Felicity Armstrong, of *Action Research for Inclusive Education: Changing Places, Changing Practices, Changing Minds*.

Gill Richards has worked in schools, further education colleges and higher education with learners identified as having special educational needs. She currently works at Nottingham Trent University in the School of Education as Director of Professional Development. Her research interests focus on 'learner voice' and inclusive education.

Raphael Richards works for Sheffield's Children and Young People's Direct-orate. His work involves supporting schools, young people and local communities to raise minority ethnic pupil's attainment and promote community cohesion across the city. He has extensive experience in developing and managing mentoring programmes, in education, social justice and business settings.

David Ruebain, is Head of Education and Disability Law and an Accredited Mediator with Levenes Solicitors. In 2002, he won RADAR's 'People of the Year Award' for Achievement in the Furtherance of Human Rights of Disabled People in the UK, and in August 2006 was listed as one of 25 Most Influential Disabled People in the UK, by *Disability Now* magazine. He has published widely and taught nationally and internationally on education and disability law.

Joanne Steele has been Development Officer for Gifted and Talented Provision in Cumbria since 2003 and chairs the National Rural Strategic Group for Gifted and Talented Education. During the 1990s she was Senior Administrator for a Primary Care Trust and then Assessment Co-ordinator for vulnerable children in South Cumbria.

Joe Whittaker is an active campaigner for an end to segregated education and is actively involved with the Alliance for Inclusive Education. Having been expelled from school himself, he then became a teacher and now works at the University of Bolton in teacher education. He travels widely, working with colleagues in other countries to overcome the effects of segregated approaches to learning and enable disabled people to become active participants in their schools and colleges.

Margaret Wood has been interested in Traveller education since working at the Gypsy Summer School in Wisbech in the early 1970s. She taught languages in secondary schools for a number of years and is now Team Manager for Traveller Education with Cambridgeshire Race Equality and Diversity Service.

Martyn Worrall is School Improvement Officer for Inclusive Education for Cumbria Children's Services Authority, following a period as Senior Education Officer in the south of Cumbria and earlier experience as a Head teacher and as a government education adviser. Martyn has been committed to developing policy and practice in Inclusive Education for many years.

Acknowledgements

We would like to thank Alison Foyle, Senior Commissioning Editor (Education) and Lucy Wainwright, Editorial Assistant (Education) for their encouragement and invaluable support in the production of this book. We also thank Claire Smith, Subject Co-ordinator in the School of Education at Nottingham Trent University, for her vital support with the administrative work associated with the final stages of this book, and Tara Flood, Director of The Alliance for Inclusive Education, for giving permission for us to reproduce work from Alliance for Inclusive Education materials. Last, we would like to thank Ruebyn Richards for his support during the key writing periods of the book when he willingly gave up his share of time on the family computer to enable us to complete chapters and meet deadlines.

Introduction

Gill Richards and Felicity Armstrong

This book is about inclusive education, diversity and values. We hope it will be a valuable resource for all those involved in learning and teaching, and the development of inclusive education. In the process of editing and contributing to this book we have focused, in particular, on the diverse roles of teaching assistants in supporting inclusion. However, we have become more aware than ever of the importance of collaboration and discussion between all those involved in the development of inclusive learning communities. We hope this book will be of great value to teaching assistants and teachers working together, and support co-operative working and shared opportunities for discussion and planning.

In some respects it is a contradiction to produce a book about inclusive education with a focus on one group of professionals (in this case, teaching assistants), because inclusion has to be about partnership and the building of shared understandings and democratic collaboration. The kind of deep cultural transformation involved in developing inclusive education in terms of relationships, values and practices cannot be brought about by individuals acting on their own – although the work of individuals is important in the process of change. Inclusive education has to be concerned with all members of the school or college community, and must be responsive to the diversity and interests of the wider community too.

Our decision to think in a focused way about teaching assistants grew out of an awareness that the literature on inclusive education has, in general, largely ignored their crucial role and contribution in developing inclusive education. Teaching assistants have often been left out of debates about inclusion, and treated in instrumental ways, without understanding or recognition of their knowledge and experience and the crucial and active role they play in many aspects of the life of schools and colleges. Our view, and that of the contributors to this book, is that teaching assistants are often 'at the coal face' in terms of the interpretation of values and policies, and – most importantly – are often in a position to understand and respond to the rich diversity of experience, expectations and concerns of children and young people.

This book is underpinned by an interest in issues and values and their relationship to the processes and practices of inclusive education. In exploring values and the possible differences and contradictions in policies and beliefs, we hope that a deeper understanding will emerge of the fundamental principles of inclusive education and the way these work their way through different relationships and practices in schools and colleges.

In editing this book we have been confronted by a range of different interpretations and perspectives about the meaning of inclusive education, and the underlying causes of barriers to participation and the ways these may be overcome. Inevitably, we all bring our own values and perceptions to our work, and this is very much the case for the contributors to this book. We do not all speak with one voice and it has not been our intention to iron out differences or impose a uniform interpretation of inclusion. To do this would be to deny the richness and diversity in perspective and experience of the individual contributors. However, we *did* ask authors to provide in some form:

- An overview of topical debates, current research and initiatives.
- Some discussion of issues relating to values and professional practice for teaching assistants, emphasizing inclusive approaches and the importance of understanding the perspectives of others.
- Some issues and questions for further reflection.

In editing the book we have engaged with a number of questions that have arisen in relation to the varied interpretations, values and experiences of contributors. We have had numerous discussions – usually by email – about the arguments put forward or the reasons for particular positions. This has been a learning experience for us as we have sometimes had to reflect critically on our own assumptions and values. We hope the different chapters in the book, and the questions they raise, will be a rich resource and basis for critical debate for independent readers as well as groups working together on professional development and academic courses.

Teaching assistants are a rapidly growing group of paraprofessionals (over 200,000 currently employed within education settings), supported by government initiatives for training. As these initiatives gather momentum, there have been an increasing number of universities offering foundation degrees for teaching assistants and local authorities providing courses to validate the Higher Level teaching assistant (HLTA) status. All of these programmes require underpinning with knowledge of education values and their impact on practice. In this book, there is an emphasis on support for inclusion of all learners and the promotion of positive values and attitudes about diversity, through challenging stereotypes and all forms of exclusion.

It explores a range of issues, intending to provide a resource for all those working in education and, in particular, for teaching assistants. We hope that the book will be interesting to read and enhance personal-professional understanding as well as providing a useful course text for those following a route to professional qualifications.

Clearly, with increasing government initiatives and policy directives, as well as the perspectives of campaigning groups with different interests and ideals, parents and communities, there is a wide range of issues that can be seen as competing in importance for a book on 'current issues of diversity and inclusion'. We have not been able to cover all possible topics of this vast area in a book of this size and we regret, in particular, the absence of chapters that specifically relate to children and young people seeking asylum, the effects of poverty on questions of inclusion and exclusion in education, and the ways in which communities can work together to develop inclusive cultures and practices.

The structure and contents of the book

Key Issues for Teaching Assistants: Working in Diverse and Inclusive Classrooms is made up of 14 chapters – all addressing different aspects and issues concerning diversity and inclusive education. In general, there is a common view of inclusive education as being concerned with the participation of all learners in education on a basis of social justice and equal recognition. Many of the ideas and arguments put forward are related and overlap. We hope that the book will be interesting and enjoyable to read as a whole, but that it will also be useful to dip into to find chapters on topics of particular interest or current concern. Each chapter ends with a number of questions or statements which we hope will stimulate critical reflection and debate, followed by some suggested key readings.

In Chapter 1 Felicity Armstrong explores some of the origins and values relating to inclusive education and the way the concept of inclusion in education and 'inclusive' terminology has been used in different contexts and for different purposes. It draws out some of the contrasting meanings and contradictions involved, and considers some of their implications for relationships and practices in education. The chapter briefly discusses research issues and findings in relation to the role of teaching assistants and inclusive education. It suggests some fundamental principles which will inform the development of inclusive schools.

Chapter 2 by Gill Richards argues that inclusive education must involve listening to the voices of learners as a means of facilitating meaningful participation and the development of inclusive practices involving all those concerned. Teaching assistants play a key role in establishing good communication with learners and accessing their perspectives. Drawing on relevant research and reports, and making links with policy developments, the chapter stresses the importance of learning from the voices of children and young people to inform the process of change.

In Chapter 3 Ken Marks and Margaret Wood provide an overview of the situation of children and young people belonging to Traveller communities and explore the factors that can lead to their exclusion and marginalization in education, and the positive role which can be played by teaching assistants. It draws out the possible tensions which can arise between the rights of the child as seen through the eyes of society and as seen through the eyes of Traveller parents/communities. The chapter outlines the work of Traveller Education Services (TES) to support schools and the emergence of good practice.

Chapter 4 by Raphael Richards explores the background of black minority ethnic (BME) groups and links this discussion to individualized experiences within education settings. It reflects on current education initiatives that support these groups, raising achievement and promoting inclusive practice. Recent research studies are used to reflect on BME perspectives, identifying areas for development in schools and colleges, and the role of teaching assistants in contributing to change.

Chapter 5 by Steve Bartlett and Diana Burton is concerned with the influence of gender on achievement as part of a wider concern with inclusive education. It covers a brief review of research and initiatives on boys and girls' achievement and explores a range of gender specific initiatives supported by the government, and current curriculum and social issues that affect participation and achievement. The chapter argues that teaching assistants, and all practitioners, need to understand issues relating to gender and their implications for inclusive education, so that they can be more effective in their practice.

Chapter 6 by Micheline Mason explores the role of teaching assistants in developing good practice in relation to young people with high-level support needs, based on principles of equity, respect and inclusion. Drawing on the principles adopted in the UN Convention of Rights of Persons with Disabilities (2006) and research by the Alliance for Inclusive Education involving young people themselves, Micheline Mason demonstrates emphatically the importance for young people of full participation and control over their own lives. This involves a renegotiating of the role of teaching and support assistants and – crucially – this must involve allowing young people to speak for themselves, and taking what they say seriously.

Chapter 7 by Vikki Anderson and Maggie Finney briefly traces the historical development of teaching assistants in education settings. It explores the working relationship that teaching assistants have with teachers, using key research studies and current policy initiatives. It draws on a recent study on teaching assistants' views concerning the experience and practice of working with teachers and examines ways in which this key relationship may affect the quality of practice with learners and identifies implications for the role of teaching assistants.

In Chapter 8 Michele Moore addresses the nature and importance of the relationship of teaching assistants with children and young people, parents and carers, and examines the nature of their role. The chapter focuses on an action research project based in the only remaining special school in a particular local authority. The purpose of the research was to 'raise standards in all aspects of school life through the examining, developing and embedding of inclusive practice'. The project closely involved teaching assistants in an exploration of their role, raising questions about consultation and the key contribution they can make to improving relationships, communication and learning opportunities. The research found that teaching assistants have a key role to play in bringing parents and caregivers into closer relationships with schools.

Chapter 9 by Gill Richards traces the historical development of special schools with reference to key legislation. It presents a range of perspectives on the current role of special schools, drawing on research concerning personal experiences and educational practice. It reflects on new initiatives and government policy on diversity and inclusion, and discusses the position taken by those who support full inclusion for all. This raises some important issues about the different and often conflicting values underpinning contrasting positions on the future of special schools.

Chapter 10 by Martyn Worrall and Joanne Steele explores values, perceptions and policies in relation to Gifted and Talented provision. They argue that inclusive education must rest on a commitment to respond to diversity and difference in relation to all learners, including those identified as 'exceptionally able'. The chapter discusses recent policy initiatives and the concept and practice of 'personalized learning' and its possible contribution to enhancing the process and outcomes of learning. The chapter offers guidance to teaching assistants in their work with children who have difficulty accessing the school curriculum they are offered. It also observes that many issues discussed are relevant to all children.

This chapter raises some important issues about values and equity and the contrasting ways the concept of inclusive education is interpreted by different people in different contexts.

Chapter 11 by Joe Whittaker and Navin Kikabhai is concerned with the relationship between notions of 'challenging behaviour' and questions of values and practices in schools. It raises some difficult questions concerning the way schools themselves may contribute to the creation of challenging behaviour and stresses the fundamental importance of listening to children and young people and taking them seriously. Teaching assistants have a key role to play in their relationships with children and young people.

In Chapter 12 Neil Duncan opens a discussion on the difficult issue of bullying and draws out questions concerning the ways schools may respond to bullying. The chapter provides a brief overview of research on bullying and how it has become an area of national and international concern. It explores the multiple forms of bullying and the potential role of school ethos and adult relationships as contributors to levels of bullying in schools. Different approaches to dealing with bullying are reviewed, drawing out implications for teaching assistants' practice.

Chapter 13 by David Ruebain, covers key legislation relating to meeting diverse needs in education settings. It discusses a range of legislation and its effects, including the 1981 Education Act and the Special Needs and Disability Act (SENDA), statementing procedures, the Disability Equality Duty and other key legislation relating to Race and Gender, drawing out implications for education practice and professional responsibilities. The chapter argues that teaching assistants have an important role to play in ensuring equality in the classroom and this will be strengthened through familiarity with the legal rights of children and young people in education.

Chapter 14 by Len Barton draws together some of the overriding concerns of the book relating to social justice and inclusive education, making connections with issues of democracy and the values which underpin policies and practices in education. The chapter emphasizes the importance of building positive relationships between all those involved in working together for inclusive education, raising some contentious issues for reflection. The chapter confirms the important role of teaching assistants in developing inclusive cultures and practices in education.

Chapter 1

Inclusive education

Felicity Armstrong

This chapter begins to explore the idea, and origins, of inclusive education and some of the very different ways the term is used in different contexts. We will consider the possible meanings and values which underpin these different interpretations, and how these relate to the lives of schools and their communities. The term 'communities' is used here to mean both the communities of people who make up the internal life of the school, and to refer to a wider concept of community which encompasses the lives, cultures, practices and interests of those in the neighbourhoods associated with the school. This discussion will be linked to the often contradictory demands made on all those implicated in the complex relationships involved in the lives of colleges and schools, learning and teaching. Teaching assistants, teachers and pupils are at the sharp edge of where these contradictions are most keenly felt – in the day-to-day life of the classroom. In the course of the discussion the chapter will draw on some examples of research to raise some issues about the role of teaching assistants in developing inclusive relationships and practices. It will end with some issues and questions which may be helpful in making connections between some of the points raised in the chapter and the particular challenges faced by those committed to developing inclusive education and who work in a support role in education.

In the light of the wide range of ways in which terminology is used, it is important, therefore, to clarify the ways we use language, and we need to recognize that inclusion means different things to different people. The starting point in this chapter is that there is a dynamic relationship between schools, communities and the broader social context. Tony Booth describes participation in the inclusive classroom in the following terms:

> It (. . .) implies learning alongside others and collaborating with them in shared lessons. It involves active engagement with what is learnt and taught and having a say in how education is experienced. But participation also involves being recognised for oneself and being accepted for oneself: I participate with you when you recognise me as a person like yourself and accept me for who I am.
>
> (Booth 2003: 2)

Inclusive education is a continuous and changing process, which is deeply affected by change in society – both short and long-term. Thus, the kinds of issues which a school needs to engage with may change dramatically in the face of any of the following: the closing down of a local factory; the outbreak of hostilities with another country; the closure of a local special school; a change in the political complexion of the country or the local council; the arrival of a group of refugees in the local community; the introduction of new structures and measures reinforcing processes of testing and assessment, or the government-led revision of an aspect of the curriculum. Many of these examples are ones which those working in education can relate to quite easily, and we can think of examples from our own experience which relate quite specifically to our own communities and work contexts. Inclusive education, then, is intrinsically related to the notions of context and community and raises questions for schools about the way in which they respond to change and diversity at both national and local level.

Inclusive education: origins and rights

Education is recognized as a basic human right by a number of United Nations instruments, from the Universal Declaration of Human Rights to the UN Convention on the Rights of the Child. Such instruments are not necessarily intended as guides for practice in particular settings, which all have their own unique characteristics, but they do provide a vision, a set of goals and expectations, which we can try to interpret in ways that reflect the barriers and opportunities relating to education within our own changing social settings. If we value all our citizens equally, and recognize their fundamental rights to equal participation and access to social wellbeing, we must ensure that all have equal access to education. However, it is apparent that national education systems exclude many children and young people, either by making inadequate or inappropriate provision, or sometimes by excluding them from education altogether. We need to explore the extent to which failure to participate fully in education is an outcome of policies and practices in education systems and in schools themselves, as well as broader questions relating to attitudes, resources and wider inequalities in society.

In 1990 the challenge of exclusion from education was first taken up on a global level by world leaders at The World Conference on Education for All: Meeting Basic Learning Needs and the World Summit on Children (New York 1990) which adopted the goal of Education for All by the Year 2000. The World Declaration on Education for All emanating from the Jomtien Conference specifically refers to the need to provide equal access to education for all children, including those who have impairments or experience disadvantages. The Framework for Action adopted by the conference provided a set of principles in support of prompting inclusive education:

- the right of all children to a full cycle of primary education;
- the commitment to a child-centred concept of education in which individual differences are accepted as a source of richness and diversity, a challenge not a problem;
- the improvement of the quality of primary education including improvements in professional training;
- the provision of a more flexible and responsive primary schooling, with respect to organisation, processes and content;
- greater parental and community participation in education;
- recognition of the wide diversity of needs and patterns of development of primary school children, demanding a wider and more flexible range of responses;
- a commitment to a developmental, intersectoral and holistic approach to education and care of primary school children.

The emphasis on *primary* education reflects the fact that in many countries of the world education may be restricted to the primary level, or even denied to some groups of children altogether. It is interesting to reflect on these principles in the light of our own policies and practices, and to ask: to what extent are we fulfilling, or falling short of, these principles in our own contexts? How should these principles be interpreted, and what would be the implications for changes in school cultures and practices?

The UNESCO World Conference on Special Needs Education: Access and Quality held in Spain in 1994 focused on the practical requirements that need to be fulfilled in order for inclusive education to become a reality. It produced the Salamanca Statement which formulated a new Statement on Inclusive Education and adopted a new Framework for Action based on the principle that ordinary schools should welcome all children regardless of difference. It proclaimed that:

> Regular schools with this inclusive orientation are the most effective means of combating discriminatory attitudes, creating welcoming communities, building an inclusive society and achieving education for all; moreover, they provide an effective education to the majority of children and improve the efficiency and ultimately the cost-effectiveness of the entire education system.
>
> (UNESCO 1994)

The World Conference called upon all governments to:

- Give the 'highest policy and budgetary priority' to improve education services so that all children could be included, regardless of differences or difficulties.

- Adopt as a matter of law or policy the principle of inclusive education and enrol all children in ordinary schools unless there were compelling reasons for doing otherwise.
- Develop demonstration projects and encourage exchanges with countries with inclusive schools.
- Ensure that organisations of disabled people, along with parents and community bodies, are involved in planning decision-making.
- Put greater effort into pre-school strategies as well as vocational aspects of inclusive education.
- Ensure that both initial and in-service teacher training address the provision of inclusive education.

In particular, the Framework for Action is based on the belief that 'inclusion and participation are essential to human dignity and to the enjoyment and exercise of human rights'. In the field of education this is reflected in bringing about a 'genuine equalisation of opportunity'. Inclusive Education:

> assumes human differences are normal and that learning must be adapted to the needs of the child, rather than the child fitted to the process. The fundamental principle of the inclusive school is that all children should learn together, where possible, and that ordinary schools must recognise and respond to the diverse needs of their students, while also having a continuum of support and services to match these needs. Inclusive schools are the 'most effective' at building solidarity between children with special needs and their peers.
>
> (The UNESCO Salamanca Statement (1994), as summarized by the Centre for Studies in Inclusive Education)

This statement is now nearly 25 years old – and yet in the UK we are still a long way from fulfilling these aspirations – and some would argue that the increasing competition and selection in our education system, and the widening gap between levels of income, have actually increased divisions and restricted opportunities for many.

Inclusive education: meanings and interpretations

In this chapter, the use of the term 'inclusive education' reflects the principle that inclusion concerns everybody – all learners, and all members of the school, college and wider community. Inclusion is:

> fundamentally about issues of human rights, equity, social justice and the struggle for a non-discriminatory society. These principles are at the heart of inclusive policy and practice.
>
> (Armstrong and Barton 2007)

It is based on the belief in the rights of all to equal recognition, respect and treatment, regardless of difference. This does not mean that particular interests, learning styles, knowledge, and cultural and linguistic heritage shall not be recognized. On the contrary – inclusion recognizes, and is responsive to, diversity and the right 'to be oneself' – in an open and democratic community. This interpretation of inclusive education implies the right for all to be an equal member of their neighbourhood school and college communities. This is rather different from the concept of 'integration', which focuses on the question of how an individual child, or group of children, might 'fit in' to a school or a class, rather than focusing on the need for a fundamental transformation in the social, cultural, curricular and pedagogic life of the school, as well as its physical organization.

Integration has, traditionally, referred to a concept and practices associated with learners identified as 'having special educational needs'. Paradoxically, the term 'inclusion' is often used in the same way as integration. For example, it is common to hear children referred to as 'being included' in a certain activity for part of the week, or to mean they attend a special school or unit but attend a mainstream school or class as *visitors* on particular days. This creates some confusion, as integration and inclusion represent very different values and practices. The key difference between the concept of inclusion and the concept of integration is that *integration* focuses on the perceived deficits in the child as creating barriers to participation, whereas *inclusion situates the barriers to participation within the school or college.*

A further muddle is created by the way policy documents sometimes adopt the language of inclusion to refer to 'raising standards' in terms of improving exam results which, in turn, is linked to 'widening participation'. Over the past quarter century there has been a series of contradictory policies emanating from successive governments, which have often been deeply confusing in terms of issues of equity and participation. For example – the 1988 Education Reform Act introduced a National Curriculum and national testing of pupils at ages 7, 11 and 14 and the publication of league tables and inspection reports on schools. The effects of this major piece of legislation were to strengthen competition between schools and to sharpen processes of the selection of pupils. But there were other, more positive, outcomes of the Act because it also gave *all* pupils an entitlement to access the National Curriculum, including children and young people enrolled in special schools. Much of the legislation introduced by recent governments have been concerned with measurable performance and raising attainment as part of an overall strategy for *school improvement*. The pressures of a highly competitive global economy are one factor in creating this climate of *performativity*. Unfortunately, when 'high standards' in education are measured primarily by levels achieved in public tests and examinations, other broader educational and creative concerns and projects become marginalized, as well as creating perceptions of 'failure' in relation to children and young people whose attainment is deemed unacceptably low. The implications for students who experience difficulties in learning in the present educational regime and climate relate to low-self esteem, marginalization and a lack of recognition in terms of who they are and what they have to contribute.

Although a number of policy documents over the past decade have specifically linked school improvement and raising standards to 'inclusive education', these are not linked to questions of equity, fairness and the overall ethos and practices of the school or college. Indeed, the overriding concern with 'raising standards', which has dominated the education system at all levels (Gewirtz 2002) can create a barrier to equity, the valuing of diversity and inclusive education (Florian and Rouse 2005), rather than opening up wider opportunities for recognizing and celebrating the knowledge, cultures and experiences of all students as a central part of teaching and learning. Ainscow *et al.* (2006) show, through their research, how the 'pressure to improve scores on national tests' may *distort* the work of schools – including those that have demonstrated a strong commitment to developing inclusive policies and practices. However, Rouse and Florian (1996) found in their research that 'many schools committed to the development of inclusive practice have been able to mediate these tensions, and work creatively and successfully' (Florian and Rouse 2005: 15) to build schools which are 'effective' in terms of developing inclusive cultures and practices, and also 'effective' in terms of raising levels of attainment.

The government policy on the education of 'Gifted and Talented' students exemplifies some of the contradictions and confusions surrounding questions of participation and equity. It raises questions such as: is it 'fair' that some children should be identified as having special 'gifts and talents' and that extra resources should be released to provide 'enrichment' activities for these children? What effect does such a policy have on the 10 per cent identified, and the 90 per cent considered *not* to have 'gifts and talents'? Don't all children possess unique 'gifts' and characteristics worthy of celebration, and don't they all deserve educational and creative 'enrichment' opportunities? Does the notion that 10 per cent of children are 'gifted and talented' (the government's figure) bear any relationship to the rich diversity of 'gifts and talents' spread across all school and college populations? One argument sometimes put forward by teachers and policy makers is that this policy is justified on the grounds that more children in economically disadvantaged communities are getting opportunities to be involved in activities which they would not have had otherwise. Some schools use the money allocated for 'gifted and talented' pupils to 'enrich' the learning opportunities for *all* their pupils (see Ainscow *et al.* 2006: 66). The government's 'gifted and talented' agenda illustrates some of the possible conflicts and contradictions embedded in many policy initiatives if considered from an inclusive education perspective.

Another example of possible conflicts in values relates to one implication of the 'raising standards' agenda, which is an increase in setting in primary and secondary schools, with children being categorized and labelled at an increasingly young age, and placed in different groups according to perceived ability. Teaching assistants often work with children who experience difficulties in the classroom and find themselves placed alongside them in 'bottom sets'! Interestingly, recent research suggests that grouping students for core curriculum subjects (English, Maths and Science) according to perceived ability is not necessarily effective in raising standards of attainment overall (Ireson *et al.* 2005). Other within-school factors which may have an impact on student attainment include the type and quality of learning and teaching opportunities provided, curriculum differentiation, teacher attitudes and expectations – as well as pupils' own sense of self-worth and confidence. These factors all relate to policy and school organization, values and practices and concern the work of teaching assistants, and all those involved in teaching, learning and the life of the school.

What can we learn from research?

The rapidly increasing number of teaching assistants working in schools over recent years, and the emphasis on work-based learning as part of professional development, has led to a greater interest in this neglected area on the part of researchers. In this section some of this work will be discussed particularly with reference to the question of the development of inclusive schools and class-rooms.

In order for teaching assistants to work effectively and comfortably with other adults and with children and young people, their work and their diverse wider role, and the particular skills and knowledge which they contribute, need to be recognized. The work of those working in a 'support' role has been marginalized both in schools and in research. Sometimes even the language used to refer to those who work in a support role is devaluing or instrumental. It is quite common to come across the terms 'deployment' or 'use' of teaching assistants or learning support staff in policy documents, reports, academic articles and professional literature[1] (although rarely, probably, in schools themselves).

One of the most fundamental aspects of transforming schools and colleges is the need to challenge existing inequalities in the way different people are valued and receive recognition, and this has to be the case for *all* members of the community if inclusive cultures and practices are to be developed. In the past, those working in a 'support role' have often been the subject of 'patterns of discrimination' which are pervasive and go 'far beyond' salary levels and conditions of service (Lorenz 1998).

Significantly, there is increasing recognition of the crucial role played by teaching assistants in developing inclusive practices and cultures (Moran and Abbott 2002). This will come as no surprise to those who actually work in

---

1   For example, the report 'The Employment and Deployment of Teaching Assistants', *NFER News*, Spring 2004, p. 5.

schools! Democratic collaboration and teamwork is essential in developing inclusive practices and planning, and this involves everybody being able to express their views and recognition given to the knowledge and experience of all participants. This is not easily accomplished in schools where professional relationships are deeply hierarchical or where there is no tradition of consultation and debate.

The question of the nature of 'support' provided by both teaching assistants and teachers themselves has been the subject of much debate. Should support for learning be provided on an individual basis or does this encourage dependency and lack of motivation among pupils, as well as creating barriers to social interaction with other learners? In her study of working practices of Learning Support Assistants (LSAs) working with students identified as having 'severe learning difficulties' and 'profound and multiple learning difficulties', Lacey (2001) concluded that the most effective practices in developing 'inclusive learning' involved the following:

- allowing opportunities for social interaction to take place between students;
- making time available for LSAs and teachers to plan together;
- supporting groups of children, rather than individuals.

In this study the importance or recognizing and drawing on the knowledge and experience of LSAs emerged as an important requirement for inclusion.

Much of the research relating to learning support assistants and classroom assistants highlight the crucial importance of the *relationships* that are formed between the different groups involved in the life of the school and in teaching and learning. Hammett and Burton (2005) observe that the failure to value, and ensure the participation of, support staff can lead to feelings of demoralization and demotivation. Their research was carried out in an 'improving' 11–18 secondary school in which 'Learning Support Assistants' (the term used in the article) are seen as 'prime supporters of the renewed emphasis on improving teaching and learning' (p. 299). They argue that there needs to be more opportunities for communication between teachers and LSAs, and this means providing time and resources to make this possible (by paying LSAs for their time spent attending meetings, for example).

Another important issue is the question of *how* support workers relate to individual students and the wider class. The interpretation of inclusive education as being concerned with learners identified as 'having special educational needs' is supported by a view of the role of support staff as supporting individual students, or groups of students, identified as having difficulties (and often with a statement). Yet, research suggests that there is a general awareness among teachers, learning support staff, pupils and researchers that the practice of individual support presents a number of difficulties and barriers to inclusion. Vincent *et al.* (2005) point out that concentration of attention on students who have been identified as having special educational needs, can encourage social, academic and physical dependence. It can also prevent interaction between students, leading to the isolation of the 'supported' student and the possible creation of negative perceptions.

Earlier in this chapter we briefly considered the possible tensions and barriers to inclusion created by pressures to 'raise standards' in performance in tests and examinations. Ainscow *et al.* (2006) carried out detailed, collaborative action research with a network of 25 schools, involving three local education authorities (LEAs) and a hundred teachers, into 'ways of identifying and overcoming barriers to participation and learning' (p. 51). Although their research explores the difficulties and barriers to inclusive education with clarity and honesty, it is encouraging in that it reveals some strengths and possibilities in the development of some existing practices identified in the research process concerning collaboration within, and between, schools. Importantly, their study emphasizes the importance of discussion of questions of values, purposes of participation, social justice and the purposes of education across all sectors of the education system, and this discussion must involve *everybody*.

On a smaller scale, work carried out by practitioners in their own work contexts, reveals the importance of listening to the voices of children and young people in order to understand their experiences and the nature of the barriers which they face, or that they identify in the daily life of the classroom. Those who are determined to address inequalities may think they have a clear idea about what needs to be done, but inclusion is not something which can be imposed, but must be based on the views of all those involved, including children and young people themselves.

In her chapter 'We talk and we like someone to listen', Mary Clifton (2004) insists on the importance of listening to the voices of international children. She carried out a small project with Dell, an 11-year-old from Thailand who came to England with her sister and mother, in which she sought Dell's views on her experience of education and what she found helpful and – importantly – not helpful. A young bilingual learning support assistant also contributed to the research. By listening to Dell's views, Mary learnt a great deal about Dell's experience that challenged her existing assumptions about the needs and interests of children arriving in schools in Britain from very different cultures. First and foremost, she began to reassess the role of attitudes and practices in schools, and the way they affect opportunities for a young person who is new to England and does not speak the language. She also began to understand the importance of the role played by the peer group in developing inclusion.

In her collaborative enquiry with a group of teaching assistants, Cath Sorsby (2004) and her co-researchers identified some key factors in the development of inclusive practices, including the need for:

- a shift in the culture and the values of the school;
- understanding that barriers to participation are created by policies, practices and attitudes, rather than by 'something wrong with the child';
- a 'problem-solving' approach to creating a curriculum for success, rather than following one that highlights failure;
- a recognition of each person's strengths and learning styles as well as recognizing difference and diversity and providing a rich and responsive learning environment for all;
- joint professional development opportunities for teachers and teaching assistants and others involved in learning and teaching;
- time for discussion and joint preparation;
- a whole school commitment to bringing about change.

The inclusive school

What would the inclusive school look like? What direction do we need to be taking? What goals should we be moving towards? It is important to recognize that there is not a blueprint for inclusive education. Every school will develop their own unique cultures and responses to their particular communities, but the important thing is that there are some clearly identifiable principles at work which underpin the structure, organization and practices of the school, its ethos and its relationship with all communities in the neighbourhood. An inclusive school will:

- be accessible to all: physically, culturally and pedagogically;
- be a school in which the voices of all members are heard and listened to;
- engage critical reflection through a review of values of practices;
- develop new ways of working through consultation and with the participation of all those involved;
- critically examine the curriculum and teaching practices, and seek the views of pupils on their learning;
- value what every person brings to the school community;
- have understandable equal opportunities policies and practices that are explained in meaningful ways and which apply to everybody;
- get to know the local community, and build and develop links with all communities in the neighbourhood;
- develop democratic practices for running all aspects of the school through, for example, the setting up of school councils;
- recognize and respect differences.

Reflections on values and practice

Inclusive education is both a set of 'ideals' and a project based on values and practices which recognize the right of all to belong. The inclusive school will, for example, try and counter oppressive beliefs and behaviours relating to racism, sexuality, class and narrow notions of conformity. It will attempt to learn as a community to understand and overcome inequalities, bullying, and marginalizing practices which are part of the everyday life of many school communities. The inclusive school is democratic so everybody has a voice and contributes to decision-making and the planning of teaching and learning.

The values and principles discussed in this chapter raise questions about the policies, practices and relationships which might foster inclusive schools and colleges. With this in mind it may be helpful to reflect on the following questions:

1   What kinds of changes are needed in your own work context, or local school, in order to develop an inclusive community in which all are valued equally, and participate fully in the life of the school?
2   What are the barriers to change?
3   What contributions can teaching assistants make to creating inclusive education?

Suggested further reading

Ainscow, M., Booth, T. and Dyson, A. with Farrell, P., Frankham, J., Gallannaugh, Howes, A. and Smith, R. (2006) *Improving Schools, Developing Inclusion*, London: Routledge.

Armstrong, F. and Moore, M. (eds) (2004) *Action Research for Inclusive Education: Changing Places, Changing Practices, Changing Minds*, London: RoutledgeFalmer.

Booth, T. and Ainscow, M. (2002) *The Index for Inclusion* (2nd Edn) Bristol: Centre for Studies on Inclusive Education (CSIE).

Vincent, K., Cremin, H. and Thomas, G. (2005) *Teachers and Assistants Working Together*, Maidenhead: Open University Press.

References

Ainscow, M., Booth, T. and Dyson, A. with Farrell, P., Frankham, J., Gallannaugh, Howes, A. and Smith, R. (2006) *Improving Schools, Developing Inclusion*, London: Routledge.

Armstrong, F. and Barton, L. (2007) 'Policy, Experience and Change and the Challenge of Inclusive Education: The Case of England' in L. Barton and F. Armstrong (eds) *Policy, Experience and Change: Cross-Cultural Reflections on Inclusive Education*, Dordrecht: Springer.

Armstrong, F., Russell, O. and Schimanski, E. (2006) 'Action Research for Inclusive Education: Innovations in Teaching and Learning', *Education in the North* 13: 14–22.

Booth, T. (2002) 'Inclusion and Exclusion in the City: Concepts and Contexts' in Potts, P. (ed.) *Inclusion in the City: Selection, Schooling and Community*, London: Routledge-Falmer.

Clifton, M. (2004) 'We Like to Talk and We Like Someone to Listen': Cultural Difference and Minority Voices as Agents of Change' in Armstrong, F. and Moore, M. (eds) (2004) *Action Research for Inclusive Education: Changing Places, Changing Practices, Changing Minds*, London: RoutledgeFalmer.

Florian, L. and Rouse, M. (2005) 'Inclusive Practice in English Secondary Schools: Lessons Learned' in Nind, M., Rix, J., Sheehy, K. and Simmons, K. (eds) *Curriculum and Pedagogy in Inclusive Education: Values into Practice*, London: RoutledgeFalmer.

Hammett, N. and Burton, N. (2005) 'Motivation, Stress and Learning Support Assistants: An Examination of Staff Perceptions at a Rural Secondary School', *School Leadership and Management* 25(3): 299–310.

Ireson, J., Hallam, S. and Hurley, C. (2005) 'What Are the Effects of Ability Grouping on GCSE Attainment?', *British Educational Research Journal* 31(4): 443–58.

Lacey, P. (2002) 'The Role of Learning Support Assistants in the Inclusive Learning of Pupils with Severe and Profound Learning Difficulties, *Educational Review* 53(2): 157–67.

Lorenz, S. (1998) *Effective In-Class Support, the Management of Support Staff in Mainstream and Special Schools*, London: David Fulton.

Moran, A. and Abbott, L. (2002) 'Developing Inclusive Schools: The Pivotal Role of Teaching Assistants in Promoting Inclusion in Special and Mainstream Schools in Northern Ireland', *European Journal of Special Needs Education*, 17(2): 161–73.

Rouse, M. and Florian, L. (1996) 'Effective Inclusive Schools: a study in two countries', *Cambridge Journal of Education* 26(1): 71–86.

Sorsby, C. (2004) 'Forging and Strengthening Alliances: Learning Support Staff and the Challenge of Inclusion' in Armstrong, F. and Moore, M. (eds) (2004) *Action Research for Inclusive Education: Changing Places, Changing Practices, Changing Minds*, London: RoutledgeFalmer.

UNESCO and Ministry of Education and Science, Spain (1994) The Salamanca Statement and Framework for Action on Special Needs Education. Online: available at www.unesco.org/education/pdf/SALAMA_E.PDF, Paris: UNESCO.

Vincent, K., Cremin, H. and Thomas, G. (2005) *Teachers and Assistants Working Together*, Maidenhead: Open University Press.

Chapter 2

Listening to learners

Whose voice counts?

Gill Richards

Introduction

Engaging with children to seek their views on issues that affect them both individually and as a group, is central to initiatives such as Every Child Matters: Change for Children (2003), the 2020 Vision (2006) and the Children Act 2004. This approach built on the aims of the Children's Fund in 2000 that sought to tackle experiences of disadvantage and social exclusion in the most vulnerable children and young people. Responding to these initiatives means that schools are increasingly listening to learners to discover how their pupils experience what is provided for them. This information can then provide the basis for further developments that more accurately meet their needs, with 'users' becoming 'participants' and sharing responsibility for learning (DfES 2020 Review Group 2006). Collecting feedback from a full range of learners is an important way for education settings to demonstrate a commitment to inclusion. Being prepared to do whatever it takes to discover the views of even the most 'hard to reach' learners, indicates the value that they place on each individual.

So why is this important for teaching assistants? First, because providing opportunities for learners to express their views and supporting feedback processes is often an important part of a teaching assistant's role. Second, to do this effectively requires a range of communication skills to both draw out information and ensure that what is recorded reflects accurately what the learner was trying to say. Understanding some of the tensions that exist about expression of learner voice can help teaching assistants use their skills more effectively, and so this chapter will explore some of the complex issues involved, drawing out implications for practice.

Listening to learners' views

Many education settings have well-established systems for collecting learners' views on their services. These typically include school councils, class representatives, questionnaires, focus groups, evaluation of curriculum and access to a complaints system. In some settings these work effectively for all learners, but in others they are seen as a management tool that only seeks feedback on issues important to teaching staff rather than identifying learners' own priorities. As Salmon (2005: 5) argues, although many establishments have moved on from the completion of 'happiness sheets', which review a learning experience after it is over, 'they have yet to implement effective ways of gathering and using learner feedback'. Cullingford (2005: 210) also supports this view, suggesting that, 'We have not yet learned to listen to their voices, let alone hear them. Perhaps we do not like the implications of what they are trying to say.' This is an important point for schools to consider: how do they listen and what do they do with the information they collect?

Pollard *et al.* (2000) suggest that pupil perspectives can help teachers and others to understand the gap between provision as it is intended, and how it is actually experienced. Whose views are sought can affect this understanding, because as Rudduck *et al.* (1996) argue, there is a need for *all* voices to be heard, not just those who are more articulate and socially confident. Morrow (2006) supports this view, reporting at a Pupil Voice conference, of the strong concerns expressed by young people within her study, who criticized situations they had experienced where the 'favourites get picked and the rest get played as fools'. She also stresses the importance of needing to understand the 'rules of the game' within education settings; if young people do not grasp the wider picture of what is going on in schools, they will not know what is possible or what they can reasonably expect.

These points are key to helping us all to listen effectively to learners about their experiences. If a learner's 'voice' is viewed as tokenistic and just 'lip service' because it does not result in action, feedback may be seen as a mechanistic chore that nobody takes seriously. Similarly, feedback that is seen to just produce reams of statistical information and not result in changes is likely to affect learners' motivation to contribute and, worse still, further reinforce feelings of their disempowerment (Allan 2005; Department for Health 2001; McDowell 1991).

The way that learners' views are collected can also affect the responses they give. If questions focus on how satisfied they are about something provided, but this is done in a situation that does not offer anonymity or even confidentiality, learners are likely to only risk giving positive answers and so what they say may be of limited value for improving that service. Kaplin *et al.* (2007: 23) describe such a situation in their study, where pupils said that they were worried that 'if we say what we really think, we might get done for it'. Concerns such as this are also discussed by Clare and Cox (2003). They suggest that when this happens schools appear to enter into consultation while really they are still remaining firmly in control of the agenda. This results in tokenism, just as in other situations where staff 'interpret' views of learners who have difficulty in giving feedback just to make sure they comply with policy directives, or where feedback does not receive any official response (Noyes 2005; Klein 2003; Jones 2002).

Even where feedback mechanisms are generally effective for listening and responding to learners' voices, some individuals or groups may experience difficulties in making their views known and influence change. Traditionally, disabled learners are one such group, as they are often seen as needing to receive professional advice rather than be experts about their own lives (Mason 2005; Gwynn 2004). This perception may be further reinforced when communication is problematic (Clifton 2004). Education staff may experience difficulties in gaining disabled learners' views where communication aids are used, where learners do not yet have the skills of advocacy or where a particular impairment impedes communication skills. Compounding these difficulties can be inaccessible feedback procedures such as forms that are either impossible for individuals to physically complete or are not understood. In a similar way, learner forums may be intimidating for those who are inexperienced in voicing their opinions, particularly in front of peers or staff, and this may prevent critical comment.

Placing all learners at the heart of education services so that they can help shape their communities can provide education settings with a route towards increasingly inclusive practice (DfES 2005; Leadbetter 2004; DfEE 2001). By engaging with 'hard to reach' learners routinely, schools and colleges may use feedback in a more sustained and far-reaching way (Ruddock 2003), fulfilling *actual* rather than *perceived* needs (Gwynn 2004). Responding to feedback through decisive action can be seen as both a way of raising standards and a significant contribution towards schools' self-assessment and development planning (DfES 2005; Sherlock 2005). If this response is to be inclusive it will need to develop strategies that capture all learners' views, not only on those issues identified by management as important, but also on what the learners themselves see as priorities.

Enabling 'hard-to-reach' learners to feed back on their experiences will require all education settings to review their procedures and consider how responses are actioned. It may be that some learners need to learn self-advocacy skills first or appropriate school language for discussing their views. Teachers and teaching assistants need to recognize that some learners find it difficult to express opinions that criticize their setting because they have learned to regard themselves as powerless. Other learners may not trust either teachers or school systems to treat their views positively and feel generally disconnected from consultation processes (Pedder and McIntyre 2006). Disabled learners may require specific support or need to have a range of experiences made available, to help them understand the choices offered They may also be accustomed to lowering their expectations, being satisfied with provision, whatever its shortcomings and afraid of jeopardizing what they do have through criticism (Anderson *et al.* 2003).

The aim of the Disability Equality Duty (2006) is to improve the experiences and opportunities for disabled people. It requires public sector organizations to involve disabled people systematically and actively in this process, moving education settings beyond the requirements of the Special Educational Needs and Disability Act (2001) 'which reinforced the importance of planning for the inclusion of disabled learners but has not yet been translated into practices that foreground the views of disabled children and young people' (Gwynn 2004: 106). It expects schools and colleges to go beyond methods of consultation which 'allow choice between limited, pre-determined options or canvas opinion . . . while maintaining the power structure' (Rose 2006: 11), to enable genuine influence on shaping provision. A key element to this process is that it is to affect proactive change and develop current provision, rather than review experiences post-completion when it is too late for those taking part to benefit.

Learning to listen and respond to disabled learners' voices may in time impact significantly on the wider day-to-day practice in many settings. The process is likely to open up a whole new range of methods for collecting the views of learners who do not traditionally participate in feedback situations. Successful methods tried out in a recent study (Richards *et al.* 2007) have included 'Diary Rooms'; 'Graffiti Walls'; mobile phone texting; role play such as, 'If you were an inspector what would you say about the school?'; and pictorial approaches using photographs taken by learners about where they feel safe and unsafe, and where they learn best in school. What appeared to work best in this study was using a range of methods each time to collect the information required so that all individuals have an opportunity to contribute. This of course took time and so schools have to be prepared to give this if they genuinely want to listen to what young people have to say. Otherwise, there is a danger that staff revert back to systems that target confident and articulate learners as an easy way to meet set feedback goals and in doing so, exclude learners whose experiences might be key to creating a more inclusive setting.

Conflicts about 'voice'

Returning to Cullingford's (2005) suggestion that maybe schools are not ready to hear what learners have to say, it may be helpful for all school staff to consider how far they feel capable to deal with responses made by empowered young people. For example, if learners are enabled to express views that are not restricted to issues set by staff, schools may have to cope with completely unexpected criticisms or requests. This can involve uncomfortable decision-making and possible conflicts between different groups or between individuals and groups that will need resolving. It takes a very confident staff group to be both open to such feedback and to withstand pressure to automatically respond positively to suggestions, even when this is inappropriate.

Learners' views may challenge those commonly held by professionals. This can be seen increasingly in debates about disabled learners' inclusion in mainstream settings. Deciding on the success or otherwise of such placements and reviewing special education policy have traditionally been the territory of 'professionals'. Engaging with disabled learners about these matters could result in powerful changes as their fresh perspectives challenge organizations. This is not to suggest that disabled people's views are not currently available, but that they may sometimes be taken less seriously if they conflict with the views of more powerful education advocates. Similarly, further tensions can occur when professionals deal mainly with parents and prioritize their views over those of the young person. Again, this is not to suggest that parent – professional partnerships are not important, just that sometimes the learner's view may become subsumed and lost within adult discussions (Anderson *et al.* 2003).

A clear example of this conflict can be seen in recent debates about inclusive education. Much government documentation states support for inclusion for most learners, although it emphasizes that the quality of the experience is more important than the location (DfES 2004; Ofsted 2006). This supports a belief that there are still some learners for whom special or separate school provision would be the only viable option i.e. those identified with 'severe and complex needs' or behaviour that is viewed as too challenging for mainstream schools to deal with. In 2006 Warnock supported these ideas, gaining a large public forum in which to declare a change from her previous apparent support of inclusion. Such views directly contrast with those of a number of people who have been recipients of 'specialized' provision and have found a 'voice' through organizations such as Disability Equality in Education and The Alliance for Inclusive Education. Rieser (2003) and Wilson and Jade (1999) for example, state that it is essential for all learners to be educated together, arguing that it is the very presence of specialized settings that prevent mainstream schools from developing with the resources to fully support all pupils. For them, it is the learners seen as the most challenging who need inclusion the most. These conflicting views raise serious issues for us all about whose voice receives the greatest audience and for what reason? How are 'user' voices sought and responded to at a national level? Teachers and teaching assistants may have easier access to 'establishment' views by the very nature of their work: how can they discover wider perspectives to inform personal decisions?

School staff are expected to be at the forefront of inclusion initiatives (DfES 2004), but often their training concentrates on meeting skills criteria rather than critically examining the multiple factors involved in classroom practice. The focus of many training programmes is usually directed at legislation, professional responsibilities and practical strategies for teaching and learning. This leads us to further key questions about learner voice. If teachers and teaching assistants are to be prepared to listen effectively to learners at risk of exclusion, when should they learn the skills and how can this be incorporated into their training programmes? What about the tutors on these programmes? They may have limited experience themselves of inclusion and limited access to the views of disadvantaged groups to share with students (Richards 2002). Whose 'voices' do student teachers and teaching assistants hear on their programmes, whose research do they learn about and how does this affect their views on inclusion? If they only hear the viewpoints of professionals rather than the 'recipients' of education services how might this affect their perception of what is successful practice?

The issue of power is critical as we reflect on how and why we listen to learners' voices. A truly inclusive setting values all of its members' perspectives without placing these within a hierarchy where some are seen to be more valid or important than others. Possibly the key question for teaching assistants to ask themselves is: what voice do *I* have? Even skilled individuals may be unable to provide support for learners to be heard if the setting in which they work does not encourage them to give their own opinions or value their contributions. Teaching assistants and learners may become united by a common experience of lack of power to influence change, but this situation can be frustrating for all involved.

The operation of power within settings can impact on the success of strategies used to gain all learners' views. While it might seem to be a simple training need for staff to learn specific communication skills such as British Sign Language or basic advocacy skills, there are wider considerations required:

- Who selects someone to be an advocate? Is this genuinely the choice of the learner and how can we be sure that it is the learner's voice that is being presented by the advocate?
- Who selects which voices to hear? Do all learners have an opportunity to present their views or only a carefully selected few?
- What information is sought? Who decides? Do adult agendas override those of children and young people?
- Who controls the conversations? What language is used? Is it accessible to everyone?
- Can learners with communication difficulties express 'unfiltered' perspectives? Are *all* views recorded?
- Are opportunities for giving perspectives unthreatening?
- Who listens to learners' views and who responds?
- How are conflicts of perspectives resolved?
- Do individuals have the right to refuse to give their views?

These questions focus on the core differences between 'consultation' and empowered 'learner voice'. Where learners are able to select who advocates for them and share control of the feedback agenda with staff, the process becomes more meaningful and inclusive. Being able to give opinions in non-threatening situations and knowing that what is said will be treated respectfully and responded to, will encourage contributions from a broader range of learners. Of equal importance, although this may seem to be at odds with working inclusively, are individual learner's rights to refuse to be involved. It is easy to see why having the opportunity to voice an opinion is seen to be a 'good thing', but respect for 'voice' must also allow for those who choose not to be involved. Of course there may be many reasons for making such a decision and these may need resolving in the longer term, but if we believe that inclusion means valuing people for themselves rather than trying to fit everyone into set practices, even this can be a valuable starting point for change.

Conclusions

The themes explored in this chapter have attempted to show that the concept of 'learner voice' is complex. If schools and colleges really want to engage with all their learners, they need to understand the deeper issues involved and respond accordingly. A truly inclusive process is not easy and needs careful planning, adequate time allocated and a range of staff skills to make the process successful. It may even challenge traditional power relationships within the setting. Teaching assistants have a key role to play in this process. They often have a unique relationship with the children and young people with whom they work and so are able to support learners' advocacy. Teaching assistants do however need to consider their own position in this process. They may, for example, be too involved with a learner to be a 'detached' facilitator in feedback situations and so need to pass this role on to a colleague. In another situation they might find themselves coerced into making sure that people they support complete a particular feedback form even if they do not understand it. Such situations can create very real difficulties for teaching assistants, but if they are able to remain focused on the learner rather than processes, this can demonstrate a clear commitment to making everybody's voice count.

Reflections on values and practice

If you are going to support learners to have a voice about matters that are important to them, you will need to reflect honestly about your own role and skills in this process.

1   When you think about the methods that your setting use to gain the views of its whole community, are these successful?
2   How confident are you in expressing your own views and do you feel that these are valued?
3   When working with learners, how well are you able to support them in saying what they think?
4   Are you tempted to 'interpret' what they say? Are you able to separate your own views from those of the learners and when necessary represent views that conflict with your own?
5   Are you committed to making every voice count?

Suggested further reading

Anderson, V., Faraday, S., Prowse, S., Richards, G. and Swindells, D. (2003) *Count Me in FE,* London: Learning and Skills Development Agency.

Clifton, M. (2004) 'We Like to Talk and We Like Some One to Listen. Cultural Difference and Minority Voices as Agents of Change', in Armstrong, F. and Moore, M. (eds) *Action Research for Inclusive Education. Changing Places, Changing Practices, Changing Minds*, London: RoutledgeFalmer.

Cullingford, C. (2005) 'Lessons from Learners about Inclusive Curriculum and Pedagogy' in Nind, M., Rix, J., Sheehey, K. and Simmons, K. (eds) *Curriculum and Pedagogy in Inclusive Education,* London: RoutledgeFalmer.

Gwynn, J. (2004) 'What About Me? I Live Here Too!', in Armstrong, F. and Moore, M. (eds) *Action Research for Inclusive Education. Changing Places, Changing Practices, Changing Minds*, London: RoutledgeFalmer.

Wilson, C. and Rowen, J. (1999) *Whose Voice is it Anyway?*, London: AIE.

References

Allan, J. (2005) 'Inclusive Learning Experiences: Learning from Children and Young People' in Nind, M., Rix, J., Sheehy, K. and Simmons, K. (eds) *Curriculum and Pedagogy in Inclusive Education*, London: RoutledgeFalmer.

Anderson V., Farady, S., Prowse, S. Richards, G. and Swindells. D. (2003) *Count Me in FE*, London: Learning and Skills Development Agency.

Clare, L. and Cox, S. (2003) 'Improving Service Approaches and Outcomes for People with Complex Needs through Consultation and Involvement', *Disability and Society* 18(7): 935–53.

Clifton, M. (2004) 'We Like to Talk and We Like Some One to Listen. Cultural Difference and Minority Voices as Agents of Change' in Armstrong, F. and Moore, M. (eds) *Action Research for Inclusive Education. Changing Places, Changing Practices, Changing Minds*, London: RoutledgeFalmer.

Cullingford, C. (2005) 'Lessons from Learners about Inclusive Curriculum and pedagogy' in Nind, M., Rix, J., Sheehey, K. and Simmons, K. (eds) *Curriculum and Pedagogy in Inclusive Education*, London: RoutledgeFalmer.

DfEE (2001) *Raising Standards in Post-16 Learning*, London: DfEE.

DfES (2004) *Removing Barriers to Achievement*, London: HMSO.

DfES (2005) *Listening to the Work-Based Learner: Unlocking the Potential of Apprentice Feedback*, London: DfES.

DfES (2006) *2020 Vision*, report of the Teaching and Learning in 2020 Review Group, Nottingham: DfES.

Department for Health (2001) *Learning Difficulties and Ethnicity*, London: HMSO.

Gwynn, J. (2004) 'What About Me? I Live Here Too!' in Armstrong, F. and Moore, M. (eds) *Action Research for Inclusive Education. Changing Places, Changing Practices, Changing Minds*, London: RoutledgeFalmer.

Jones, G. (2002) *Diverging Paths to Adulthood*, report for the Rowntree Foundation, pp. 1–8.

Kaplin, I., Lewis, I. and Mumba, P. (2007) 'Picturing global educational inclusion? Looking and thinking across students' photographs from the UK, Zambia and Indonesia', *Journal of Research in Special Educational Needs* 7(1): 23–35.

Klein, R. (2003) *We Want Our Say*, Stoke-on-Trent: Trentham Books.

Leadbetter (2004) 'Personalisation Through Participation. A New Script for Public Service', London: DEMOS.

McDowell, L. (ed.) (1991) *Putting Students First: Listening to Students and Responding to their Needs*, SCED paper 64, Birmingham: SCED.

Mason, M. (2005) *Incurably Human*, Nottingham: Inclusive Solutions.

Morrow, V. (2006) 'We get played for fools. Some promises and pitfalls of community and institutional participation for children and young people'. Keynote speech, *Pupil Voice and Participation: Pleasures, Promises and Pitfalls*, National Research Conference, Nottingham University.

Noyes, A. (2005) 'Pupil Voice: Purpose, Power and the Possibilities for Democratic Schooling', *British Educational Research Journal* 31(4): 533–46.

Ofsted (2006) *Inclusion: Does it Matter Where Pupils are Taught?*, London: Crown Copyright.

Pedder, D. and McIntyre, D. (2006) 'Pupil Consultation: The Importance of Social Capital', *Education Review* 58(2): 145–57.

Pollard, A. and Triggs, P. with Broadfoot, P., McNess, E. and Osborn, M. (2000) *What Pupils Say: Changing Policy and Practice in Primary Education*, London: Continuum.

Richards, G. (2002) 'Are We All Prepared For Inclusion? A Study of Initial Teacher Training in Further Education', *The Skill Journal* 74, November.

Richards, G., Anderson, V. and Drury, P. (2007) *Responding to Learners' Views*, London: Learning and Skills Network.

Rieser, R. (2003) 'The Struggle for Inclusion: The Growth of a Movement' in Nind, M., Rix, J., Sheehy, K. and Simmons, K. (eds) *Inclusive Education: Diverse Perspectives*, London: David Fulton.

Rose, C. (2006) *How to Actively Involve Disabled People*, London: LSN.

Rudduck, J., Chaplain, R. and Wallace, G. (1996) *School Improvement: What Can Pupils Tell Us?*, London: David Fulton.

Rudduck, J. (2003) *Pupil Voice and Citizenship Education*, report for the QCA Citizenship and PSHE Team.

Salmon, M. (2005) 'Foreword' in Berkeley, J. (ed.) *Listening to the Work-Based Learner: Unlocking the Potential of Apprentice Feedback*, Sheffield: DfES.

Sherlock, D. (2005) 'The Adult Learning Inspectorate' in Berkeley, J. (ed.) *Listening to the Work-Based Learner: Unlocking the Potential of Apprentice Feedback*, Sheffield: DfES.

Wilson, C. and Jade, R. (1999) *Whose Voice is it Anyway?* London: Alliance for Inclusive Education.

Wilson, J. (2000) 'Doing Justice to Inclusion', *European Journal of Special Needs Education* 15.

Chapter 3

Supporting Traveller children

Ken Marks and Margaret Wood

> Traveller pupils are still the group most at risk in the education system. They are the one minority ethnic group which is too often 'out of sight and out of mind'.
>
> Ofsted 2003: 21

Why has it proved so difficult to build effective bridges between our schooling systems and the communities that constitute our Traveller populations, and what are the inclusive challenges for classroom practice? How can teaching assistants play their part? This chapter is intended to raise awareness about cultures and lifestyles which are all too often misunderstood, and to explore implications for practitioners.

In numerical terms, the main traditional UK Traveller groupings are Gypsies, Irish Travellers, Showmen (fairground families) and, north of the border, Scottish Travellers. These are distinctive communities, each with their own strong identity. They have all, however, been shaped by a common heritage of mobility offering one of the best ways to begin understanding some of the key needs of Traveller pupils, and here it is helpful to focus on three themes.

In a sense the most fundamental of these themes is the mobile lifestyle itself. The system of schools which we all take for granted was set up to serve local catchments. Large numbers of Traveller families will be away from their home base for extended periods, especially between April and October. What challenges does this present for schools as well as for Traveller families?

The second theme is cultural. Over the generations mobile lifestyles have played an important part in reinforcing strong and distinctive community identities and values, which remain central for families even if they cease to travel and settle in one locality. These partly reflect the central role of the family as a living-working unit, and the self-sufficiency and independence which are a fundamental part of a heritage of life on the road. They also reflect norms which are important for a mobile caravan/trailer lifestyle. This second, cultural, theme raises an important set of inclusive challenges for staff in schools with implications for awareness and practice in terms of both teaching and support.

The third theme relates to prejudice. There is a variety of evidence which suggests that nomadic communities tend to attract suspicion and hostility, and Danaher (2000) has suggested that this is a worldwide phenomenon. It is certainly the experience of our UK Travelling communities and has played its part in moulding ways in which they think about and react to 'authority', as well as to the educational opportunities open to their children. Prejudice all too often continues to be an issue even for families who settle with their trailer on a recognized local site or are housed by a local authority. Such negative, and sometimes racist, reactions pose another dimension of challenge for work with both pupils and parents.

This chapter will consider each of these themes in turn before inviting readers to reflect on some aspects of emergent good practice, both from within the school sector and from specialist local authority based Traveller Education Services (TES).

The mobile lifestyle

Compulsory schooling was first introduced in the late nineteenth century. It was an immediate problem for a variety of itinerant and 'journeyman' families and continues to be a fundamental issue for the main Traveller communities. Most mobile Traveller families over-winter in one place and children can then go to a local 'base' school. Attendance is often problematic, however, during the main work-travel season. Families are encouraged to try to link up with local schools wherever they can during this period, and official guidance also encourages local authorities (LAs) and schools to respond pragmatically. However, there are clearly inherent learning coverage and continuity issues for the children and sadly families don't always receive an inclusive welcome from schools.

The majority of fairground families and those of the smaller circus community move frequently, often transferring from one site to another in a different part of the country on a weekly basis during the travel season. The main problem here is that school attendance is often impracticable with the potential for significant gaps in the learning process.

This is also an issue for large numbers of children from the other traditional communities, but here travel patterns are much more varied, partly reflecting the changing range of economic activities pursued by Traveller families (Office of the Deputy Prime Minister 2003). Some families, for example, now come and go more frequently from their winter base during the travel season, while others reflect a more traditional seasonal-labour pattern; spending months away from base but in a relatively small number of locations. In such situations there is better potential to build local and inclusive bridges. Sadly, however, it is also important to be aware of the other extreme. There are something of the order of 2,000 Gypsy and Irish Traveller families who have no established winter-base site and are currently forced into a transient lifestyle throughout the year.

Travel patterns have also been affected by the loss of traditional stopping places over the years and by the current dearth of official and recognized transit sites. Following the 1994 Criminal Justice and Public Order Act families now face potential criminal prosecution if they stop on an unauthorized site.

Being away from your base site, if you have one, can therefore be a daunting experience and arrangements for schooling may not be top of the family agenda. So what can schools do to encourage inclusive practice?

Clearly those which have winter-based families within their area have an important part to play in working with their local TES to make best use of pupils' time in school. Many have also become involved in the design and support of personalized distance learning packs which children can use while away. Something of the order of 1,200 children now travel with such packs, and while this approach has mainly developed within the fairground and circus communities there are also some significant examples of good practice with Gypsy, Irish and Scottish Traveller children. Following initiatives from the DfES, with some parallel developments in Scotland, many Traveller children are also beginning to use laptops and the internet to link back to their base schools. This has added a new and exciting dimension to the possibility of such distance learning support.

At the same time, *all* schools need to be sensitive to Traveller families who are temporarily in their area; even more so for those families forced into a highly mobile lifestyle. It can take courage and effort for a family to try to link up with a school, as many have a legacy of rejection. It can, of course, take courage for the school as the arrival of Traveller families can cause hostile local reaction. Fortunately there are some excellent examples of good practice, often supported by TES, which show just what can be achieved in this important dimension of community bridge building.

Cultural values

In this section of the chapter we will attempt to highlight some aspects of Traveller cultures which have particular relevance to schooling including areas where community perspectives, norms and values can be at odds with assumptions which are often taken for granted in terms of school practices and expectations. This is an important focus for the inclusive classroom and not just for families who maintain a mobile lifestyle. Over the years many Traveller families have, in effect, 'settled'. However, although they may now live on a fixed site or be housed (often with the trailer close by), their community heritage remains an integral part of their identity, and this sense of identity is reinforced by both extended family ties and traditional community events.

It is therefore important to appreciate Traveller families as part of communities which value their independence and freedom to travel, and have a strong emphasis on the family as a living-working unit. From the school perspective it is also important to appreciate how this impacts on priorities for learning, initially through patterns of play and then through example and role modelling. As Holmes and her co-authors have noted:

> The travelling communities historically have sought to be self sufficient, independent and resourceful. They have largely operated in extended family groups providing a mobile workforce and/or organising around . . . business interest(s) . . . Child rearing practices and skills have focused on children as trainee adults learning alongside adults and being inducted into the family work from a young age (11/12-years-old). Strong family education and work skills have been transferred from generation to generation in this way, ensuring continuity of the community and its work traditions.
>
> (Holmes *et al.* 2001: 75)

In this context, Liégeois (1998) has made a helpful and important distinction between this form of community-based 'education', and the 'schooling' process required by society. Fortunately there is a convergence of interest at the primary stage as the communities increasingly see the value of literacy skills as part of their own view of educational and economic priorities, and this has been an important factor in enabling many schools to work with families to begin to develop successful inclusive practice.

However, large numbers of families remain cautious about potential hostility towards their children and about negative influences, and these concerns take on an even greater significance when children transfer to the secondary sector where Traveller parents often express worries about aspects of peer culture such as permissive sexual behaviour and drug taking. Transfer also coincides with the beginnings of the informal apprentice model when the expectation is that children will be taking on adult roles in the family rather than being at school. Commitment to secondary schooling has improved within the fairground community, partly because families are increasingly taking a broader view of the value and relevance of qualifications. However, secondary attendance remains a major issue for the other traditional mobile groupings and Derrington and Kendall (2004) have provided an insightful commentary on this challenge, based directly on the experiences of children and families.

There is clearly a way to go in building creative and positive bridges with the communities, especially for the secondary phase, and part of the challenge is also to encourage greater awareness of some important and more specific issues for school-based practice.

First, in terms of early learning, children will be used to distinctive, community-orientated, patterns of play with differing acceptable 'inside' and 'outside' behaviours. Cleanliness will also be at a premium within the home and there are important modesty codes. When children first attend school they can be thrust into a dissonant world in which they are separated from siblings, and with very different rules, structures and patterns of play/learning interaction. Parents and children may also be especially sensitive about modesty issues such as changing for PE. In addition it is important to remember that many parents will have had negative and limited experience of school, and some may have missed out on schooling entirely. Children will then be making their own sense of a world that seems alien not just to them but often to the whole family. Both children and parents can need considerable encouragement and reassurance.

Second, certainly from the primary phase, it is vital to appreciate that these are oral cultures, a tradition which they value, and although parents do increasingly see the functional value of literacy skills they are all too often unable to support their children with reading and writing practice, nor do they model these skills. In addition it needs to be born in mind that Gypsies, Irish Travellers and Scottish Travellers will often use distinctive dialects in the home; drawing from traditional Romani, Gammon or Cant. Children will need support to accommodate to the language of the classroom and there is again the need for a proactive awareness.

Finally, at the secondary phase, it is important to appreciate that Traveller families have had to develop resilience over the generations and value a sense of independence within which they have to be prepared to 'stand up for themselves'. This is part and parcel of taking on young adult roles but these emphases can cause conflict at school. Where Traveller children become targets for abuse they are all too likely to react, and this reaction needs sensitive handling. Secondary-age Traveller children can also find it difficult to switch between young adult recognition at home and the child/pupil role they are expected to maintain with teachers at school. This can cause conflict with staff who are unaware of the difficult balance that these children have to maintain.

Having focused on potential dissonances, it seems important to round off this section by reiterating that there are encouraging signs of progress within the primary sector, partly driven by a common concern with literacy, and partly by approaches which acknowledge and celebrate Traveller cultures. It is also important to draw attention to the strong practical, problem-solving orientation of the communities which is also part of their 'apprenticeship' culture. Families across all the communities are increasingly interested in many of the vocational pathways available in further education colleges as these are, again, seen as part of their own educational and economic priorities. Hopefully the new 14–19 vocational curriculum structure will begin to provide a platform for a more flexible and creative synthesis between schools and families.

Prejudice: awareness and action

> All the evidence shows that Travellers and Gypsies are some of the most vulnerable and marginalized ethnic minority groups in Britain. 'No Travellers' signs in pubs and shops can still be seen today . . .
>
> Gypsy and Traveller children are taunted and bullied in school, local residents are openly hostile to them, and scare stories in the media fuel prejudice and make racist attitudes acceptable.
>
> (CRE 2004: 2)

Since the introduction of the amended Race Relations Act in 2000, Gypsies and Irish Travellers have a degree of legal protection against discrimination, and there are parallel developments in Northern Ireland. However, these opening sentences from the three-year strategic plan developed by the Commission for Racial Equality in 2004 are a stark reminder of continuing levels of hostility towards Traveller communities. Prejudice is an ever present reality for Gypsies, Irish and Scottish Travellers,[1] and to a lesser degree for fairground families. It has deep historical roots and seems to have been, at least in part, an endemic reaction to nomadic lifestyles that did not fit neatly with local systems of control and accountability, and where it would have been all too easy to blame transient families for local ills, even local crimes. Kenrick and Clark (1999) provide a brief but useful overview, which emphasizes the way in which scapegoating and stereotyping have continued to reinforce prejudice, especially through the press, and sadly through some children's literature.[2]

In this context, these authors are also right to draw particular attention to current conflicts over land use. The lack of recognized base sites and transit sites in some parts of the country sometimes forces Traveller families into using unsuitable and unofficial sites, or into settling on their own privately purchased land prior to gaining planning permission. Such occurrences often cause local hostility and lead to negative press coverage, which almost always ignores the underlying causal issues while reinforcing prejudice. Recent changes in local authority strategic planning requirements should improve this situation over time as more sites become available, but the legacy of local hostility over land use has clearly added to negative attitudes towards the communities.

We would argue that successful inclusive work with Traveller children therefore needs a proactive awareness of the deeply ingrained historical impact of prejudice that can affect us all, as well as an understanding of contemporary issues. We also need an understanding of the impact on families. This is especially true for the Gypsy, Irish and Scottish Traveller communities where

---

1   The CRE sees its remit as also covering Scottish Travellers as a community 'defined by national or ethnic origins'.
2   See, in particular, Chapter 4 which is entitled 'Gypsies and race relations-theory and practice'. Clark and Greenfields (2006) also provide an updated perspective.

most parents will have grown up within a climate of hostility and rejection. Here, as already noted, one immediate consequence is that parents and children may be especially concerned about potential bullying. Indeed, one response may be 'passing' – i.e. the families and pupils not revealing their cultural identity.

Actual incidents of bullying can quickly lead to children being withdrawn, but at the other end of the spectrum, resistive behaviours can and do emerge and contribute to the high proportion of exclusions affecting Traveller pupils. As again noted above, it is vital to appreciate that standing up for yourself, your group and your community is an essential part of an identity shaped by historical experience, and that such reactions need to be dealt with from an informed perspective. It is, however, also important to appreciate that fears are not just about bullying. As Kiddle (1999) has pointed out, parents are likely to be very sensitive to the impact of a variety of aspects of their children's reception and experiences at school; the welcome they receive, the empathy and sensitivity of staff and interactivity with other pupils. They will be ever-cautious about any manifestation of potential prejudice and in this context recent trends suggest a worrying retreat into 'elective home education', which some Traveller families have begun to misuse partly as a means of justifying the withdrawal and protection of their children (Ivatts 2006).

Reflections, resources and further sources of information

What can schools do to overcome potential barriers to learning related to mobility, cultural diversity and prejudice or racism? How can teaching assistants contribute? We have suggested that one prerequisite is awareness, but how do schools develop from broad awareness to effective action and how can classroom-based staff play their part? These are questions we will consider in this final section, beginning with the more general school perspective where the best starting point will normally be contact with local specialist TES staff.

Most local authorities have such specialist staff although they may be assigned to a team with a broader local title and remit.[3] Services vary in size and often employ both teachers and teaching assistants. They may also employ home school liaison officers, youth workers, early years' professionals, mentors and adult outreach workers. Their purpose is generally twofold. First: to provide awareness raising and training to enable schools and local authorities to develop the necessary expertise to meet the needs of their Traveller pupils

3   Almost every English LA and most Scottish LEAs have designated specialist staff. Some have separate TES units while others embed Traveller staff within other teams. We use the shorthand 'TES staff' for both situations in this chapter.

within mainstream settings. Second: to raise pupil achievement by supporting access, attendance, continuity, secondary transfer and parental involvement. Increasingly, TES staff are also involved in helping schools to evaluate the effectiveness of their policies and everyday practice with regard to Traveller pupils, planning targeted interventions based upon a careful analysis of pupil level data, developing a broad and inclusive curriculum that reflects cultural diversity, building effective partnerships with parents and the community and creating a positive ethos for learning that centres firmly on equality.

Clearly such services offer a very important 'live' resource to schools. Their work is grounded in outreach to the communities and they usually have strong and positive contacts with families in the area, including those who are newly arrived and living on unofficial sites. Here the basis of trust is sometimes reinforced through signposting to health care and services such as refuse disposal, water, benefits, accommodation and legal advice.

Outreach also gives TES staff the potential to build and reinforce bridges between Traveller families and schools and means that they develop informed insights about individual needs and concerns. TES staff involvement can include helping to arrange matters such as transport, uniform, school dinners and additional curriculum support. Additional support may involve the initial assessment of pupils, and help with developing appropriate teaching strategies that will enable them to learn alongside their peers.

Where children have an established pattern of attendance, TES staff input may, at times, involve mediation between schools and families and support for parents to raise any concerns or to attend meetings relating to pupil progress, special educational needs or behavioural matters. At the same time, TES staff can help schools to consider the practicalities of how they can work more closely with parents to address their very real anxieties about a range of issues, some of which have already been highlighted. These include bullying and name calling, the sometimes negative attitudes of other pupils and parents, sanctions and rewards, the wearing of traditional jewellery, changing for PE, sex education, drugs, school trips and homework.

There are also many good examples of TES support for schools in the development of distance learning for their more mobile pupils. As noted earlier in the chapter, something like 1,200 children now travel with personalized materials to enable them to keep up with as much as possible of the mainstream curriculum. A series of E-LAMP (e-learning and mobility project) developments funded by the DfES and coordinated by the National Association of Teachers of Travellers (NATT) means that more than 250 of these children now have laptops that give them access to the internet, both to enrich learning and so that they can keep in contact with their schools. This has proved an effective enhancement and over 90 English schools are now involved. The DfES has issued a guidance document to encourage further development (Marks 2006), and parallel developments are being planned in Scotland, with Glasgow leading the way during 2005 (MTN 2006).

The breadth and wealth of successful school–TES partnerships is perhaps best illustrated by a series of examples highlighted in the DfES publication *Aiming High: Raising the Achievement of Gypsy Traveller Pupils A Guide to Good Practice* (2003). However, as this report stresses, the child 'belongs' to the school while the TES has a supportive role. Part of the challenge is therefore to transfer the personalized dimension which TES staff can offer into the school and classroom setting. In practice, teaching assistants are often key players in making school a safe and welcoming environment for potentially vulnerable pupils. It is therefore not surprising to find many excellent examples in schools across the country where teaching assistants have already taken on a key role in building up trust with both pupils and Traveller parents.

When mobile children return to school after a long period away, or when they arrive at a new school, the welcome they receive is all important. What they need is a friendly and smiling face and someone who will create strategies to help them settle in and become integrated not segregated. The teaching assistant is often the adult who works most closely with the children and who needs to be particularly alert to the possibility of some children being left out, picked upon or discriminated against. It may also be possible for schools to encourage positive relationships between children in a more structured way, through the personal, social and health education (PSHE) curriculum, through buddying systems and guided playground activities, by involving parents and by making sure that children know what they can do if things go wrong. Here again teaching assistants can play an important part. In one Cambridgeshire school a teaching assistant helped to train Year 6 pupils, including Traveller children, who then acted as mentors for younger pupils during playtimes and lunchtimes. Many teaching assistants have also helped to support extra curricular activities targeted at Traveller pupils including IT, dance, karaoke and drama. They have supported Key Stage 4 pupils attending local further education colleges on day release vocational programmes. On occasions, where a good relationship has been established between a teaching assistant and a Traveller child, this has encouraged the parents to allow the child to take part in school trips. In early years settings teaching assistants have helped raise awareness and address discrimination, similarities and differences through, for example, using Persona Dolls.[4]

Clearly more direct forms of learning support are also crucial at every stage, especially as many parents have had negative, and sometimes minimal, experience of schools. It is interesting to note some recent research which suggests that Traveller pupils across a broad age range (4–15) were positive in their own views about learning, even though they were clearly affected by the continuing prevalence of prejudice within their schools (Warrington 2006). TAs are well placed to reinforce such positive attitudes towards learning in sensitive ways, especially through extra literacy support and help with differentiated activity

4   See Brown (2001) for details.

across the curriculum. They can also, and sometimes do, take on more proactive roles in terms of seeking out appropriate Traveller-related resources, many of which have been produced by TES in collaboration with the communities themselves.[5] These clearly have relevance for support work but they can also be recommended to class teachers as a basis for whole class activity.

Resources such as *Melissa to the Rescue* and *Where's My Teddy?*[6] have recently, for example, been used in Cambridgeshire in this way and Traveller children who had previously been reluctant to join in, rapidly developed in confidence as, for once, the stories included areas in which they were experts. These examples mirror practice in many schools across the country and clearly such resources need to be used sensitively, i.e. without asking direct personal questions or identifying that particular children are Travellers unless it is clear that they are comfortable with sharing their identity. In addition, they are important as a way of celebrating Traveller lifestyles, something which can also be achieved by drawing on resources such as Traveller story tellers and artists, or local Travellers with particular skills who are able to contribute to the curriculum. Such initiatives often have a very powerful impact on the perceptions of staff, governors, pupils and parents alike. In this celebratory context it is important to note that some TES have teaching, and indeed teaching assistants, staff who are themselves Travellers and can bring a unique role-modelling dimension to work in schools.

As both DfES and local data relating to attendance, attainment and exclusions continue to demonstrate, the gap between Gypsy and Traveller pupils and the whole pupil cohort at all key stages from Foundation onwards is very much wider than for any other ethnic group. However, there is clear evidence that where schools and systems are sensitive to their needs, Gypsy and Traveller pupils can and do progress within our schools, and from this perspective it may be helpful finally to consider your own school situation.

Reflection on values and practice

1   Are Traveller cultures and issues considered within the curriculum in your school?
2   If Traveller pupils arrived how would your school respond?
3   If the school is already working with Traveller communities, what are the respective influences of mobility, culture and prejudice on your Gypsy and Traveller pupils?
4   What are your school's strengths in ensuring that they provide positive support rather then presenting barriers to learning?

5   One useful starting point is the list provided on the DfES Standards website. See www. standards.dfes.gov.uk/ethnicminorities/resources/gypsytravellerresourcesnov05.xls.
6   Details of both texts are given on the DfES site mentioned in the previous note.

5   What more needs to be done to develop awareness and challenge preju-
    dice?
6   Last but not least, how can TA roles contribute to the bridge-building
    process?

Suggested further reading

Details of your local TES can be found on the NATT website at www.natt.org.uk, and
one good starting point for developing an overview of issues faced by the communities
is the CRE site www.cre.gov.uk/gdpract/g_and_t_facts.html. Another useful source
of information is the Leeds TES website www.travellersinleeds.co.uk. This site also
provides hyperlinks to a number of other useful websites.

The following books are also recommended (for full details see the list of references):

Kenrick and Clark (1999) and Clark and Greenfields (2006) give a historical overview
    and a discussion of racism and contemporary issues faced by the communities.
Kiddle (1999) An excellent overview which has a particular focus on the perspective
    of Traveller pupils themselves, as well as some excellent ideas for developing
    practice.
Tyler (2005) and O'Hanlon and Holmes (2004) are books which discuss both issues
    and aspects of practice.
Warrington (2006) which builds from the voices of Traveller children, as does
    Derrington and Kendall (2004) in the secondary context.

References

Brown, B. (2001, reprinted 2005) *Combating Discrimination: Persona Dolls in Action*,
    Stoke-on-Trent: Trentham Books.
Central Advisory Council for Education (1967) *Children and their Primary Schools* (*The
    Plowden Report*), London: HMSO.
Clark, C. and Greenfields, M. (2006) *Here to Stay: The Gypsies and Travellers of Britain*,
    Hatfield: University of Hertfordshire Press.
Commission for Racial Equality (2004) *Gypsies and Travellers: A Strategy for the CRE,
    2004–2007*, London: CRE.
Danaher, P.A. (2000) Guest Editor's Introduction, *International Journal for Educational
    Research* 33(3): 221–30.
Derrington, C. and Kendall, S. (2004) *Gypsy Traveller Students in Secondary Schools:
    Culture, Identity and Achievement*, Stoke-on-Trent: Trentham Books.
DfES (2003) *Aiming High: Raising the Achievement of Gypsy Traveller Pupils A Guide to
    Good Practice*, London: DfES.
Hawes, D. and Perez, B. (1995) *The Gypsy and the State: The Ethnic Cleansing of British
    Society*, Bristol: SAUS publications.
Holmes, P., Knaepkens, L. and Marks, K. (2001) 'Fighting Social Exclusion
    Through ODL: the Development of Initiatives With the Children of Traveller
    Communities' in Trindade A.R. (ed.) *New Learning*, Portugal: Universidade Aberta,
    pp. 74–86.

Ivatts, A. (2006) *Elective Home Education: The Situation Regarding the Current Policy and Practice in Elective Home Education for Gypsy, Roma and Traveller Children*, London: DfES.

Kenrick, D. and Clark, C. (1999) *Moving On: The Gypsies and Travellers of Britain*, Hatfield: University of Hertfordshire Press.

Kiddle, C. (1999) *Traveller Children: A Voice for Themselves*, London: Jessica Kingsley.

Liégeois, J.P. (1998) *School Provisions for Ethnic Minorities: The Gypsy Paradigm*, Hatfield: University of Hertfordshire Press.

Marks, K. (2006) *School Supported Distance Learning*, Nottingham: DfES Publications.

MTN (2006) *Laptops for Travellers*. Online: available at www.mtnonline.co.uk/laptops fortravellers (accessed January, 2007).

Office of the Deputy Prime Minister (2003) *Local Authority Gypsy/Traveller Sites in England: Housing Research Summary Number 195*, London: The Office of the Deputy Prime Minister.

Ofsted (2003) *Provision and Support for Traveller Pupils*, London: Ofsted.

O'Hanlon, C. and Holmes, P. (2004) *The Education of Gypsy and Traveller Children: Towards Inclusion and Educational Achievement*, Stoke-on-Trent: Trentham Books.

Tyler, C. (ed.) (2005) *Traveller Education: Accounts of Good Practice*, Stoke-on-Trent: Trentham Books.

Warrington, C. (2006) *Children's Voices: Changing Futures (The Views and Experiences of Young Gypsies and Travellers)*, Ipswich: Ormiston Children and Families Trust.

Chapter 4

Not in my image

Ethnic diversity in the classroom

Raphael Richards

- In 2006, the minority ethnic population in maintained schools was 17 per cent and 21 per cent in secondary and primary respectively. By 2010 over 20 per cent of the total maintained school population will be from minority ethnic communities.
- The General Teaching Council (GTC) reported that 7.8 per cent of the teaching population was from minority ethnic groups. It is estimated that the percentage of teaching assistants from minority ethnic groups is between 10 and 15 per cent.
- While Chinese, Indian, Irish and Mixed White and Asian pupils consistently performed above the national average for all pupils, Black, Pakistani, Bangladeshi and Mixed White and Black Caribbean pupils consistently performed below the national average for all pupils.
- Working-class minority ethnic pupils are making better progress in secondary schools nationally than working-class White British pupils.
- In England, 686,000 pupils are recorded as having a mother tongue other than English. More than 200 languages are spoken in the homes of children attending school. Over 41 per cent of Bangladeshi and 27 per cent of Pakistani pupils reported that English was not their first or main language.

Introduction

Imagine that throughout your years in primary school, none of the tall people interacting with you as teachers, teaching assistants or support staff looks like you. Now, imagine spending five to six hours each day in lessons doing History, Geography, Science and English without seeing or hearing positive things about adults who might reflect you. What subconscious pictures would this create for the child about the adult world and school?

On setting out to write this chapter, I asked several teachers and teaching assistants what they would expect from an article about ethnic diversity. They said I should start by explaining what diversity and ethnicity are, why people needed to know this and how they would benefit from having the information. It was important to find out before starting, because in my experience it helps if you ask the people you are supporting, what they need. In asking the question I recognize that most of our services are about helping individuals and that people's experiences, although often similar, can be significantly different.

In schools across the country, the ethnic diversity of the classroom will vary widely depending on where you are in the country and in which city you live. In fact the ethnic diversity of neighbouring schools can be very different. The level of single ethnic group access and usage of educational, residential and social facilities can be stark in some communities. The Cantle Report into the 2001 disturbance found that:

> Separate educational arrangements, community and voluntary bodies, employment, place of worship, language, social and cultural networks means that many communities operate on a basis of parallel lives. These lives often do not seem to touch at any point, let alone overlap and promote any meaningful interchanges.
>
> (Cantle 2001: 9)

In 2005 Trevor Phillips, the then Chair of the Commission for Racial Equality (CRE), reminded us of the Ted Cantle Report on the troubles in Oldham, by saying that children continued to live 'parallel lives' being educated in separate schools where there are either predominantly Black or predominantly White pupils (Phillips 2005). While this is the case, what is more predictable is the lack of ethnic diversity of the teaching staff, support staff and senior management and governance of schools. The diversity of pupil population in schools is increasing. In 2006 the minority ethnic population in schools nationally stood at 18.5 per cent. The Department for Education and Skills (DfES) predicts that by 2010 over 20 per cent of pupils would be of minority ethnic heritage in maintained schools (DfES 2006). In 2005, the GTC reported that less than 7.8 per cent of training teachers in maintained schools were from minority ethnic communities (GTC 2005; Runnymede Trust 2003b).

In this chapter I want to explore the varied characteristics that make up the diversity of minority ethnic children and young people likely to be in school classrooms. This I hope to achieve by highlighting some of the key issues around an ethnically diverse classroom and then setting out a sound background from which readers can expand their understanding of diversity and ethnicity.

What is 'diversity'?

The term diversity has increased in usage since the mid 1990s and today, hardly a day will pass without us reading or hearing the term. However, the context within which we hear it changes regularly. You will hear on the news and elsewhere about diversity in relation to a company's workforce, about the mix of people served in a demographic area, about the pupil population in a school or the curriculum being taught and certainly about the languages in local communities.

The dictionary shows the word diversity as having multiple meanings with the two most common being, *variety:* a variety of something such as opinion, colour or style; and *social inclusiveness:* ethnic variety, as well as socio-economic and gender variety, in a group, society or institution (Oxford 2002). Our focus in this chapter is on ethnic diversity. Within the scope of ethnic diversity, there are factors that people generally cannot change about themselves, for example ability/disability, age, ethnicity, gender, religious beliefs and sexual orientation. Recognizing ethnic diversity does not detract from the reality that people are in many ways similar and that people often have more to unite than divide them.

Diversity encompasses human aspects such as culture, gender, heritage, religion, personality, thinking style, educational background, and the myriad of qualities, visible and invisible that make each of us different. People are diverse in other ways. We live in different places, have different kinds of heritage, and experience different cultural influences. We speak many different languages and have a variety of ethnic backgrounds and religious beliefs. That said, many believe the level of similarities between individuals, groups and communities is far greater than any differences (Rowley and Moore 2002).

What is 'ethnicity'?

The UK Race Relations Act 1976 defined a 'racial group' as 'a group of persons defined by reference to colour, race, nationality or ethnic or national origins'. Thus the term race and ethnicity are commonly interchanged. 'Ethnicity' and 'ethnic group' became more formally defined in UK law by a House of Lords decision (*Mandla v. Lee* 1983) as relating to those with 'a long shared history and a distinct culture'. Other 'relevant' characteristics were 'a common geographic origin or descent from a small number of common ancestors; a common language; a common literature; a common religion and being a minority within a larger community'. The ethnic groups identified by the Office of National Statistics in the decennial UK Census are usually adopted. Comparing the categories in the 1991 Census with those of 2001 there are some significant differences, for example 'Mixed' was added to identify people having two or more ethnic origins. While the 2001 Census uses the term 'ethnic group', it also makes it clear that this is seen as a matter of 'cultural background' (Census 2001).

In recent years, attempts have been made to acknowledge that ethnicity is a characteristic of all individuals and groups, majorities and minorities alike. In the past, the term 'ethnic minority' tended to suggest that the minority or marginalized status of such a group arose from its 'possession' of ethnicity itself, rather than to the low value ascribed to its particular ethnicity in the wider, 'majority' cultural/ethnic environment (Mason 2000; Dadzie 2000). It is important to recognize that definitions that are 'social constructs', such as Black community, refugees or asylum seekers, can change.

The term 'minority ethnic' is mainly used to describe people who are in the minority within a defined population on the grounds of 'race', colour, culture, language or nationality. In the past, those referred to as 'ethnic minorities' were mainly identified as those groups of people who have come from the 'New Commonwealth' to live in the country since the 1950s, that is, visible minorities (people of colour). The term was less associated with the many 'ethnic minorities' from Old Commonwealth countries and Europe who settled in Britain before and since the 1950s. Currently the term is used increasingly to refer to all who have arrived to live and/or work in Britain, including, for example, migrant workers from new European member states.

Ethnic diversity in Britain

Little is known about the first people who inhabited Britain, except that they came from somewhere else. According to historians (Nicolson 1974; Merriman 1993) early stone, bronze and ceramic findings suggest that the culture of migrants to this land shared common features with people from as far away as the Mediterranean and Near East. In the first century AD, Celtic Britain south of Hadrian's Wall became part of the vast Roman Empire, which extended deep into the Middle East and North Africa. The Romans ruled Britain for 400 years, building cities, roads and ports throughout the island. Land and sea trades linking Britain to the Mediterranean were well established in this period. The demise of the Roman Empire saw many large-scale invasions from what is now our European partner countries including, Germany, Denmark and Netherlands. They all left cultural footprints on what is Britain today (Holmes 1978; CRE 1997).

The British Empire, by the end of the nineteenth century, covered large parts of the globe and had 'subjects' in far-flung places (Adams 1987; CRE 1997). Following the end of slavery the Empire's success was sustained by over 2 million Indian and Chinese indentured labourers working on plantations, mines, docks, ships and railways in Commonwealth countries (Claire 1996). Their labour was crucial to the prosperity and industrial expansion Britain achieved during the nineteenth century. As British subjects, people from the Empire were expected to fight in all of Britain's wars, including in wars of colonial expansion (Fryer 1989).

Faced with the massive task of reconstruction after the Second World War, and acute labour shortages, the British government encouraged immigration, first from among European refugees displaced by the war, then from Ireland and the Commonwealth countries. Before long, in some factories, mills and plants, the overwhelming majority of workers were Asian or Black. By the end of the 1970s, strict controls on immigration had been introduced and only relatives (sons, daughters and spouses) were allowed into Britain. Most immigrants to Britain today come from other parts of Europe or arrive as asylum seekers or refugees. Immigrants have often met hostility and resentment, yet even a quick study would show that they have brought skills and qualifications, set up businesses and created jobs, not only for themselves but also for local people. Many have been willing to do jobs that have been difficult to fill locally.

At any one time, immigrants have only been a small proportion of the British population. In 2006, only about 7 per cent of the population were not born in Britain. What is remarkable and often not understood is that the contributions immigrants and their immediate descendants have made to the country's economy and infrastructure, and continue to make, are out of all proportion to their numbers.

Pupils' ethnicity in schools

If only 7 per cent of people living in Britain were not born in the country, how can we report that by 2010, 20 per cent of the school pupil population will be of minority ethnic heritage? Being born in Britain makes you British by nationality but your ethnicity may be stated differently such as Bangladeshi, Black Caribbean, Pakistani or White Other (DfES 2006). The schools' population is measured yearly through the Pupil Level Annual School Census (PLASC). The 'Schools Census', as it is now commonly known, captures information about children, provided by their parents. When a child enters a school, his or her parents or legal carer fill out a form declaring the child's ethnicity, first language and other information.

From the 2006 Schools Census, it was reported that 21 per cent of the maintained primary schools population and 17 per cent of the maintained secondary schools population were from minority ethnic groups (DfES 2006). Comparisons with the 2004 School Census indicate a sustained rise in minority ethnic population, due in part to a decreasing White pupil population and increasing Asian, Black African and Mixed heritage pupils. In many cities the minority ethnic school population is greater than 30 per cent (for example, London, Birmingham, Leeds, Manchester). In other areas such as Cumbria, Norwich and Plymouth the minority ethnic school population is less than 6 per cent. Schools with less than 5 per cent minority ethnic population are deemed 'predominantly White'. Within many schools are what is termed 'isolated minority ethnic pupils', where teachers often have little or no experience of working with minority ethnic pupils. Regardless of the setting, the support needs of minority ethnic pupils must be met (Knowles and Ridley 2006; DfES 2004). At some point in their careers, the majority of teachers and teaching assistants across Britain are likely to work with minority ethnic pupils.

Minority ethnic attainment characteristics

The key purpose of Children's Services is to deliver on the 'Every Child Matters' agenda. This may suggest that the need for focusing on ethnic diversity has become redundant, particularly when schools are being encouraged to focus on the needs of the whole child. I would argue that ethnicity is an integral part of individual pupils and impact to varying degrees on how they view their environment. More importantly, they react to the way teachers and teaching assistants engage with them. There are high achievers in all minority ethnic groups, with Chinese and Indian pupils out-performing all groups at all Key Stages.

High achieving pupils regularly cite supportive teachers, parents or other significant adults, including mentors. They tell of people inspiring them and believing they would achieve and talk about wanting to attain a particular goal. Some talk about overcoming adversity and defying teachers and other adults who told them they would not achieve. One of the major features of minority ethnic pupils' under-achievement is 'low expectation', stemming from teachers and sometimes parents. The commonly agreed position is that the stigma of under-achievement needs to be removed from all groups. This means tackling low expectation, creating an inclusive environment and responding to individual needs (Green 2000).

The Every Child Matters agenda combined with the five outcomes helps us to look at the individual child's experience. That said, group data provides useful indicators in schools as to how specific groups fare in the classroom and wider school community. By looking at trends over time we can see if specific groups are under-achieving or consistently failing to make progress. The DfES now report yearly on 'Ethnicity and Education for Maintained Schools Nationally'. In the 2006 edition the following attainment and socio-economic characteristics were identified:

- Minority ethnic pupils, especially Pakistani, Bangladeshi, Black African and Black Caribbean pupils, are more likely to experience deprivation than White British pupils. For example, 70 per cent of Bangladeshi pupils and almost 60 per cent of Pakistani and Black African pupils live in the 20 per cent most deprived postcode areas, compared to less than 20 per cent of White British pupils.
- Indian, Chinese, Irish and White and Asian pupils consistently have higher levels of attainment than other ethnic groups across all Key Stages.

- White Other, Pakistani, Bangladeshi, Black Caribbean, Black African and Black Other pupils have consistently performed below the average for all pupils on every scale of the Foundation Stage profile.
- Gypsy/Roma, Travellers of Irish Heritage, Black, Pakistani and Bangladeshi pupils consistently have lower levels of attainment than other ethnic groups across all Key Stages.
- Even when allowing for prior attainment and other variables, most ethnic groups make more progress than White British pupils with similar characteristics and levels of prior attainment. However, Black Caribbean, White and Black Caribbean, Black Other, Pakistani, Gypsy/Roma and Travellers of Irish Heritage pupils make less progress at primary school than similar White British pupils.
- While all ethnic groups are less likely to achieve the expected level in the teacher assessment than in the test in English at Key Stage 2 and 3, there are larger than average differences between English teacher assessment and test results for Asian and Black pupils and for pupils for whom English is an additional language.
- In 2006 it was found that for 41 per cent of Bangladeshi and 27 per cent of Pakistani pupils English was not their first or main language. English as an Additional Language (EAL) plays a significant part in the outcomes for some minority ethnic groups.

The above data confirms the reality, that while some minority ethnic groups are out-performing their White counterparts, others such as Caribbean, Pakistani and Bangladeshi pupils are significantly under-performing. It's also important that we recognize that regional and local outcomes vary significantly. For example Caribbean pupils do well in a few cities at GCSE, while in others their progress is slow throughout secondary schooling (DfES 2006). However, the topical attainment debate in 2007 is focusing on White working-class boys' progress in secondary schools compared with minority ethnic pupils' progress. This reflects the complex interconnectedness of issues of attainment and progression when comparing and reviewing groups by either class or ethnicity.

For teachers and teaching assistants, the challenge is to identify how their own individual actions and continued professional development can be shaped to impact on the underachievement of individuals and groups in their classroom, particularly those from minority ethnic communities. According to the GTC (2006): 'Teachers believe that for pupils, the most important issues to address are social class, race/ethnicity and gender. Asked what is needed to tackle underachievement, the overwhelming majority of teachers believe that "the achievement of each individual child needs to be maximised".' They identify a mix of measures to help, including raising parental and school expectations of the child.

Predominantly White staff

Over the last 20 years, the call has been for the education workforce to become more diverse to reflect the full range of ethnic population in Britain's schools and local authorities (Ross 2002; Modood 1988). Alistair Ross argues that the character, ubiquity, pervasiveness and duration of school make it particularly important that teaching is a profession that reflects the population of multi-ethnic Britain. Teachers from the ethnic minorities are certainly under-represented. In 1983 it was reported that 2 per cent of teachers were from minority communities. The Training Development Agency for schools reported in 2006 that current recruitment to training courses achieve 6.7 per cent applicants from minority ethnic communities across England. In 2003, the proportion of Black pupils, at 19.6 per cent, was more than six times the proportion of Black teachers. The proportion of Black, Asian and minority ethnic pupils in London schools was 43.5 per cent, but the proportion of Black, Asian and minority ethnic teachers was just 7.4 per cent. The figures for teachers from minority ethnic backgrounds are often treated with caution as response to questions asking for ethnic origins in surveys are often incomplete (DfES 2006). Nationally, there is a drive to increase the representation of minority ethnic staff in the classroom. Researchers are suggesting that initial teacher training is not putting enough emphasis on the needs of pupils from different cultural, faith and linguistic backgrounds and that teachers and teaching assistants are often emerging from training without the knowledge, skills, understanding or attitudes needed for successful work in multicultural schools (Runnymede Trust 2003a).

There are several debates running, including the need for more role models from minority ethnic communities (Baez and Clarke 1990). In writing the foreword for *Made in Britain* Gary Phillips said 'Black and minority ethnic (BME) young people, like all other young people, need role models from every area of society but in particular role models from BME background' (D'Souza 2005: vii). Others highlight the need to challenge racism and promote diversity by having more BME representation in schools (Arora 2005; Cline 2002). For the foreseeable future we are unlikely to achieve the level of BME adults' representation in the classroom that would reflect current future minority ethnic pupil population in schools.

Increasing proportions of students from minority ethnic communities are entering Higher Education, however they are not studying to enter the teaching profession. In the teaching workforce, teachers from minority ethnic communities are less likely to be in the positions of headteacher or deputy than White teachers, even when allowance is made for length of service. Teachers from minority ethnic communities are more likely to be on the basic scales. The Higher Education Statistics Agency report for 2004/5 shows that universities are not attracting enough students from minority ethnic communities on to education courses (HESA 2004/5); teacher training and teaching assistant courses indicate significant under-representation of candidates from minority ethnic communities; and the poor retention and progression of minority ethnic teachers and teaching assistants are cause for concern (Osler 1997; Jones 1999; Ross 2001). In light of this, the emphasis on creating a whole school ethos where pupils from minority ethnic communities can feel included, valued and able to participate becomes increasingly important.

Gary Howard in his book *We Can't Teach What We Don't Know* (1999), suggests that teachers need to know themselves very well in order to take on knowing others in an open and respectful way. He advocates teachers spending time getting to know the backgrounds of children they are teaching, a journey he highly recommends. When we explore ethnic diversity we are mostly talking about people with origins in significantly different lifestyles and cultural experiences from us. Research shows that as significant adults in the classroom (teachers or teaching assistants), rarely do we explore who we are, how we come to believe the things we take for granted and use for forming our assumptions and intuitions. In *A White Teacher Talks About Race*, Julie Landsman outlines her heritage and the influences it brings to her work as a teacher in a school where 60–80 per cent of students are non European Americans. She said 'my culture is: East Louis jazz, Southern cooking and the work ethic from my father's side; New England Puritanism, pot roast, classical music on my mother's side' (Landsman 2001). Knowing what we bring to the classroom helps us to shape pupils' experiences. The debate today is not about individual or institutional racism, it is more focused on our level of self-awareness, our ability to take ownership and responsibility for our day-to-day engagement with our environment (Hooks 1989; Delgado and Stefancic 2000). This should lead to our never making assumptions about an individual based on the racial, ethnic, or cultural group to which he or she appears to belong. We can then get to know and treat each student first and foremost as an individual.

Conclusion

The classroom must be an inclusive environment, where difference does not displace or undermine each individual's sense of self. Significant adults within the classroom have a duty to ensure equality of outcome for all pupils, regardless of race, gender, ethnicity, ability or sexual orientation. Educators and support staff have an important role in ensuring pupils' equal access to an opportunity to learn and develop. To this end they must work to avoid unwittingly discriminating against individuals or groups. In promoting equality of opportunity and good race relations, the starting point is to emphasize similarities rather than differences and the strength that having things in common brings to the classroom, so that differences can be seen to provide opportunities for learning exciting and interesting things about other cultures.

Given the growing opportunities for teachers to engage with increasing numbers of minority ethnic groups of pupils, their training and continuing professional development must include greater emphasis on what can be done to maximize the outcome for minority ethnic children and young people in the school environment. Clearly there is a challenge for teachers and teaching assistants on an individual level to be reflective and build their own understanding of the minority ethnic groups within the school and classrooms where they are working. The Every Child Matters agenda is very much about how we contribute individually to collective networks that will help individual children stay safe, enjoy, achieve and maximize their life chances.

Reflecting on values and practice

1   Often we achieve success with one or two children through building an effective rapport and just getting on well with them. Reflect on what helps you to make those successful relationships.
2   What would it mean to *challenge yourself* to overcome any barriers to building good relationships with minority ethnic pupils?
3   Take time to find out the ethnic diversity of your school and how it has changed over the last 5 years.

Suggested further reading

Commission for Equality and Human Rights: www.cehr.org.uk.
Ethnic Minority Achievement Unit: www.standards.dfes.gov.uk/ethnicminorities.
Refugee Council: http: www.refugeecouncil.org.uk.
Runnymede Trust: www.runnymedetrust.org/projects/education/resourcesforSchools. html.
Teachernet English as an Additional Language: www.teachernet.gov.uk/teachingand learning/library/EALteaching/.

References

Adams, C. (1987) *Across Seven Seas and Thirteen Rivers: Life Stories of Pioneer Sylheti Settlers in Britain*, London: Eastside Books.
Arora, R.K. (2005) *Race and Ethnicity in Education*, Aldershot: Ashgate.
Beaz, T. and Clarke, E. (1990) 'Reading, Writing and Role Models', *Community, Technical, and Junior College Journal* 60(3): 31–4.
Cantle, T. (2001) *Community Cohesion: A Report of the Independent Team*, London: Home Office.
Claire, H. (1996) *Reclaiming Our Pasts*, Stoke-on-Trent: Trentham Books.
Cline, T., de Abreu, G., Fihosy, C., Gray, H., Lambert, H. and Neale, J. (2002) *Minority Ethnic Pupils in Mainly White Schools*, Nottingham: DfES.
Commission for Racial Equality (1997) *Routes of the Future: Ethnic Diversity in the Making of Britain*, Northampton: Bemrose Press.
D'Souza, S. and Clarke, P. (2005) *Made in Britain – Inspirational Role Models from British Black and Minority Ethnic Communities*, Harlow: Pearson Education.
Dadzie, S. (2000) *Toolkit for Tackling Racism in Schools*, Stoke-on-Trent: Trentham Books.

Delgado, R. and Stefancic, J. (eds) (2000) *Critical Race Theory: The Cutting Edge*, Philadelphia, PA: Temple University Press.

Department of Education and Skills (2006) *Ethnicity and Education: The Evidence of Minority Ethnic Pupils Age 5–16*, Nottingham: DfES.

Fryer, P. (1984) *Staying Power: The History of Black People in Britain*, London: Pluto Press

General Teaching Council (2005) *Mapping Opinion*. Online: available at www.gtce. org.uk/research/tsurvey.

Greater London Authority (2006) *Black Teachers in London*, London: GLA.

Green, P. (2000) *DIECEC Raising the Standards – A Practical Guide to Raising Ethnic Minority and Bilingual Pupils' Achievement*, Stoke-on-Trent: Trentham Books.

Higher Education Statistics Agency (2006) *Students in Higher Education Institutions 2004/5*, London: HESA.

Holmes, C. (1978) *Immigration and Minorities in British Society*, London: George Allen & Unwin.

Hooks, B. (1998) *Taking Back: Thinking Feminist. Thinking Black*, Cambridge: South End Press.

Howard, G. (1999) *We Can't Teach What We Don't Know – White Teachers, Multicultural Schools*, New York: Teachers College Press.

Jones, R. (1999). *Teaching Racism or Tackling it? Multicultural Stories from White Beginning Teachers*, Stoke-on-Trent: Trentham Books.

Knowles, E. and Riley, W. (2006) *Another Spanner in the Works – Challenging Prejudice and Racism in Mainly White Schools*, Stoke-on-Trent: Trentham Books.

Landsman, J. (2001) *A White Teacher Talks About Race*, Lanham, MD: Scarecrow Press.

Mason, D. (2000) *Oxford Modern Britain – Race and Ethnicity in Modern Britain*, Oxford: Oxford University Press.

Merriman, N. (ed.) (1993) *The People of London: Fifteen Thousand Years of Settlement From Overseas*, London: Museum of London.

Modood, T. (1988) *Not Easy Being British, Culture and Citizenship*, Stoke-on-Trent: Runnymede Trust and Trentham Books.

National Statistics (2003) *2001 UK Census*, London: Home Office.

Nicolson, C. (1974) *Strangers to England: Immigration to England 1100–1945*, London: Wayland Publisher.

Osler, A. (1997) *The Education and Career of Black Teachers – Changing Identities, Changing Lives*, Buckingham: Open University Press.

Oxford University Press (2002) – *Concise English Dictionary*, Oxford: Oxford University Press.

Phillips, T. (2005) 'After 7/7: Sleepwalking into segregation', speech given to the Manchester Council for Community Relations. Online: available at www.cre.gov.uk.

Ross, A. (2001) *Ethnic Minority Teachers in the Teaching Workforce*, London: IPSE Occasional Paper.

Ross, A. (2002) *Classroom Assistants Won't End Teacher Shortage*, London: Institute for Public Policy Research.

Rowley, S.J. and Moore, J.A. (2002) 'When Who I Am Impacts How I Am Represented: Addressing Minority Student Issues in Different Contexts', *Roeper Review* 24: 63–7.

Runnymede Trust (2003a) *Complementing Teachers – A Practical Guide to Promoting Race and Identity on the Agenda*, Stoke-on-Trent: Trentham Books.

Runnymede Trust (2003b) 'Black and Minority Ethnic issues in teaching and learning', London. Briefing Paper.

Chapter 5

The influence of gender on achievement

Steve Bartlett and Diana Burton

Introduction

We are all affected in some way by issues of social class, ethnicity and gender in our society. In this chapter we look specifically at the influence of gender on the achievement of pupils in our education system. We consider how, for much of the twentieth century, research concentrated on the inequality of opportunity for girls and the social changes that have attempted to rectify this. We then look at the current debates surrounding the apparently poor achievement of boys and the culture of underperformance accompanying this. We conclude by suggesting that any examination of the self-perception, motivation and achievement of children and young people needs to include a consideration of social class, ethnicity and gender issues. It is only by being aware of such factors that policies promoting social inclusion can have any hope of success. All classroom practitioners, including teaching assistants, need to understand these significant forces in pupils' lives in order to make their practice more effective.

Sex and gender

Before we consider the impact of gender on pupil achievement it is important to examine the terminology that is used in such debates. The term 'sex' is usually used when referring to our biological make up. It identifies us as male or female. Biological differences include chromosomes, hormones and physical sexual characteristics such as sexual organs, body hair, physique, etc. Gender refers to the social construction of masculine and feminine. It is what we expect males and females to be 'like' in terms of behaviour, appearance, beliefs and attitudes. There has been a continuing debate as to how much of our maleness and femaleness is biologically determined and how much is socially constructed.

A biological determinist position holds that our biological sex is significant in determining us as individuals. Thus mothering and caring are presented as female traits while aggression and protecting are male. While we are all individuals and we live in different social environments, our biological make-up plays the major part in determining who we are and how we behave. This biological base can be seen as underpinning many social explanations for the structure of families and the conjugal roles within them. An alternative view is that although there are certain biological differences between males and females, it is society and the culture that we live in that creates the notions of masculinity and femininity.

Early feminist writers such as Oakley (1975) wished to highlight the significance of cultural as opposed to biological factors in explaining the ongoing socially inferior position of women in society. Their argument was that it was the social constructions of gender and sexuality that led to the oppression of women. The biological accounts were seen as part of male social control that perpetuated the myth of male superiority. The whole notion of masculinity and femininity from this perspective was socially rather than biologically determined and could thus be challenged. What still remains unclear is the dividing line between biological and social influences on an individual's gender construction. There are physical differences between males and females and these become more obvious as we grow up and move through adolescence and into adulthood. However, there is a wide variation both within and across the genders in terms of individual physical characteristics. What is deemed as attractive to the opposite sex is different from society to society and changes over time with fashion. Clothing, diet and body building/reducing exercises to change our appearance are all used and with advances in medical science people can radically alter their physical characteristics and even biological sex. In modern societies and across a range of cultures any presentation of a clear uncomplicated sexual divide would be an over simplification.

Influences upon the creation of gender

If we were to consider different societies in history and around the world we see many differences in gender roles. In her now classic anthropological account, Mead (1935) found great variation in the roles of men and women in a study of three tribes in New Guinea. In western culture the representation of gender as a binary split between masculine and feminine make them appear as opposites with everyone falling either side of the sexual binary line. In this way stereotypes of male and female can be presented as completely opposed e.g. male versus female, hard versus soft, rational versus emotional (Kehily 2001). Thus from birth we are brought up to be male or female, and to be mistaken for being of the opposite sex from that with which you identify, is a significant concern as we seek to maintain our self-identity.

While teenagers strive to be independent from the older generation they are also subject to strong peer pressures. Gender characteristics that stereotype appropriate physical appearance and behaviour can cause pressure to conform, particularly on young people who are coming to terms with themselves as they develop. To be identified as different or 'other' can have a significant effect upon the self-image of young people. Kehily (2001) examines the issues of sexuality in school and how identities are negotiated and created. Pupil interaction and perceptions are significant in the 'othering' process. Labels become attached to pupils and some are more difficult to resist or counter than others. Language plays a very powerful part in this process and use of sexual insults such as 'gay', 'queer' or 'slag' may have lasting repercussions on the identities, future inter-actions and sexual behaviour of the young people involved (Vicars 2006).

Masculinities and femininities

Stereotypical images of boys in school include loud, boisterous behaviour, lack of interest in studying and generally taking a rushed and untidy approach to work. Images of stereotypical girl behaviour include being quiet, hard work-ing, neat and careful in appearance. If we look at real groups of young people and consider the broad range that exists, for example, in terms of behaviour, beliefs, values, appearance, we see how inappropriate it is to use such stereo-types. Actually the majority of boys are not disruptive in the classroom and all girls do not get on with their work quietly. We should be wary of using too rigid a definition of what constitutes female or male behaviour of young people. Some writers, such as Paechter (1998), Mac an Ghaill (1994) and Swain (2004), speak of a range of masculinities and femininities thus allowing for greater variation. Reay (2001: 153) suggests that femininity is 'dynamic, various and changing' and it is more useful to think in terms of multiple femininities.

Swain (2004) says that pupils live within the context of their own com-munities and that these wider contexts influence the individual school policies and cultures. Thus schools are influenced by local employment opportunities, housing type, religious and ethnic mix of the area. Within this Swain says that each school also has its own *gender regime*. This 'consists of . . . individual personnel expectations, rules, routines and a hierarchical ordering of particular practices' (p. 182). It is interesting to consider the integral part that gender relationships play in school life and how these vary depending upon the ethos of the school. School uniform, lining up in the playground or outside the classroom, class lists that separate boys and girls, and how pupils and teachers are addressed are all instances where gender may or may nor be highlighted in formal school procedures. There are many ways in which gender is also part of informal school processes, e.g. the arrangement of each individual classroom and where pupils sit, who children play with at break times and what they play, the number of pupils choosing different subjects at secondary school, the number of male and female adults employed by the school and their positions of responsibility. Since schools are a key part of the wider socialization process they both influence and are influenced by, gender relationships.

A historical view of recent developments in gender relations in Britain

The way in which the roles of men and women and their relationships to each other vary over time can be illustrated by considering the comparatively short period from Victorian England to the present day. In the early 1800s Britain was very much a patriarchal society. Women were not able to vote, own property or obtain a divorce. Within the middle classes women were effectively either under the control of their father or their husband. It was men who governed the empire and the society, ran businesses and supported the family. Women did not work and were confined to a life that revolved around the home. Boys from the more affluent classes would be educated at public and grammar schools but the education of girls would be primarily left to governesses, conducted in the home based upon the knowledge suitable for a lady. For the working classes life was much harder and both men and women worked though women did the more menial factory work and were paid less than men. In the early educational provision for the working classes girls were able to attend school as well as boys though both were taught appropriately to the social expectations of the time.

It has taken many years of political and social pressure for women to gain legal equality with men. They gained the right to divorce and importantly to retain their own property upon divorce. Women gained the vote in the early 1900s and the Sex Discrimination Act of 1975 outlawed discrimination on the grounds of gender.

From this date women, legally at least, had equality with men. However while there had been these legal changes there were still economic and social differences that were strongly influenced by gender. In employment terms women remained very under-represented in many, usually more highly paid, professions and the average earnings of women remained well below that of men. It has actually proved very difficult for women to 'break into' male dominated areas such as medicine, law and engineering. At the time of the Sex Discrimination Act it was still widely accepted that a woman's place remained in the home and that the man was the main 'breadwinner'. In this way women's employment was largely seen as temporary before starting a family or as a way of supplementing the family income when the children were older. Changes in attitude have continued to take place and over the years women have increasingly taken up careers in many areas that previously they did not. However, while many women now have more demanding jobs their average earnings still lag behind those of men and they remain under-represented in many areas of higher paid employment (www.statistics.gov.uk).

Social and political attitudes are reflected in education. State education has been provided throughout the twentieth century to all pupils regardless of gender. In the early part of the 1900s the elementary schools were co-educational. While primary schools have always been co-educational, the introduction of a selective secondary system saw the development of single sex grammar schools and often, though not always, single sex secondary modern schools. It was the development of new large comprehensive schools from the 1960s onwards that saw boys and girls taught together in their secondary education. From this time it could be argued that there was gender equality in state education.

Gender and achievement

Being taught in the same school did not remove the impact of gender upon a pupil's experiences. In the 1960s the inequalities in society were reflected in the classroom where teachers, peers and parents treated boys and girls very differently. At that time it was usual to have gender specific stereotypical expectations of pupils, so curricular activities were unashamedly contrived around them, e.g. needlework and typing for girls, and metalwork and technical drawing for boys.

In the 1970s and 1980s much feminist research in education was concerned with the perceived underachievement of girls and how the education process worked to maintain this through discrimination and marginalization. The gender differences were maintained and highlighted through the processes of schooling, which involved the separation of the genders through school uniform, a gender-specific curriculum and differential expectations of behaviour. This was further enforced through the attitude of teachers, peers, parents and later, their usually male, employers. Feminist researchers were interested to show how the ambitions of female students remained low and how they were discouraged in a variety of ways from choosing the 'hard' mathematical and scientific subjects so important to future employment prospects in favour of the more 'feminine' arts and humanities.

Oakley (1975) looked at the socialization of young children and how they acquire their gender roles from home, school and peers. Children learn gender expectations from the society surrounding them and these lessons are reinforced through play. Whyte (1983) looked at gender stereotyping and bias in the primary school curriculum. This was displayed through reading schemes and lesson content that emphasized the different positions of men and women in society. Sharpe (1976) considered the influence of gender stereotypes in secondary schools and how this encouraged teenage girls to behave in 'feminine' ways and to develop gendered career aspirations. Spender (1982) investigated interaction in the classroom, language and the curriculum. She noted the marginal position of girls in the classroom and the message this gave about their future roles in society.

Curriculum strategies

In the 1970s and 1980s strategies were developed to make the curriculum more girl-friendly in response to such concerns and there have been many initiatives designed to improve the achievement of girls by raising awareness, altering attitudes, increasing ambition. Consideration was given to the curriculum and teaching methods. The Girls into Science and Technology (GIST) project, for example, was a four-year project begun in 1979 that investigated the reasons for girls' underachievement in science and technology, and encouraged teachers to develop classroom strategies to change this (Smail 2000). Similarly, Genderwatch was a practical evaluation pack that promoted an action research approach enabling teachers to monitor gender in all areas of the daily life of their schools. By using and adapting a proforma teachers were able to examine curriculum content, their teaching practices and how pupils were treated in all aspects of their school experience. The pack was designed to raise awareness and encourage the adoption of positive anti-discriminatory action (Myers 1987). These initiatives tended to be individual rather than coordinated and Murphy and Gipps (1993) suggested that although they worked for many, mainly middle-class, girls, they were singularly unsuccessful for a great many others and, in fact, provoked a male backlash.

Raising girls' achievement

While the raising of awareness and the development work that accompanied it were all based on the belief in the underachievement of girls relative to boys, the actual figures show that the reality was not that straightforward. Even in the 1970s girls were outperforming boys in English and modern foreign languages. Also more girls were achieving five or more O-level passes (equivalent to A*–C, GCSE) than boys. However, because these included subjects that were seen as low status such as home economics and because boys were doing better at maths and sciences, which were regarded as 'hard' subjects of high status, then girls were perceived as underachieving (Francis 2000). Also it should be noted that the selective system of grammar and secondary modern schools, in operation before the development of the comprehensive system, had favoured boys due to the larger number of places available in boys' grammar schools as opposed to those admitting girls. Thus boys did not need to score as highly as girls in the 11+ to secure a grammar school education. It was not the case then that girls were necessarily underachieving but that their success was not being recognized and that they were not offered the same opportunities or encouragement as boys in order to pursue the more rewarding economic options. Girls' futures were still being perceived as domestically based.

The Conservative government came to power in 1979 emphasizing competition, individual achievement and success. They did not trust the liberal education establishment and sought to reform the education system. While not being concerned with the promotion of equal opportunities, one of their reforms, the introduction of the national curriculum, had what is now often regarded as a significant impact on the achievements of girls (Francis 2000). From its inception all pupils were required to study the national curriculum. Thus it was no longer possible for boys or girls to 'drop' some subjects in favour of others. The Conservatives were also responsible for the introduction of testing of all pupils at different stages in their compulsory education and the production of league tables based on GCSE, A level and the earlier Key Stage test results. These were and are used to judge overall school performance, making the achievements of boys and girls more transparent then ever. They show how the performance of both boys and girls has steadily improved. What has caught the public attention though is that the improvement in the results of girls has been greater than that of boys. While continuing to outperform boys in language subjects, girls have caught up boys in maths and the sciences. Concern is now focused on the performance of boys.

Current performance of boys and girls

While being aware that Gorard (2000) and Hammersley (2001) have stressed a need for caution when interpreting statistics on gender and examination performance, using the statistics from the DfES (www.dfes.gov) we can see that from 2001/2 to 2005/6 the percentage of all pupils gaining five or more GCSE grades at A*–C has increased. Girls have continued to attain a higher percentage of five or more passes at A*–C than boys. This had previously been noted to be the case with O levels (Francis 2000). What is significant is that girls are now doing better than boys in all the core subjects of maths, English and science, apart from single sciences when taken separately.

When looking at national curriculum assessment a similar picture also appears of a general trend towards increasing achievement of both boys *and* girls over the years since national testing began. Girls are on average doing better than boys and this is particularly noticeable in the older age groups at Key Stage 3 (www.dfes.ac.uk).

However, it is important for teaching assistants to realize that though girls' overall average scores have perhaps always been higher than boys', the difference in performance is not that great with high percentages of boys continuing to perform well. Also, within both boys and girls there is a wide range of achievement with many young people continuing to experience academic and behavioural difficulties at school. It is these pupils that need the support of education professionals.

Explanations for boys' underachievement

Elwood (2005) notes that over the last twenty years the debate has shifted from being about the creation of equal opportunities and improving the educational experiences of girls to concerns about male underachievement and disadvantage (p. 337). Connolly (2004) suggests that the panic surrounding the underachievement of boys has been rather an overreaction. The media has portrayed boys as falling behind and homed in on an apparent growth of a 'laddish' culture among teenage boys that is anti-study, against school values and leads to underachievement. Various explanations have been offered to explain why girls are performing better than boys.

Genetic differences

Historically the assumption has been, perhaps due to male dominant views, that women were the weaker and thus the inferior sex that needed to be protected. The consistently higher level of achievement by girls academically may now lead some to the conclusion that this is due to genetic differences, i.e. the intellectual superiority of women. Noble *et al.* (2001) point out that, interesting though this notion is, the evidence supporting it is currently very thin. They also warn against the taking up of stereotypes that ignore the fact that difference in achievement between genders is not that large and more importantly that great variations in achievement occur within the genders. Feminist analysts would suggest that the 'moral panic' that has accompanied this perceived failure of boys and the demand to rectify the situation is a reflection of the fear within the male dominated political establishment.

Social and economic change

In recent decades there have been enormous changes in the economy that have had repercussions on how people earn their living, the organization of the family and the amount of leisure time and disposable income available. The traditional occupations based upon heavy industry dominated by male workers that involved strength and training in traditional skills have disappeared. This has had significant effects upon communities based around these industries such as mining, ship-building, steel and deep sea fishing (Noble *et al.* 2001). Newer forms of employment are service based and seen as being more tradi- tionally female. The male is now no longer the only, or even the major 'breadwinner' in the family. Thus the traditional masculine image in working- class communities is no longer applicable as it was even 20 years ago and many working-class boys see no particular role for themselves. They see no need to work hard at school as it will make little difference to their future. At the same time these boys emphasize and play out their masculinities at school where it is important to be seen as 'hard', 'cool', not a 'poof' or a 'swot' (Smith 2003). It can of course be argued that working-class boys could always get masculine jobs in the past and so have never really had reason to work hard at school. Significantly, Connolly (2006) suggests that masculin- ities and femininities are not just about gender alone but must be seen as combining with social class and ethnicity to 'produce differing and enduring forms of identity' (p. 15). It is this complex mix that teachers and teaching assistants need to be aware of.

School culture

It is suggested that schools have become more female oriented in recent decades and that school culture now works in favour of girls and against the achievement of boys (Noble *et al.* 2001 and Smith 2003). It is assumed that the assessment regimes have developed to favour girls with more emphasis on coursework rather than final exams. However, this trend has reversed in recent years with no significant falling back of girls' performance.

The curriculum is said to favour girls with little to excite boys and the type of learning is considered not to suit boys' learning approaches. This point ignores the many areas of the curriculum where the content has been specifically chosen to attract boys. Also learning approaches do vary between girls as well as between boys and girls. Arnot and Miles (2005) suggest that the increasing emphasis on a performative school system has led to greater resistance from working-class boys who have a history of low achievement. This they say is being misinterpreted as a new development, termed 'laddishness'.

Jones and Myhill (2004) noted how beliefs about identity can inform teachers' perceptions resulting in a tendency to associate boys with under-achievement and girls with high achievement. This labelling process may contribute to the low expectations of boys thus creating a self-fulfilling prophecy. Elwood (2005) says that for many teachers, teaching assistants and policymakers boys are now seen as 'poor boys' or that 'boys will be boys' or as 'problem' boys. Proposed solutions to low achievement arising from these stereotypes involve shifting classroom practices in order to engage boys' interests. She points to a whole raft of initiatives and policies and associated publicity involved in tackling the problem of boys' underachievement.

Conclusions

In summarizing the arguments concerning gender and achievement we can say that the performance of boys and girls overall has improved throughout the 1990s and the 2000s, that girls have been improving faster than boys and that they are now outperforming boys in many subjects and are at least performing more or less equally in all. However, to portray girls as achieving and boys as underachieving is too simplistic a view (Arnot and Miles 2005; Gipps 2006; Elwood 2005). It should be noted that the differences in overall performance of boys and girls are not that great. It is the improvement in performance of girls from the more middle-class backgrounds in all subjects that has caused the rise in girls' performance overall. Boys from middle-class backgrounds continue to generally perform well. Boys and girls from the lower socio-economic groups continue to under perform when compared to their more affluent peers. Thus, as Connolly (2006) says, while gender does exert an influence on GCSE attainment, this is overshadowed by the effects of social class and ethnicity.

In conclusion we can say that there are many influences on the achievement of pupils with social background, ethnicity and gender all being significant.

Effective teaching assistants must take account of these while endeavouring to treat pupils as the individuals they are.

Reflection on values and practice

1   Reflect on all the different jobs done by adults in your school and the gender of those who do them. What conclusions can you draw from the results of this exercise in terms of gender and employment in your school? Do your findings have any policy implications?

2   Keep a log of all the pupils you work with on an individual basis during one school day. In this record note the age and gender of the pupil, why you were working together, and what you both did. When analysing your log are there any gender related factors that you notice? If this exercise was extended over a longer period of one week, would this impact upon your findings? What strategies might you need to consider in light of your finding?

3   Observe pupils working in class. How do different groups and individuals work differently over a period of time? How long is spent on task, in cooperative behaviour and what is the quality of work produced? Is gender a factor in any of the variations you notice? How might you intervene to change things?

Suggested further reading

Browne, N. (2004) *Gender Equity in the Early Years*, Maidenhead: Open University Press.

Oakley, A. (1975) *Sex, Gender and Society*, London: Temple Smith.

Skelton, C. Francis, B. and Smulyan, L. (eds) (2006) *The Sage Handbook of Gender and Education*, London: Sage.

References

Arnot, M. and Miles, P. (2005) 'A Reconstruction of the Gender Agenda: The Contradictory Gender Dimensions in New Labour's Educational and Economic Policy', *Oxford Review of Education* 31(1): 173–89.

Connolly, P. (2004) *Boys and Schooling in the Early Years*, London: RoutledgeFalmer.

Connolly, P. (2006) 'The Effects of Social Class and Ethnicity on Gender Differences in GCSE Attainment: A Secondary Analysis of the Youth Cohort Study of England and Wales 1997–2001', *The British Educational Research Journal* 32(1): 3–21.

Elwood, J. (2005) 'Gender and Achievement: What Have Exams Got to do With It?' *Oxford Review of Education* 31(3): 373–93.

Francis, B. (2000) *Boys, Girls and Achievement. Addressing the Classroom Issues*, London: Routledge.

Gipps, C. (1993) 'The Structure for Assessment and Recording', in O'Hear, P. and White, J. (eds) *Assessing the National Curriculum*, London: Paul Chapman.

Gipps, C. (2006) 'Gender, Performance and Learning Style', Public Lecture, University of Wolverhampton, 10 May 2006.

Gorard, S. (2000) *Education and Social Justice: The Changing Composition of Schools and its Implications*, Cardiff: University of Wales Press.

Hammersley, M. (2001) 'Obvious, All Too Obvious? Methodological Issues in Using Sex/Gender as a Variable in Educational Research', in Francis, B. and Skelton, C. (eds) *Investigating Gender: Contemporary Perspectives in Education*, Buckingham: Open University Press.

Jones, S. and Myhill, D. (2004) '"Troublesome Boys" and "Compliant Girls": Gender Identity and Perceptions of Achievement and Underachievement', *British Journal of Sociology of Education*, 25(5): 547–61.

Kehily, M. (2001) 'Issues of Gender and Sexuality in Schools', in Francis, B. and Skelton, C. (eds) *Investigating Gender: Contemporary Perspectives in Education*, Buckingham: Open University Press.

Mac an Ghaill, M. (1994) *The Making of Men: Masculinities, Sexuality and Schooling*, Buckingham: Open University Press.

Mead, M. (1935) *Sex and Temperament in Three Primitive Societies*, London: Routledge & Kegan Paul.

Murphy, P.F. and Gipps, C.V. (1993) *Equity in the Classroom*, London: Falmer Press.

Myers, K. (1987) *Genderwatch: Self-Assessment Schedules for Use in Schools*, London: Schools Curriculum Development Council.

Noble, C., Brown, J. and Murphy, J. (2001) *How to Raise Boys' Achievement*, London: David Fulton.

Oakley, A. (1975) *Sex, Gender and Society*, London: Temple Smith.

Paechter, C. (1998) *Educating the Other: Gender, Power and Schooling*, London: Routledge.

Reay, D. (2001), 'The Paradox of Contemporary Femininities in Education: Combining Fluidity with Fixity', in Francis, B. and Skelton, C. (eds) *Investigating Gender: Contemporary Perspectives in Education*, Buckingham: Open University Press.

Sharpe, S. (1976) *Just Like a Girl: How Girls Learn to be Women*, Harmondsworth: Penguin.

Smail, B. (2000) 'Has the Mountain Moved? The Girls into Science and Technology Project 1979–83' in Myers, K. (ed.) *Whatever Happened to Equal Opportunities in Schools? Gender Equality Initiatives in Education*, Buckingham: Open University Press.

Smith, E. (2003) Failing Boys and Moral Panics: Perspectives on the Underachievement Debate, *British Journal of Educational Studies*, 51(3): 282–95.

Spender, D. (1982) *Invisible Women: The Schooling Scandal*, London: Writers and Readers.

Swain, J. (2004) 'The Resources and Strategies that 10–11-Year-Old Boys Use to Construct Masculinities in the School Setting', *British Educational Research Journal*, 30(1): 167–85.

Vicars, M. (2006) 'Who Are You Calling Queer? Sticks and Stones Can Break My Bones But Names Will Always Hurt Me', *British Educational Research Journal* 32(3): 347–61.

Whyte, J. (1983) *Beyond the Wendy House: Sex-Role Stereotyping in Primary Schools*, York: Longman.

Chapter 6

The inclusion assistant

Young people with high-level support needs in mainstream schools, colleges and universities: developing good practice[1]

Micheline Mason

The most exciting aspect of educational change over the last decade or so has been the inclusion of children with high-level support needs into mainstream provision. Rising to this challenge has brought about the beginnings of a seismic change in the values and culture of the establishments in which it has happened. However, the numbers of such children are relatively small, and much is still to be learned before all disabled children can be certain of a warm welcome and appropriate support in their local mainstream provision.

Although the move towards greater inclusion has been attributed to progressive government policies, it has in fact been driven by parents of disabled children and disabled people themselves. This has been an international phenomena and has led to the right to inclusive education being adopted in the UN Convention of Rights of Persons with Disabilities in New York 2006 which states that parties shall ensure that:

a   persons with disabilities are not excluded from the general education system on the basis of disability, and that children with disabilities are not excluded from free and compulsory primary education, or from secondary education, on the basis of disability;
b   persons with disabilities can access an inclusive, quality and free primary education and secondary education on an equal basis with others in the communities in which they live;
c   reasonable accommodation of the individual's requirements is provided;
d   persons with disabilities receive the support required, within the general education system, to facilitate their effective education;
e   effective individualized support measures are provided in environments that maximize academic and social development, consistent with the goal of full inclusion.

---

1   Much of the material in this chapter is based on action-based research carried out between 2003 and 2006 by Micheline Mason and Christine Burke when they developed a training course for adults who work one-to-one with young people with high-level support needs (AIE 2007).

I have documented the rationale for this movement in a recent book *Incurably Human* (Mason 2005), which includes the history of the Special Education System, its roots in Eugenics and the development of the medical model of disability. The medical model of disability attributes all the problems faced by disabled people to the impairment itself. In this model disabled children, especially those with high-level support needs, are prepared for a life dominated by therapy and segregated services in the shape of special schools, residential homes, sheltered workshops, adult training centres and day centres. The book recounts the rise of the disability movement, and the development of the social model of disability. This model comes from disabled people. It acknowledges the difficulties inherent in living with a significant impairment, but places the factors that actually disable a person as outside of the individual onto the physical and social barriers within society, which can, by definition, be removed. This model makes links to the move towards inclusive education by identifying that the key barriers, and therefore the solutions, are based within the way that education is currently conceptualized and arranged.

The long-term goal of the inclusion movement is to create a different type of society which can embrace both the gifts and the needs of all its citizens without recourse to segregation or institutionalization.

Although springing from the struggles of people who are personally affected by these issues, increasing numbers of people, including teachers and teaching assistants, have been inspired by the potential benefit to everyone of an inclusive society. Many have become passionate supporters of change, basing their beliefs on the successes they have experienced within their own schools. All supporters of inclusion come to understand that the change needed requires the nurturing of real connections between children across the full diversity of their community. For example, Nigel Hutton a head teacher and chair of 'Heading for Inclusion' (a group of head teachers and senior staff who are dedicated to developing the practice of inclusive education) argued in a Heading for Inclusion press release (6/7/06):

> Inclusive education is the future of education. In order for us to live in a safe, sustainable world we need to encourage our young people to build local communities based on mutual respect and human values. Those of us working in inclusive schools know that the only way to achieve that is to create a new kind of school – neither mainstream or special – but a school which effectively addresses the needs of all its pupils. The ills of the world today are due to a lack of understanding of difference whether that be cultural, linguistic, political, religious or physical! Segregated education serves to deepen that misunderstanding.

Ideological stances are very different from the day-to-day experiences of disabled children and young people, parents, teachers and teaching assistants.

Many families have started out passionately wanting an inclusive placement for their son or daughter only to retreat in defeat, battered into the comparative safety of a special school, from where, in their disillusionment, they have argued that this is a reason for the permanent existence of special schools, especially for children with high-level support needs. At the same time, however, some children have been enabled to belong to a mainstream school, progress to Further Education or Higher Education and emerge at the end as an extraordinary group of young adults, knowing how to achieve lives for themselves possibly unknown in their degree of 'ordinariness' by any previous generation of disabled people, i.e. living independently, being in control of their own lives and the supports they need to live it; having relationships; following hobbies and interests; having a voice in the world (AIE 2005a). For most of these young people, the support of their teaching assistant was crucial to the success of their school placements.

The teaching assistant debate

In the early days of integration, disabled children were only allowed into mainstream schools if they brought a full-time 'minder' with them in the form of what was then called a 'Learning Support Assistant'. They generally took complete responsibility for the physical care and safety of the children, and also, to a large degree, for helping the children to do their work by adapting it. The teachers themselves took varying degrees of responsibility for planning their lessons so that the children were included. Some left all of that to the learning support assistant, the special educational needs co-ordinator and any specialist advisory teachers. Depending on the personality and understanding of the learning support assistants and the children, they could act also as the children's 'friend', spending their entire time close by; or they could act as *facilitators* of friendships, drawing children into collective activities and standing back when peer relationships started to form.

The good side of this was that parents were confident that even children with high-level support needs who could be very vulnerable in a school situation would be cared for. The learning support assistants often became very skilled at meeting individual needs, including the use of specialist equipment, administering medication, implementing therapies such as physiotherapy or speech therapy (under the guidance of a qualified professional). They often learnt 'emergency procedures' and when to recognize that they were needed. All together this made possible the integration of children with a range of impairments including those labelled as severe, complex or profound.

The difficulty is that it did not lead to the real inclusion of children, especially those with high-level support needs. Teachers did not necessarily include them in their lessons; if the learning support assistant was away the child was told to stay at home; if the learning support assistant/child relationship was not good, they both became very unhappy; it was exhausting and isolating for the learning support assistant and there was a very high turnover of staff.

The most common criticism was that the learning support assistant became a barrier to the child becoming part of their peer group. It singled them out and made them feel 'different'.

Developments then took place, which attempted to address this issue, including the restructuring of the role of learning support assistant to teaching assistant. However, this left many pupils with high-level support needs without the one-to-one facilitation they needed, consequently undermining their success in mainstream schools.

The independent living movement grew from an 'uprising' of young adults living in Cheshire (residential) Homes in 1966 (Mason 2005). They felt they had no control over their lives and were being made to waste their time. They identified the main barrier they faced as having no financial means to buy in the physical support they needed to leave the homes and live in ordinary houses in the community. They invented the role of 'personal assistant', and fought for the right to choose either a statutory service to provide care, or money in the form of direct payments to hire and manage their own staff.

This battle was eventually won and since 2003 all local authorities now have to provide a direct payments scheme for those who choose it and this is used to employ personal assistants. Recently this entitlement was extended to disabled young people aged 16–17 and to younger disabled children via their parents. This has allowed many disabled people the chance to live full and exciting lives outside of institutional walls or control. The role of personal assistant is now also used by young people with learning difficulties to explore life in ways which are unique to this era and generation. The benefits for disabled people are that they choose who gives them support, and they direct the nature of that support and the goals to which they are working. For disabled people with the highest level of need, personal assistants are part of a package of carers, often including parents and other relatives.

Many disabled people say it is often not understood by the non-disabled world how tiring it is to have to keep training new people to meet their basic needs, or how insecure they feel when they do not have reliable and familiar helpers, or how vulnerable to abuse they are when they have no say over who provides intimate care. The skill to manage personal assistants is one which needs to be learnt. It is a life skill of utmost importance for disabled people.

In a school situation it is a challenge to think about a young person 'directing' an adult, but the change of role from 'minder' to 'assistant' or facilitator, is what needs to happen.

What young people are saying

In a unique study carried out by the Alliance for Inclusive Education in 2001 (AIE 2007), twelve young people who used one-to one support in mainstream schools were asked what they liked, and what they found difficult about the support they were given. The consultation showed that young people wanted assistants in school who are more like the personal assistants employed by disabled adults under the direct payments scheme. They saw the role as that of a facilitator where both their educational and social inclusion would be supported. They invented what is essentially a new post within schools, that of the 'inclusion assistant'.

In further research completed by the Alliance for Inclusive Education (AIE) (2005c), using young consultants with young people identified as having special educational needs in a large, inclusive secondary school in East London, one young disabled person described this role as an 'ally':

> They need to be someone who has good knowledge of the social and medical models of disability, someone who realises that the relationships of the young people is central to their job, so supporting friendships between young people is really very key. Participation is at the centre of what they are doing, that they have particular skills to do with having access to things like facilitated communication, interpreters, they don't necessarily have to go through all these things themselves, but they will be connected to people that do and will know about these systems and independent living and personal assistants. They have good attention for the young people themselves to work things out however challenging it gets. They are committed completely to the young people. Their role has to be there for the support of the child and the dreams of that young person.
>
> (Lucy Mason, AIE 2005c: 3)

In related research a parent of a child identified as having 'severe learning difficulties' made similar points looking back on her son's experience of school (AIE 2005c: 9):

> A learning support assistant's job is to facilitate. You're there to support the young person but you've also got to respect that he needs time with his friends – you have to bring the two together but then let it happen . . . knowing when to let go.
>
> I would say that James's learning support assistant at secondary school didn't see encouraging relationships as part of her job, let alone her main job. I think it would be a good idea to have some sort of continuity, the same or similar support between what you get at school and later. Because if you look back now from what you would want now, like an ideal personal assistant, you could see what needed to be done in school, in retrospect.

The role of the inclusion assistant

The role of inclusion assistant would require very particular personal attributes, as well as knowledge and skills which could be learned. In particular it would require a personality that positively enjoyed the company of young people and who was committed to empowering them – helping them to make their own decisions and use the resources around them, including other people, to achieve their own goals. It would need someone who was sympathetic to the struggles young people have within a society which affords them little respect or power, especially if they come from poor backgrounds, minority ethnic groups, are gay or lesbian, or are disabled. They would need to have some confidence in supporting the relationships between young people, especially when these are difficult or volatile.

As well as the basic attitudes and social skills a person would need to bring to the job, some background information would be essential. This would be to do with the context within which young people with high-level support needs are living. It would include the law as it relates to them, for example, The Disability Discrimination Act (1995); the resources available to them both at school, at home and into adult life; the politics of disability as a rights based issue; the history of segregation and the rise of the disability movement; the perspective of parents who themselves struggle within the medical and social models of disability.

The skills needed by an inclusion assistant fall into several areas, based on certain assumed rights, set out below, of the young people concerned. Inclusion assistants need to be aware of these and incorporate them into their practice to maximize inclusion for the young people with whom they work.

The right to a positive future

Unless a positive future is imagined, we will not know why we are doing certain things, or why we should be trying to bring about change. We will not be able to judge success or failure. Children with high-level support needs are often limited by the low expectations of those who care for them. These expectations need to be challenged and therefore a goal, a desired outcome, for all the work that is entailed in building inclusive communities and supporting people with high-level support needs to be consciously adopted.

The most useful training for teaching assistants and potential Inclusion Assistants will involve meeting role models – disabled adults who have active lives in the community, including people identified as having learning difficulties and/or 'complex needs 'and who are (with assistance if necessary) in control of their support, systems and resources.

The right to be valued

Inclusion is more than a placement in a mainstream classroom, especially for children with high-level support needs. Being valued by his or her friends and teachers and supporters is what makes the placement work.

An inclusion assistant will need to find ways to help everyone value children who have historically only been seen in a negative light, as problems and drains on the resources of society. This may even include the child's parents who may have had years of negativity from medical professionals. The example of a classmate's statement below from *Snapshots of Possibility* (AIE 2005b: 11) demonstrates the importance of friends:

> What we most enjoy at playtime is when we push William up the hill in his wheelchair and come down really fast – we run down all holding on because we must not let go or he will roll off and get hurt. We hold on really tight in case he gets frightened. We enjoy reading with William. We hold out two books and he looks at the one he wants. We follow his eyes. He likes Kipper books. Lucy and Vita hold the book and turn the pages. Natasha reads the words. When he is out of his wheelchair he lies down to take part in activities and we lie down with him. When William goes to soft play a group of us go with him and we all roll around together. The best thing about having William in the class is his hugging and giving big cuddles.

The right to be safe

Children who rely on others for assistance with personal and intimate care have a particular need for their right to safety to be protected. This example demonstrates how this can work effectively in practice:

> When you are thirteen it's a real drag for your birthday to fall on a school day. But for my daughter Clare this turned out to be a blessing in disguise. I couldn't have foreseen what a powerful and illuminating moment was going to occur in the local burger bar where she and her friends had decided to assemble that Tuesday after school. They had settled down to munch into their choice of fries and shakes, when one of them said, 'Diana, Clare has something important to tell you.' They all went a bit quiet, and turned to Clare. Clare was a little hesitant; she has learning difficulties and a speech and language impairment. This wasn't going to be easy. But with their gentle help and encouragement the story unfolded of how her current Learning Support Assistant was mistreating her. Ignoring her in class – even reading a magazine if she could get away with it and most devastatingly had hit Clare on the way back from swimming one day. I just had the presence of mind to reassure Clare, and all of them that action would be taken immediately, but most of all to thank them for making sure that Clare told her own story and not gone behind her back. They had made sure that this behaviour, carefully hidden from the teachers, had been exposed and Clare got to understand how wrong it was. Their actions and

thoughtfulness led to changes that empowered Clare for the rest of her school days. No learning support assistant was ever again recruited unless Clare gave the go-ahead at the interview and was completely comfortable with them after a few weeks trial. All this was possible because her friends had witnessed some wrong doing and been able to deal with it the way they would have wanted for themselves. Respectfully. There is no greater protection in life than having friends that can look out for you.

(Parent, AIE 2007)

However careful we are, children are vulnerable to abuse from people bigger and stronger than themselves. Disabled children who need intimate care from adults are particularly vulnerable. One of the main safeguards for disabled children is being surrounded by non-disabled children. Their presence will inhibit most abusers, and if one manages to mistreat a disabled child, it is likely that their friends will tell and will be taken seriously. This alone is enough to make an argument for inclusive schools rather than herding all the most vulnerable children together, out of sight, with numerous adults in places known to attract abusers (Utting 1997).

Another important safeguard is that every child should choose who carries out their intimate care procedures. Like Clare, most children, even with the most severe impairments, can and do indicate when they are not happy with the care they are receiving from certain people.

The right to have physical needs met

Children with additional physical needs will only be safe if they have one or more people available to them at all times who know how to meet those needs. Every child will be different and their individual needs will have to be taught by the child, the parents or other regular assistants together with advice from professionals such as paediatric occupational therapists, and aids advisers. These skills can range from lifting and transferring, dressing/undressing, assisting with the toilet, assisting with eating and drinking or tube feeding, use of specialist equipment such as standing frames, wheelchairs, speech machines, back-braces and portable ventilators.

It should not be assumed that all these needs must be met by adults. Children with such needs often prefer some of them to be met by their friends, especially as they grow older.

The right to have communication needs met

Some children with high-level support needs have impairments that affect their ability to hear, understand and use language. Unfortunately there has been a long history of mistreatment of these children based on the false idea that the inability to speak is the result of an inability to think, or understand. Because of this children have been left in silent places, under-stimulated and ignored, yet it is fundamental to our human nature to engage in two-way communication with each other.

Every effort should be made to give every child a communication system, even if that can only involve body language. A dependable 'yes' and 'no' can also make a big difference to the exchange of information between two people. Learning how to facilitate or use speech technology is a vital skill for many inclusion assistants, and all teaching assistants should make themselves familiar with the speech/communication systems of all the pupils with whom they work.

The right to have learning needs met

Children with high-level support needs often need their work to be adapted or made accessible for them. A teacher assistant or an inclusion assistant should not seek to replace the role of the ordinary classroom teacher in doing this preparation, even if the teacher wants them to. The assistant is there as much to help the teacher to teach as the child to be a student. The teacher should plan their lessons to include all their pupils and have given thought to how the lesson might need modifying, adapting or accessing for each child. The assistant's role is to make sure that the teacher has the necessary information about the child, to make sure the child is comfortable, has understood what is expected of them, has all the resources they need and has the physical help they need either from themselves or a fellow pupil. They are not there to do the child's work for them!

The right to allies

Children who have difficulties with communication, or behaviour, or who lack social skills, or are simply shy, may have a struggle to make and keep friends. The building of children's skills in how to make friendships is crucial to the development of an inclusive environment. Learning to facilitate 'Circles of Friends' (Newton and Wilson 2005) is an invaluable skill for an inclusion assistant and will require some specialist training with someone who already uses this tool.

The right to have a voice within the school

Children with high-level support needs often have unusual perspectives on things and can make very important contributions to everyone's picture of the world. They may need help to find a place in which they can be heard with respect. As Charlotte (1999) argues:

If anyone were to ask me what message I might have for others I would tell them that they should listen to, believe and respect young people. In my experience it is very difficult to tell anyone how you feel when they won't listen; if you are not believed then you stop believing in yourself; if you are not respected then you lose self respect and everyone needs self respect.

(Charlotte, JRF 1999)

Further considerations

As the role of inclusion assistant develops and is required in more and more schools and colleges, the serious question of training, accreditation and pay scales must be addressed on a national level. As can be seen, the role is very different to the traditional model of 'care' with its notorious low level of pay and status. The inclusion assistant is a highly skilled person. Their input into both the educational lives of the young people with whom they are assigned to work, and the whole school as they help develop relationships among pupils and between their pupils and teachers, parents, health professionals and the local community, cannot be underestimated. They are an essential part of a team, which is creating a huge shift in culture within our education system towards full inclusion.

Reflecting on values and practice

1   Think about your own practice. How would you feel if you were to be directed by a child?
2   How much could you find out about someone if they could only answer your questions with a 'yes' or 'no'?
3   How would you feel if a stranger took you into the toilet and started to undress you?
4   Do you think anyone has a limited ability to learn?
5   Can you see conflicts between adults in school needing to be in control and a disabled child's need for autonomy?
6   Can you imagine children with high-level support needs growing up to have full and meaningful lives outside of an institution?

Suggested further reading

AIE (2001) *The Inclusion Assistant Report and Video*, London: The Alliance for Inclusive Education.
AIE (2007) *The Inclusion Assistant Training Pack*, London: The Alliance for Inclusive Education.
Mason, M. (2005) *Incurably Human*, Nottingham: Inclusive Solutions.

Newton, C. and Wilson, D. (2005) *Creating Circles of Friends, a Peer Support and Inclusion Workbook*, Nottingham: Inclusive Solutions.

Tashie, C., Shapiro-Barnard, S. and Rossetti, Z. (2006) *Seeing the Charade: What We Need To Do and Undo to Make Friendships Happen*, Nottingham: Inclusive Solutions.

Contact and online bookshops

AIE: www.allfie.org.uk.
Inclusive Solutions: www.Inclusive-solutions.com.

References

AIE (2001) *The Inclusion Assistant Report and Video*, London: The Alliance for Inclusive Education.

AIE (2005a) *Where Are They Now?*, London: The Alliance for Inclusive Education.

AIE (2005b) *Snapshots of Possibility*, London: The Alliance for Inclusive Education.

AIE (2005c) 'The Case for the Inclusion Assistant'. Report for the DfES, London: The Alliance for Inclusive Education.

AIE (2007) *The Inclusion Assistant Training Pack*, London: The Alliance for Inclusive Education.

JRF (1999) 'Transition to Adulthood for Young Disabled People with Complex Health and Support Needs', *JRF Findings*, York: Joseph Rowntree Foundation.

Mason, M. (2005) *Incurably Human*, Nottingham: Inclusive Solutions.

Morris, J. (1999) *Hurtling into the Void: Transition into Adulthood for Young Disabled People with Complex Health and Support Needs*, Brighton: Pavilion.

Newton, C. and Wilson, D. (2005) *Creating Circles of Friends, a Peer support and Inclusion Workbook*, Nottingham: Inclusive Solutions.

Utting, W. (1997) *People Like Us. The Report of the Review of the Safeguards for Children Living Away From Home*, London: HMSO.

Chapter 7

'I'm a TA not a PA!'

Teaching assistants working with teachers

Vikki Anderson and Maggie Finney

The move towards inclusive education has led to a greater need for additional support in the classroom, resulting in a significant rise in the number of teaching assistants in schools. The recent drive by the government to raise standards and reduce teacher workloads has increased the variety and complexity of tasks carried out by teaching assistants but research indicates that there is considerable variation in the deployment, pay, conditions and training of this body of staff. In this chapter we will explore existing research in which teaching assistants have expressed their views and will also focus on our recent small-scale study of teaching assistants' perspectives on working with teachers, examining how this relationship can affect the quality of inclusive practice and identifying the implications for your future role.

The role of support staff has changed considerably over the years. Initially assistants functioned as classroom auxiliaries who relieved teachers of care and housekeeping-type duties (Clayton 1993) but government initiatives in inclusion, curriculum development and workforce remodelling have resulted in them taking on an ever-increasing variety of tasks, with many playing a significant part in the learning and teaching process. The DfES (2000) has identified 'teaching assistant' as the government's preferred term for paid support staff in primary, special and secondary schools, including those with a general role and others with specific responsibilities for a pupil, subject area or age group. The term aims to 'reduce the confusion of different titles denoting the same function' and acknowledge 'the contribution which well-trained and well-managed assistants can make to the teaching and learning process and to pupil achievement' (DfES 2000: 4). The past decade has seen a rapid growth in the number of teaching assistants employed in English primary and secondary schools. Government statistics indicate that in 1997 there were 24,000 full-time equivalent 'learning support assistants' working in mainstream schools in England, whereas more recent figures stand at 148,500 (DfES 2005).

Although the DfES (2000) has identified four strands of the teaching assistant's role: support for the pupil, the teacher, the curriculum and the school, these can be widely interpreted and there appears to be little consensus regarding the duties they are expected to perform. Kerry (2005: 377) examined the roles of teaching assistants documented in the literature and proposed 11 different types, from 'Dogsbody' and 'Routine administrator/teacher's PA' to 'Teacher support and partial substitute', and 'Mobile paraprofessional', the latter being required to plan and deliver learning activities in a similar way to higher level teaching assistants (TDA 2007).

Research published in the 1990s highlighted a number of challenges faced by teaching assistants, including uncertainty about roles and responsibilities, low status and pay, and lack of involvement in, or time for, planning. The focus here is on studies carried out in England across a range of local education authorities (LEAs) that incorporated the views of teaching assistants themselves.

In a questionnaire survey of classroom assistants and teachers in a range of Key Stage 1 settings, 81 classroom assistants and 70 teachers gave their perceptions of classroom assistants' working roles and responsibilities (Moyles and Suschitzky 1997). There was no indication of any greater involvement with the preparation of resources and materials by classroom assistants than teachers, raising the question of who should perform the more routine tasks. In the interview phase of the research, one headteacher commented: 'The school has such good CAs that we are now looking for someone to do the more mundane tasks – I'm talking to governors about it right now!' (Moyles and Suschitzky 1997: 57).

Classroom assistants reported high-levels of job satisfaction, particularly with regard to working with children but many said they had little involvement in planning for pupils' learning experiences, resulting in them being unaware of the learning objectives set by the teacher. These findings were echoed in a study by Farrell et al. (1999) involving a wider range of education providers. One hundred and forty-nine learning support assistants and 113 teachers were interviewed during case study visits to 21 sites, including LEA support services, mainstream and special schools across the primary and secondary phases of education. The vast majority of learning support assistants were committed to their jobs and enthusiastic about their work. However, a consistent problem in the mainstream sites was the lack of time for day-to-day planning meetings when the learning support assistant could receive advice from, and give feedback to, the teacher. An exception was in mainstream primary schools where learning support assistants supported teachers in implementing the National Literacy Strategy. Here the level of prescription resulted in everyone sharing clear objectives and the learning support assistant's role being more clearly defined. In the majority of schools visited in this study, the learning support assistants felt supported by senior management and part of the whole school team. They were nevertheless concerned about the lack of career structure and felt that differences in pay between themselves and teachers were too great given the work they were expected to do. Most of the learning support assistants had job descriptions but many did not refer to them and often did completely unrelated work. This mirrors the dissatisfaction about status and pay expressed by classroom assistants in Moyles and Suschitzky's (1997) study, again in relation to their changing roles.

Farrell *et al.* (1999) found that in some cases, the distinction between the role of learning support assistants and teachers was unclear. Some assistants were involved in adapting programmes of work and in planning new programmes, partly because they did not have regular contact with support teachers. Overall, learning support assistants were happy to implement Individual Education Plans that had been devised by the teacher but did not want to take full responsibility for the pupils' progress. A lack of certainty about roles and responsibilities can also be seen in Moyles and Suschitzky's (1997) study, in which classroom assistants viewed working with children identified as having special educational needs as being a major part of their role but almost half the teachers disagreed, perceiving general support for the teacher to be more important.

Lee and Mawson (1998) conducted a questionnaire survey of 767 classroom assistants across a range of mainstream primary schools in England and found that while most were satisfied with their jobs, they were unhappy about pay and the lack of time and information available to do the work properly. Many said they felt undervalued and that teachers needed to communicate with them more, include them in their lesson plans in advance and involve them in staff meetings. Shaw (2001) obtained similar results in her study of 'learning supporters' in primary and secondary schools in London and the North of England. Many reported the enjoyment and satisfaction gained from working with pupils but some said they did not feel appreciated and thought that although teachers welcomed them into their classrooms, they often regarded them as little more than helpers. One teaching assistant remarked: 'Teachers don't understand our role. They think it is useful to have another pair of hands' (Shaw 2001: 11). Assistants were often told that they were valued but this was not supported by good wages, permanent employment and a clear career structure.

More recent research by Smith *et al.* (2004) reflected a number of the issues raised in previous studies. The results of a questionnaire survey completed by 264 headteachers, 535 teachers and 568 teaching assistants in 327 primary and secondary schools in England and Wales revealed that a major difficulty affecting the working relationships of teachers and teaching assistants was lack of time to plan and prepare lessons together. Only 54 per cent of the teaching assistants in this study reported that their schools had policies on their roles and responsibilities and again there were concerns about pay and conditions of service: 'My job description grew, the workload doubled . . . my salary stayed the same' (Smith *et al.* 2004: 8). These issues are reiterated in our study outlined and discussed below, indicating that unfortunately for some teaching assistants, experiences do not appear to have changed despite the weight of evidence demonstrating concerns about everyday practice.

In the USA, Riggs (2004) asked a group of 35 paraeducators from special and mainstream schools to identify what they wanted newly qualified teachers to know about working with them. The large number of responses was clustered and ranked, leading to a 'top ten' of things they thought teachers should know. These were later included in a set of suggestions for pre-service teaching programmes and incorporated into teacher competences. The themes that arose were: valuing paraprofessionals, clarification of the paraeducator's role, team working, effective communication with paraeducators, learning and teaching within the classroom, and supervision and guidance of paraeducators. We conducted a similar study with 33 teaching assistants working in primary, secondary and special schools in the Midlands, all of whom were studying for a Foundation degree. They identified 30 statements that they wanted to make to the teachers with whom they worked and their conversations about the reasons for their choices were recorded. The following themes emerged: valuing teaching assistants' opinions, experience and skills; conditions of service; clarity of the teaching assistant's role; joint planning and effective communication with teaching assistants; training for teachers, and learning and teaching. Most of these themes mirror the findings of Riggs (2004) and the larger scale studies highlighted above.

It was noticed that many of the statements appeared negative. This could be an accurate reflection of how the teaching assistants were feeling or because they had already made positive comments to teachers, leaving unvoiced issues in the forefront of their thoughts when responding to the study. Several statements referred to the lack of clarity of teaching assistants' roles, for example:

[We want a] clear indication of the role within the classroom.

I'm a TA, not a PA.

These were accompanied by the comment:

We sometimes assume a role and are told 'no', that is not what I want you to do.

These statements reflect the dilemma identified by Moyles and Suschitzky (1997) and lead to two key questions. First, if administrative and routine tasks are allocated to teaching assistants to reduce teachers' workloads, how much time will they have to play a part in teaching and learning? Second, if experienced teaching assistants are to plan and deliver learning activities, who will carry out the routine duties? There is clearly a danger that tensions will arise as the impact of workforce remodelling (DfES 2003a) is felt in schools. This was apparent in Smith *et al.*'s (2004) study, in which some teaching assistants found themselves spending less time supporting learners to enable them to cover teachers' routine tasks. A typical response was:

The new workplace agreement has put back the cause of teaching assistants greatly. Now we have all the jobs the teacher wants to rid him/herself of – mainly unskilled labour, too, such as photocopying, and collecting money. We don't mind this as part of our role but this is beginning to supersede our usual work.

(Smith *et al.* 2004: 22)

The distinction between higher-level teaching assistant and teaching assistant may help to deal with the challenges presented by workforce remodelling but schools may need to find more concrete solutions, such as those illustrated in case studies documented by Teachernet (2007). Salmestone Primary School developed a new, clearly defined 'teacher assistant' role in order to relieve the administrative burdens on teaching staff without detracting from the school's drive on numeracy and literacy, in which most specifically trained support staff were engaged. In the secondary phase of education, Mosslands School attached 'resource assistants' to departments to assist with the type of administrative and clerical duties included in the 24 tasks identified in the Workload Agreement (WAMG 2003), giving teachers more time to focus on raising the standards of learning and teaching.

Many teaching assistants work with more than one teacher, the challenges of which are outlined by Lee (2002). It is therefore essential that they have detailed job descriptions and most importantly, that these are adhered to. Gerschel (2005) reports that many teaching assistants at training sessions felt their job descriptions were irrelevant or out of date and that the most useful job descriptions were those they had helped draw up themselves.

In the Midlands study, the concepts of feeling valued, respected and gaining recognition for their contributions were reflected in a third of the statements produced by the teaching assistants. These included:

[We want to be] valued more, respected as individuals,

which was supported by the comment

so that we can perform our jobs better.

I would like some recognition.

Make me feel included.

[We want] greater recognition through pay.

This last statement was accompanied by the comment: 'We are expected to do more than we are paid for.'

Workforce remodelling (DfES 2003a) identifies the need for opportunities for career progression and recognizes the contribution made by teaching assistants to the learning and teaching process but the issues of pay and conditions have yet to be addressed. There is clearly a need for a national pay structure, as wage rates are set by each Local Authority and salaries may differ on a regional basis, with some teaching assistants being paid during term time only.

It is, however, clear from the statements that being valued does not rest solely with financial rewards. When learning support assistants in Mistry et al.'s (2004) study raised this issue, they commented that they would appreciate 'being thanked occasionally'. Mistry et al. refer to the significance of this in human resources management, whereby: '. . . people are not going to work to their optimum level unless they feel valued and appreciated' (Mistry *et al.* 2004: 134). This links to other statements made by teaching assistants in the Midlands study, such as:

> Please ask for my opinion – it counts!
>
> Don't underestimate the experience I have to offer.
>
> Acknowledge our skills.

indicating that they felt teachers should identify and make more use of their skills and experience. This could involve giving them a role in areas of the curriculum other than core skills, for as one teaching assistant remarked:

> I heard teachers say: 'We didn't know she could speak French fluently.'

The DfES (2003b) acknowledges that teaching assistants have abilities and skills that have been underused. Some schools have introduced performance management and appraisal procedures for teaching assistants similar to those of teachers in order to raise the professional status of support staff. This appears to have been welcomed by teaching assistants as a formal but supportive means of gaining recognition and appreciation for their work and engaging in discussion about professional development (Groom 2006).

In line with other research findings, a number of statements in the Midlands study emphasized the need for joint planning, information sharing and effective communication between teachers and teaching assistants. These included:

> [We need] effective communication between all staff.

accompanied by the comments:

> I am never invited to a meeting, and I go to meetings but I'm unpaid.
>
> Please make time in order to plan collaboratively with me.
>
> Give us lesson plans.
>
> Give us more information [about the lessons/students' needs].

When discussing this, one teaching assistant said:

> We are going into every lesson cold – I would like to know what I am doing for each lesson.

The DfES (2000) argues that the quality of teaching is enhanced when teachers provide clear guidance to teaching assistants and involve them in planning. Partnership working is key to the Every Child Matters (DfES 2004a) initiative, which identifies the need for a more coherent and flexible workforce, supported by appropriate training and professional development. It is therefore crucial that this occurs with adults who are working together in the classroom.

An example of good practice is provided by Fox *et al.* (2004) who describe a situation in which a primary school teacher informed the teaching assistant about the whole day's planning, focusing on the work of the entire class, together with specific planning for a child identified as having Down Syndrome. The teaching assistant recorded her views in the teacher's planning and assessment book at the end of the morning and afternoon sessions, and the teacher used these to differentiate the next day's lessons. In a different school in which a child who carried a similar label was supported by two teaching assistants, the class teacher met with them at lunchtimes to plan for the following week. The teaching assistants knew in advance what they had to do in relation to the whole class and to support the child, resulting in this pupil being regarded as a full member of the class by peers and staff alike.

Teachers must share their planning with teaching assistants so that they know what is expected of them and have opportunities to air their views. If teaching assistants do not have a forum for expressing their opinions, the 'voice vacuum' described by O'Brien and Garner (2001: 3) will restrict the growth of a fruitful professional partnership aimed at improving the quality of learners' experiences. It is important, however, that joint planning is not carried out at lunchtime or after school, relying on the good will of teaching assistants but that structured, paid time is allocated to it. The responsibility for collaborative partnership does not therefore rest solely with the class or subject teacher but is a management issue that requires a whole school approach.

The teaching assistants in the Midlands study made a number of comments about learning and teaching in the classroom. Some of these focused on communicating with pupils:

> Why do you treat her like she can't communicate because she is in a wheelchair?

> Why don't you listen to what they have to say?

Others referred directly to teaching approaches:

> I think there is a better way of teaching that.

> [We want] more differentiation – especially at secondary level

> And there is the issue of teaching assistants assuming responsibility for pupils identified as having special educational needs.

> Don't assume the lower ability group should only work with the TA.

> Why don't you use your expertise to take the lower ability group and I'll take the rest?

An accompanying comment highlighted the negative effect that this could have on pupils:

> Children are often labelled because we are known to work with the 'SEN' [special educational needs] group.

With increasing demands being placed on teachers, learning support assistants can be received with relief. However, some teachers may detach themselves from pupils identified as having special educational needs when they have additional support in the classroom. This practice is described by a teaching assistant in Shaw's research: 'The teacher looks at you and thinks there is an LSA [learning support assistant], let them get on with it. They hardly have any contact with the child' (Shaw 2001: 11).

Gerschel (2005: 71) refers to 'the 'Velcro' model' of a teaching assistant being attached to a single pupil and cautions against a culture in which the pupil may become emotionally dependent on the assistant and therefore less likely to be fully included in the class or to form relationships with peers. As an alternative, Gerschel cites the example of a small, mixed comprehensive school where teaching assistants work with groups rather than individuals but also operate a system in which a key worker provides a point of contact for each pupil identified as having special educational needs.

Observations within a mainstream junior school (Rose 2000) revealed that learning support assistants played an important role in supporting the whole class rather than concentrating on individuals with statements of special educational needs. For example, a learning support assistant was used to monitor the work of the rest of the class while the teacher worked intensively with a pupil with speech and language difficulties. Learning support assistants were seen to be skilled in making decisions about when and where support was necessary and all six pupils focused on in the study saw the assistant as a supporter of the whole class.

However, Rose (2000: 194) stresses that: 'Defined roles and management responsibilities are clearly an essential factor in ensuring that classroom support is both unobtrusive and focused upon addressing the most urgent needs at a given time' – implying that additional training is required if all teachers are to acquire appropriate skills for the effective deployment of teaching assistants.

Teaching assistants in the Midlands study reinforced this by referring to the professional development of teachers:

> [You need] teacher training on how to use TAs effectively.

> Teachers need more training in SEN.

There was clearly some concern about newly qualified teachers' lack of expertise, as one teaching assistant commented:

When I hear that a newly qualified teacher is coming and I have to work with her, I really worry.

Skills in developing effective working partnerships with teaching assistants may not be well honed in all teachers. Although preparation for working with teaching assistants is included in the teaching standards, the Initial Teacher Training (ITT) curriculum is so full that there may be little time to attend to this (Watkinson 2004).

The Special Educational Needs Code of Practice (DfES 2001) makes it clear that every teacher should expect to teach children identified as having special educational needs. However, as the House of Commons Education and Skills Select Committee (2006) points out, it would be unrealistic to expect educators to be able to meet the needs of these pupils if they have not received appropriate training. The Audit Commission (2002: 36) states that:

> Many teachers feel under considerable pressure, on the one hand to meet the needs of individual pupils, and on the other to deliver a demanding national curriculum and achieve ever-better test results; research suggests that many feel ill-equipped for this task.

The DfES (2004b) acknowledges the need to equip teachers with the practical skills for working effectively with pupils but the Training and Development Agency for Schools agreed with the Select Committee that there was 'not a big emphasis on SEN in initial teacher training' (House of Commons Education and Skills Select Committee 2006: 70). The Select Committee recommends not only that training in special educational needs should become a core, compulsory part of ITT for all teachers but also that: 'Good quality, appropriate continuing professional development should be made available for all teachers and schools should be resourced to fund them. Compulsory in-service training should include SEN if it is to be given sufficient priority in schools' (House of Commons Education and Skills Select Committee 2006: 71).

The teaching assistants in the Midlands study voiced key issues arising from their experiences of working with teachers, some of which may have been difficult to express face to face. Many of these issues are reflected in previous research, indicating that they still need to be addressed if good practice is to occur. It is evident that together with government-led changes related to occupational standards, qualifications, pay and conditions of service, an ongoing process of clear, supportive communication and reflective practice is needed between teachers and teaching assistants. Roles and responsibilities must be clearly defined in order to resolve the 'TA versus PA' dilemma. Collaborative teamwork, focusing on an understanding of the perspectives of learners is fundamental to inclusive classroom practice and all teachers need to assume a shared responsibility for the success of pupils identified as having special educational needs. However, this will only be possible if both teachers and teaching assistants are properly equipped to meet the wide range of needs in the classroom. Training for teachers and teaching assistants in inclusive practice is essential, together with training for teachers in the effective deployment of teaching assistants. There is also a need for a national pay structure and a system of management and appraisal that will enable teaching assistants to use their own strengths and identify areas for development, while following a clear career progression route. Finally, it can be seen throughout this chapter that the issue of valuing teaching assistants is of supreme importance and must be addressed if they are to play an integral part in improving educational opportunities for all learners, regardless of difference.

Reflection on values and practice

1   Reflect on the relationships you have with teachers. Can you identify aspects of your work together that could be improved upon? Is there anything that you can do to move towards these changes?
2   What are the possible implications of the workforce agreement for you, the teacher(s) you work with and the pupils you support?
3   What joint training would you and a teacher benefit from and how can this be pursued?

Suggested further reading

DfES (2000) *Working with Teaching Assistants: A Good Practice Guide*, London: DfES.
Fox, S., Farrell, P. and Davis, P. (2004) 'Factors Associated with the Effective Inclusion of Primary-Aged Pupils with Down's Syndrome', *British Journal of Special Education*, 31: 184–90.
Gerschel, L. (2005) 'The Special Educational Needs Coordinator's Role in Managing Teaching Assistants: The Greenwich Perspective', *Support for Learning*, 20: 69–76.
Lee, B. (2002) *Teaching Assistants in Schools: The Current State of Play*, Slough: NFER.
Riggs, C. (2004) 'To Teachers. What Paraeducators Want You to Know', *Teaching Exceptional Children* 36: 8–12.

References

Audit Commission (2002) *Special Educational Needs: a Mainstream Issue*, London: Audit Commission.
Clayton, T. (1993) 'From Domestic Helper to "Assistant Teacher" – the Changing Role of the British Classroom Assistant', *European Journal of Special Needs Education* 8: 32–44.
DfES (2000) *Working with Teaching Assistants: A Good Practice Guide*, London: DfES.
DfES (2001) *Special Educational Needs Code of Practice*, London: DfES.
DfES (2003a) *Raising Standards and Tackling Workload: A National Agreement*, London: DfES.
DfES (2003b) *Developing the Role of Support Staff – What the National Agreement Means For You*, London: DfES.

DfES (2004a) *Every Child Matters: Change for Children*, London: DfES.

DfES (2004b) *Removing Barriers to Achievement – The Government's Strategy for SEN*, London: DfES.

DfES (2005) *School Workforce in England*, London: DfES.

Farrell, P., Balshaw, M. and Polat, F. (1999) *The Management, Role and Training of Learning Support Assistants*, London: DfEE.

Fox, S., Farrell, P. and Davis, P. (2004) 'Factors Associated with the Effective Inclusion of Primary-Aged Pupils with Down's Syndrome', *British Journal of Special Education*, 31: 184–90.

Gerschel, L. (2005) 'The Special Educational Needs Coordinator's Role in Managing Teaching Assistants: the Greenwich Perspective', *Support for Learning*, 20: 69–76.

Groom, B. (2006) 'Building Relationships for Learning: the Developing Role of the Teaching Assistant', *Support for Learning*, 21: 199–203.

Kerry, T. (2005) 'Towards a Typology for Conceptualising the Roles of Teaching Assistants' *Educational Review*, 57: 373–84.

House of Commons Education and Skills Committee (2006) *Special Educational Needs Third Report of Session 2005–6, Vol. 1*, London: The Stationery Office.

Lee, B. (2002) *Teaching Assistants in Schools: The Current State of Play*, Slough: NFER.

Lee, B. and Mawson, C. (1998) *Survey of Classroom Assistants*, Slough: NFER.

Mistry, M., Burton, N and Brundrett, M. (2004) 'Managing LSAs: an Evaluation of the Use of Learning Support Assistants in an Urban Primary School', *School Leadership and Management* 24: 125–36.

Moyles, J. and Suschitzky, W. (1997) *Jills of All Trades? Classroom Assistants in KS1 Classes*, London: ATL.

O'Brien, T. and Garner, P. (2001) 'Tim and Philip's Story: Setting the Record Straight', in O'Brien, T. and Garner, P. (eds) *Untold Stories: Learning Support Assistants and Their Work*, Stoke-on-Trent: Trentham Books.

Riggs, C. (2004) 'To Teachers. What Paraeducators Want You to Know', *Teaching Exceptional Children*, 36: 8–12.

Rose, R. (2000) 'Using Classroom Support in a Primary School: a Single School Case Study', *British Journal of Special Education* 27: 191–6.

Shaw, L. (2001) *Learning Supporters and Inclusion (Roles, Rewards, Concerns and Challenges)* Bristol: CSIE.

Smith, P., Whitby, K. and Sharpe, C. (2004) *The Employment and Deployment of Teaching Assistants*, Slough: NFER.

Teachernet (2007) *Case Studies*. Online: available at www.teachernet.gov.uk/Case Studies (accessed 21 March 2007).

TDA (2007) *Higher Level Teaching Assistants*. Online: available at www.tda.gov.uk/support/htla.aspx (accessed 11 March 2007).

Workforce Agreement Monitoring Group (WAMG) (2003) *Raising Standards and Tackling Workload: Implementing the National Agreement*, London: DfES.

Watkinson, A. (2004) 'To Teach or Not To Teach?', *Managing Schools Today* 13: 17–21.

Chapter 8

Inclusive relationships

Insights from teaching assistants on how schools can reach parents

Michele Moore

Context

This chapter reports on research in a school in central England which caters for around 170 pupils aged between 3 and 19 years, described as 'children with significant and complex special educational needs'. The area the school is in was identified in 1999 as one of the poorest regions in Europe. Since 2002, when our three year involvement with the school began, there has been constant talk of 'urban renaissance'. Local and regional government strategic effort has been aimed at reducing deprivation in the area to create a better quality of life for the people who live there. Pittlesden School is the only 'special' school left in the local authority, but in keeping with local emphasis on new and higher aspirations for all citizens, it comes as no surprise that this segregated school, for some of the most deprived and excluded children in Europe, has an explicit commitment to promote inclusion for all of its pupils.

This chapter reports on research commissioned by the school management team to raise standards in all aspects of school life through examining, developing and embedding inclusive practice. The model for supporting school improvement described in this chapter seeks to promote positive change through embedding a culture of everyday research action, involving participants in continual reflection and evaluation of what happens in the processes of inclusive teaching and learning (Armstrong and Moore 2004). Anyone can get involved in research action – not just teachers. Teaching assistants are allies in this task for any thinking school. We argue that best practice emerges when everyday reflections and observations are constantly pooled and questioned so that practice can be challenged and shifted on a day-by-day basis, which culminates in consistent – and continual conditions for – inclusion and thereby excellence. In our work at Pittlesden School, teaching assistants were identified as key to the development of more inclusive working practices.

Inclusion of teaching assistants

In line with previous researchers, we stress the importance of fully including teaching assistants in a whole school approach to school improvement (Moran and Abbott 2002; Sorsby 2004). It is imperative that emphasis is placed on building inclusion in all aspects of school life and that everyone a child meets in school who supports their learning shares this view. That is to say, everyone who works at a school should be included – in a manner which best suits and develops their skills – in a collective agenda for shaping improvements in teaching and learning. Thus, at the heart of the work we were doing in Pittlesden School was the assumption that inclusion of all of a school's stake-holders enhances the participation and learning of all pupils and is key to the raising standards agenda (Dunn and Moore 2004).

This chapter reports and analyses data from a part of the research which looked at the views of a group of teachers and teaching assistants on the development of inclusive practice through improving contact with parents and caregivers. The group felt that improving consultation could open up new avenues through which they could work to reduce exclusion. They considered teaching assistants as having a unique role to play in bringing parents and caregivers into closer relationships with schools which is often underestimated; in particular, they are often in a position to build bridges with those schools they find 'hard to reach'.

When the project first began, these issues were discussed in terms of 'hard to reach parents and caregivers' but it soon became clear that this term was in danger of becoming a label that erroneously places responsibility for difficulties over consultation with families. Those involved in the research preferred to focus on barriers to consultation that might stem from the school itself, rather than seeing parents as 'the problem'. And it was realized that some staff in schools are 'harder to reach' than others; specifically, the view surfaced that parents and caregivers may find teachers 'harder to reach' than teaching assistants. The chapter draws on what happened next as the group decided to concentrate their efforts to support school improvement on closer inclusion of parents and caregivers in their work.

Challenging assumptions around the role of teaching assistants

When participants began to explore what would be involved in developing and implementing a more proactive role for teaching assistants in consultation, the first thing that happened was that an implicit recognition that teaching assis-tants had been undervalued, had to be acknowledged. This exposed deep-felt and enduring struggles concerning professional contribution and identity:

> I've never been asked to get involved with any consultation with parents. I've often felt I've been chucked on the scrap heap in terms of what I could offer – but I've got a lot to give these children and their families.
>
> (Teaching assistant)

Several researchers have noted the need to raise the self-esteem of teaching assistants and other support staff (Hammett and Burton 2005; Rhodes 2006) and we realized if we were to ignore these tensions, and fail to open up the question of the impact of underlying concerns, then the degree to which significant change could be brought about would be limited.

Critical questions had to surface and be grappled with about why teachers and teaching assistants had tended not to work together on consultation issues. What factors explained why some teachers and teaching assistants did manage to work collaboratively on facilitating communications with parents and caregivers yet others felt excluded from the consultation process? Sources of discontent – and sometimes disagreement – were not easy to work through. But some examples help to illustrate that enabling outcomes could be derived from the uncomfortable process of jointly recognizing that, mostly, the teaching assistants felt that their contribution to communication with parents and caregivers had counted for less than the contribution made by their teacher colleagues. This was part of a wider tension: teaching assistants were stressing the importance of what they do, in any aspect of their job, being given equal value to that of anyone else's work.

The examples are taken from focused group discussions involving members of the school management group as well as teachers and teaching assistants. To begin with, several teaching assistants said they found aspects of their work demoralizing and undermining. In the words of one, endorsed by others, 'I don't want to be treated as a glorified toilet assistant or relegated to washing paint pots.' As far as most participants were concerned, 'if the school really wants to improve consultation with parents then teaching assistants can help to do it'. Recognition of this would mean teaching assistants could contribute to school improvement, feel they could do their jobs more effectively and in turn, increase their sense of 'being valued'.

Teaching assistants talked about wanting to share more in planning around consultation. They felt their skills and experience were not being best utilized. They were keen to operate across different domains of school life and saw themselves as ideally suited to play a pivotal role in bringing parents and caregivers into closer relation with the school. They were candid about not necessarily experiencing comfortable levels of inclusion in consultation on school life themselves and felt what they had learned from their own sense of exclusion gave insights into how they might work to raise the voices of parents and caregivers.

Through airing and sharing dissatisfaction concerning the role of teaching assistants it became possible to envisage new horizons. Sometimes views expressed made for rather bleak discussions, but by working through these, the participants came to see themselves as doing something that enabled new and more inclusive practices to evolve; not only for themselves, but for other stakeholders too. It is worth noting that it takes a courageous school management group to trust the action research process to constructively illuminate such difficult issues. The headteacher who commissioned our involvement with the school allowed these processes to take place because she was determined that the entitlements to high quality inclusive education for pupils at the school would be met.

And so, as the project to improve consultation with parents and caregivers began to take shape, it soon became evident to everyone involved that 'inclusive thinking and practice is hard work' Barton (2004). Yet from the earliest days of the project, teaching assistants showed real commitment to putting in the hard work required to bring to fruition a link between inclusion of the voices of parents and caregivers and school improvement. Nevertheless, everyone involved had realized that improving consultation with parents and caregivers as part of a strategy for embedding a new inclusive culture would not be brought about through one-off 'quick fix' solutions.

Widening inclusion of parents and caregivers

The group had established that better communication with parents and care-givers would enhance confidence for innovation and draw on the expertise of a group not routinely involved in supporting school improvement. A recurrent conviction was that 'parents know their children best and we need to share this knowledge'. Yet different perspectives on this emerged. Some participants felt consultation may be hard because often people do *not* actually feel they 'know best' in relation to their child's education. As Reay and Ball (1998: 434) point out: '. . . underpinning the sense of "not knowing best" in relation to children's education, are difficult issues of adult passivity, lack of wider social power and educational knowledge.' Participants were tapping into these 'difficult issues' as they interrogated how they might facilitate links with parents and care-givers. A process of questioning assumptions unravelled:

> Over the years I've noticed some parents prefer to talk to teaching assistants. They are nervous about seeing teachers. They often seem more comfortable talking to teaching assistants about how the student is doing regarding personal needs or about the child's general experience of school life.
>
> (Teaching assistant)

> [T]eachers might be the last people parents feel they can communicate comfortably and easily with . . . teaching assistants might be better placed to communicate with parents – often support staff are used as conduits for getting messages between parents and the class teacher.
>
> (Teacher)

And from this:

> [T]here might even be personality clashes – at least we could give parents the choice and say in letters or when we see them *'you can talk to your child's*

teacher or any of the teaching assistants . . .' make it clear that talking to support staff is just as important and useful.

(Teaching assistant)

It was emerging that a relatively under-utilized resource lay in the willingness of teaching assistants to access the views of parents and caregivers. While it may appear self-evident that teaching assistants should play an active part in consultation, there had been reluctance to put this into words. Teaching assistants said they worried that asserting their skills for effective communication with parents and caregivers might appear critical of the teacher. Conversely, some teachers felt asking teaching assistants to consult with parents might be unreasonable, or expose personal limitations. The opportunity for teaching assistants and teachers to work collaboratively on the difficulties of consultation in the context of an exploratory research project enabled them to take apart assumptions about 'who is the expert on communication with families?' – and 'whose job is it?' in a non-confrontational context. From this point on, teachers and teaching assistants were encouraged to reconsider their assumptions and to revise any limitations these assumptions placed on the part teaching assistants were playing in consultation.

Acknowledging that teaching assistants are key to successful consultation between parents and school prompted new suggestions for good practice. Someone pointed out 'it could be that the teacher is the best one to talk to about curriculum and 'work' matters' and this was not disputed, but a shift in control over communications between school and parents and caregivers was immediately seen to be helpful. Once the assumption that teachers had an exclusive role to play in communications with parents and caregivers was challenged it became possible to put forward ideas about how teaching assistants could extend or complement consultation processes without implied or explicit critism.

Practical matters

Participants were then asked to think about the practical question of *how* to enhance the role of teaching assistants in consultation with parents and caregivers. They began to share ideas, frequently based on observational narratives about the reality of everyday life in the school. These are presented next.

An insight from the research discussions was that first steps towards bringing parents and caregivers into closer relationships with schools can come from anyone – not necessarily needing to be initiated by teachers. Teaching assistants are indispensable here and, we found, are keen to develop this role. In practical terms, teaching assistants pointed out it is worth remembering that routine communications with parents and caregivers – not necessarily on the scale of formalized consultations – build confidence and helps establish relationships. For those parents and caregivers who may feel they have relatively little to contribute to a discussion with a teacher, for example, teaching assistants might be able to use their skills to glean seemingly small insights that can contribute to improved teaching and learning.

Many examples came to light, of things parents had mentioned while strapping a child into their bus seat or handing over a child in the cloakroom. For example, one mum had mentioned to a teaching assistant that her daughter had been to a cathedral to be confirmed. Inclusion of this parent's brief input later enabled the teaching assistant to raise the pupil's voice in class and help scaffold her learning:

Teacher: your mum told me you went to the Cathedral, Holly . . .
          (no response)
TA: you went to be . . . co . . .
          (no response)
TA: con . . . .
          (no response)
TA: . . . conf . . .
Holly   confirmed!

The group came to realize that teaching assistants had significant ongoing access to communication with parents and caregivers. Recognition of the importance of these 'fragments of consultation' greatly encouraged them to see opportunities to include the voices of parents and caregivers in the project of supporting school improvement. One member of the group observed:

> I hadn't realized that sort of chitchat was an example of consultation with a parent that could improve teaching and learning.

Teaching assistants then raised the question of 'can we go to parents, rather than them coming to us?', which opened up potential for new sites of intervention and practice. Hammet and Burton (2005) similarly suggest scope for expanding the role teaching assistants can play both within and beyond the school. It was recognized that communication and consultation with parents does not necessarily take place, or need to take place, in school:

> We can't force parents to come into school – some parents have problems with transport – students come from a wide area, and some parents do not drive.
>
> (Teaching assistant)

> If some parents are reluctant to come to the school, could the school go to the parents? Problems with this might arise – such as the question of taking up parents' time and the question of who could do such visits? Teaching assistants would be ideal because they could maintain links

between teachers, parents and any other agencies involved, but would this put loads more work on them?

(Teacher)

Complicated issues come up over *sites* of consultation: on the one hand home visits might help raise participation of parents and caregivers in school life, but they might also create disenfranchisement:

Some parents may see something like this as intrusive, while others might use it as a further reason to *not* come in to the school or as an excuse *not* to see a teacher.

(Teacher)

This is an example of where it became clear through the research that one-off 'quick fix' solutions are rarely available to those seeking to advance an agenda for inclusion. The Management Group agreed to convene a working party, including representative teaching assistants, to consider these issues further.

One factor which complicates consultation for Pittlesden School is that its pupils have complex impairments which can constrain a family's participation in school life. As a critical backdrop to the research we had offered participants the social model of disability as a constructive theoretical position which helps focus on practical ideas of how we can work to develop inclusive practice without being straitjacketed by what we feel we do or do not know about impairment (Oliver 1996). This approach does not deny that some children and their families are harder to include than others but instead helps us to evolve clear and consistent thinking about how the consequences of any child's impairment – including its impact on how families can get involved in school life – can be managed in comfortable and enabling ways.

We encouraged participants to think in terms of what it takes to be inclusive (Allan 2003) in order to reach new positions on what it might take to draw closer links between parents with complex commitments and their children's school.

Focus on the consequences of impairment had certainly become part of the discussion:

A problem parents face if they are invited to something after school is finding someone to look after children who have special needs.

(Teacher)

Another factor as to why parents might not come to evening or after school events is the disruption this causes to their child's routine. A lot of the students have problems coping with even slight disruptions in their normal routines – for instance if their bath is late – and this can have further repercussions later on, or the next day.

(Teaching assistant)

Yet commitment to a social model approach to dismantling those barriers which shore up exclusions proved inspiring:

[T]eaching assistants could help here by providing crèche facilities, or other activities to keep students and their siblings occupied.

[W]e could use an SMS TXT service to bring in the views of families.

[W]e may be able to gear some of our strategies around informal contact so not all of the emphasis around communication with families means they have to come into school for meetings with a teacher.

(Teaching assistant)

As the group then looked back over recent events which might have been better utilized in terms of opportunities for parents and caregivers they observed scope for changing practice:

[T]he idea of having meetings with parents 'tagged on' after a school event has been tried, but even though parents turned up to the event, and refreshments were provided, very few stayed for the meeting.

(Teaching assistant)

Informal gathering time was then scheduled *before* the next big event and did indeed create opportunities for meeting more families than usual in a relaxed way. Recognition was given to the active part teaching assistants should play in talking to parents and caregivers during this gathering so that their role in the process of consultation was explicitly established. Now when they chatted to parents they had a brief to treat conversation as a *consultative mechanism*. Afterwards, when snippets of consultation were fed back it was immediately obvious that parents and staff shared real concern over inclusion of children who come to school on buses which frequently arrive late. Late arrival clearly impedes children's participation in teaching and learning and staff had been frustrated about this for some time. As the voices of parents and caregivers were added to the picture, the need to tackle the issue became more urgent and the possibility of involving parents as allies in the school's campaign to improve punctuality of buses became clear. Staff felt they were beginning to recognize the real improvements that could be made to teaching and learning through maximizing consultation with parents and caregivers – and the substantial role that teaching assistants could play in making this happen was easy to see.

Opening up dialogue around new possibilities for teaching assistants to support consultation with parents and caregivers revealed many strands of opportunity. Some extended current practice. For example, it was noticed some parents liked being invited into their child's classroom to help out. In these situations scope for 'consultation' exists:

> Perhaps class teachers could release teaching assistants for a few minutes to chat to parents and listen to their concerns and help let them know the school is interested in what they think.
>
> (Teaching assistant)

Added to this was an important perception of parents and caregivers as having sometimes encountered oppressive practices in communications with school:

> [W]e need to find out what parents think when we invite them in to discuss how their child is doing. Many automatically think something is wrong, or that their child is in trouble. Making it clear to parents why we want to meet them is important and being invited to meet a teaching assistant might be less worrying.
>
> (Teaching assistant)

The importance of putting into place structures that encourage parents and caregivers to be involved in communications with the school early on in a child's school career was something teaching assistants felt could prevent distance building up:

> [I]t is vital we get a positive start with parents of children coming to us as this marks the beginning of a long relationship.
>
> (Teaching assistant)

Observations of school routines helped generate ideas on expanding the role of teaching assistants in consultation:

> [R]eceiving class teachers often visit children in other settings to liaise with staff and carers and establish good communication – teaching assistants could do this as well.
>
> [A]ny visit a parent makes to school could include a separate opportunity to talk to their child's class TA – so they have time to reflect and get a chance to ask questions about things they might not have thought of with the teacher. Teaching assistants could do 'follow up' discussions on the way out with parents to add to the feeling that we are trying to connect with them.
>
> (Teaching assistant)

Changing practice

As part of the 'action' cycle in the research project, participants were tasked with developing ideas for new types of consultation. They saw the importance of creating an event or activity which would enable them to find out the views of parents and caregivers about what makes communication and consultation work. It would provide important insights about possible barriers to communication with school, and help establish shared understanding of why improving communication is vital for school improvement. Different ideas were proposed:

> What about 'fun' activities to encourage whole families to participate? We could try and get reluctant parents to realise we're not just there for the 'official' school stuff – we are human and approachable and interested in them.
>
> (Teaching assistant)

> The school website could have a parents area which could contain links to information sites, other agencies, free software and invite responses.
>
> (Teaching assistant)

Debate then opened up about how to avoid marginalizing families without access to computers, what to do about ensuring access for parents who don't read or write and how to include people who find English difficult. New critical questions were constantly coming up:

> What will we do about the views of parents who seem to be presenting a barrier to their child's learning?
>
> Who will have access to knowledge gained through consultation with parents?
>
> [W]hat boundaries will be placed around the sharing of information from, and about, parents?
>
> (Teaching assistant)

And so it transpired that the participants were realizing the importance and complexity of inclusive approaches for all, regardless of the determinants of difference.

Arguably what we have seen in this chapter is that for Pittlesden School, learning through shared engagement in research has promoted inclusion at a variety of levels. The inclusion of teaching assistants in developing consultation with parents and caregivers through action research proved an extremely interesting exercise, which offers insights for any school improvement team. Evidently, an inclusive school is characterized by support staff being actively involved in its development.

Areas for reflection

The research has demonstrated that teaching assistants who are engaged with the day-to-day reality of implementing inclusive practice, and have the opportunity to reflect upon the ideology and the detail of inclusion, are key agents for change. It has shown that consultation with parents can be usefully approached as problem sharing for teachers and teaching assistants to work on collaboratively, and that best practice comes from sustained efforts to get to know what parents and caregivers feel would enable them to come into closer communication with the school. Teaching assistants have a contribution to make in gathering information and talking with parents and caregivers about this. A number of points for further reflection can be usefully considered.

First, through this project we realize the critical importance of teaching assistants being brought into a relationship of collaboration in order to advance school improvement. Working in a climate of openness with teaching colleagues enables widespread professional development to take place, improves morale and enhances individual practice. The evidence presented in this chapter shows teaching assistants have a central role to play in supporting school improvement when they work closely with each other and with teachers and other allies including parents.

Second, a question for schools is 'how can a culture of constant reflection to promote research action involving teaching assistants be encouraged and sustained?' This question is important. The chapter has shown how a research project provided an opportunity for teaching assistants to observe and examine a range of divergent and sometimes troubling dilemmas involved in making their work with parents more inclusive that have not typically been thought of as belonging to their world of work. Through their research engagements it became possible for teaching assistants to develop understanding of the different strategies they can bring to school improvement and to reveal the potential impacts of their work on the parents and caregivers they seek to include. This chapter shows a great deal was achieved. Following on from the research findings it seems important for schools to:

- identify possibilities for teaching assistants to pioneer changes in respect of inclusive working with a range of family stakeholders;
- reflect on the challenges and barriers that working to improve communication with parents throw up for teaching assistants, and think about whole school approaches to overcoming these;
- identify and drive through projects for developing the role of teaching assistants to further enhance the project of consultation and inclusion.

This chapter has charted the difference teaching assistants made in bringing parents into relation with a school and makes recommendations for inclusive practice. Hopefully it signifies the importance of positioning teaching assistants at the cutting edge of initiatives to advance the agenda for inclusion.

Reflection on values and practice

1   What contribution do teaching assistants make to communications between families and the school in your own work context?
2   What kinds of values underpin inclusive relationships between home and school?
3   Are there any issues about confidentiality in relation to information teaching assistants may learn about from parents and caregivers, and should all information be shared with the teaching staff and/or headteacher?

Suggested further reading

Moran, A. and Abbott, L. (2002) 'Developing Inclusive Schools: the Pivotal Role of Teaching Assistants in Promoting Inclusion in Special and Mainstream Schools in Northern Ireland', *European Journal of Special Needs Education*, 17(2): 161–73.
Sorsby, C. (2004) 'Forging and Strengthening Alliances: Learning Support Staff and the Challenge of Inclusion', in Armstrong, F. and Moore, M. (eds), *Action Research for Inclusive Education: Changing Places, Changing Practices, Changing Minds*, London: RoutledgeFalmer.

References

Allan, J. (2003) 'Productive Pedagogies and the Challenge of Inclusion', *British Journal of Special Education*, 30(4): 175–9.
Armstrong, F. and Moore, M. (eds) (2004) *Action Research for Inclusive Education: Changing Places, Changing Practices, Changing Minds*, London: RoutledgeFalmer.
Barton, L. (2004) 'Foreword' in Armstrong, F. and Moore, M. (eds) *Action Research for Inclusive Education: Changing Places, Changing Practices, Changing Minds*, London: RoutledgeFalmer.
Dunn, K. and Moore, M. (2004) *Report on Supporting School Improvement – Enhancing Satisfactory Teaching*, confidential report to Commissioning School.
Hammett, N. and Burton, N. (2005) 'Motivation, Stress and Learning Support Assistants: an Examination of Staff Perceptions at a Rural Secondary School', *Leadership and Management* 25(3): 299–310.
Moran, A. and Abbott, L. (2002) 'Developing Inclusive Schools: the Pivotal Role of Teaching Assistants in Promoting Inclusion in Special and Mainstream Schools in Northern Ireland', *European Journal of Special Needs Education* 17(2): 161–73.
Oliver, M. (1996) *Understanding Disability: from Theory to Practice*, London: Macmillan.
Reay, D. and Ball, S. (1998) '"Making their Minds Up": Family Dynamics of School Choice', *British Educational Research Journal*, 24(4): 431–48.
Rhodes, C. (2006) 'The Impact of Leadership and Management on the Construction of Professional Identity in School Learning Mentors', *Educational Studies* 32(2): 157–69.
Sorsby, C. (2004) 'Forging and Strengthening Alliances: Learning Support Staff and the Challenge of Inclusion', in Armstrong, F. and Moore, M. (eds) *Action Research for Inclusive Education: Changing Places, Changing Practices, Changing Minds*, London: RoutledgeFalmer.

Chapter 9

A new role for special schools?

Gill Richards

The Green Paper *Excellence for All Children* (1997) announced that there would be a new role for special schools within its vision for meeting children's special educational needs in the changing education sector. It accepted that there would still be a need for special schools to provide for a small number of pupils whose needs could not be met within the mainstream sector (p. 49), but argued that a new role was required to take account of the current context. In particular, it identified that moves towards inclusion and meeting increasingly complex learners' needs would impact on the traditional categories of special schools and expectations of the way that their staff worked. This notion of retaining special schools with a role that develops in line with current initiatives has been key to later government policy discussions and their strategy, 'Removing Barriers to Achievement' (2004).

So, what were the 'old' roles for special schools and how should these change as our schools respond to meeting the educational needs of increasingly diverse learners? Should special schools be expected to continually develop 'new' roles as mainstream schools improve their capacity to educate learners previously seen as requiring specialist teaching and facilities? What does the future hold for special schools? What are the implications for teaching assistants and their roles?

Teaching assistants are often viewed as the solution to difficulties encountered when pupils identified as needing special education are moved into different environments. Understanding the social history of special schooling, where we are now and how we arrived there, is important for all staff as these factors do affect our work even if this isn't immediately obvious. This chapter will attempt to explore these issues and reflect on the impact initiatives in the past and present have had on those associated with special schools.

What was the 'old' role for special schools?

Armstrong (2003: 1) argues that: 'the history of special education is for the most part a hidden history. Rarely are the voices of those who were schooled in this system heard.' Swain (2005: 787) supports this view, suggesting that historical views were presented mainly by 'non-disabled professionals . . . the history of those in power'. Indeed, many historical details of special education provision have originated from official reports, medical practitioners' studies and information from other professionals involved with maintaining special education. This reflected the culture of the times where disabled people were seen as 'defective' and requiring others to decide how their needs should be met.

Historical 'facts' that originate in this way mean that our understanding of early special schools and their development is one-dimensional, drawn only from the perspectives of the 'establishment', those who worked in and managed the schools, rather than including the views of those who received the schooling. As in other areas of history where only one dominant perspective is presented (for example, one country's view of a war they fought in), careful reflection may be needed on what is presented as uncontested 'truth' about the success, or otherwise, of special school provision.

Early special schools, towards the end of the nineteenth century, were rooted in the ideology of the Eugenics movement. Eugenicists believed that the quality of the population would be improved if it contained more intelligent, educated and skilled workers. They argued that this could be achieved first, by encouraging 'superior' groups to have more children and second, by preventing 'inferior' groups from having any children. This led to policies across the world of sterilization, segregation and in its extreme version of Nazism, extermination, affecting the lives of many seen as undesirable by those in power because of their race, skin colour, religion, sexual preferences or impairment. The roots of this movement can be seen in some practices with disabled people today, for example where terminations are routinely offered to expectant mothers whose baby is likely to be born with Down Syndrome; where disabled people are 'encouraged' to be sterilized or use contraception to prevent them becoming parents; and where adults with the most severe learning difficulties may still live in group settings that are organized in ways reminiscent of past asylums.

During this time, intelligence was believed to be bred rather than nurtured (Kevles 1985) and so this led to commonly held views that there was no point in educating disabled people (Thomas and Loxley 2001) or allowing them to have children. Consequently, disabled people were commonly viewed as defective, needing to be controlled and segregated from the rest of society. This led to significant numbers of children and adults with learning difficulties or complex needs being placed in institutions such as asylums and colonies, with the sexes kept carefully apart. Placement in these establishments required diagnosis by medical practitioners of an individual's 'defect', for example, 'lunatic', 'idiot', 'imbecile' and 'feeble-minded'.

Being able to work and not be a drain on society were also important values held by Eugenicists, so in contrast to people with learning difficulties, other groups of disabled children, for example those who were categorized as blind, deaf or feeble-minded, were provided with education to enable them to gain future employment (Armstrong 2003: 11). This early form of special education was offered in a range of special schools, classes within institutions and other settings outside of the mainstream system. Teachers were relatively free to decide on the curriculum they provided, although some School Boards gave them direction, such as the School Board for London (1891), which stated that teachers should offer an 'extended type of kindergarten instruction, giving special emphasis on manual occupations' (Read and Walmsley 2006: 459). At this time, many special schools catered for classes of about 20 pupils while their mainstream counterparts had classes of at least 50, so despite the curriculum appearing to be a contradictory mix of childlike lessons and preparation for work, it did indicate an attempt to meet individual needs.

Generally in these times, most special schools were expected to teach the '3 'Rs' (reading, writing and arithmetic) to enable pupils to gain the skills to transfer into mainstream schools. This was supplemented by work skills and scripture lessons. Work skills tended to be gender specific with boys studying woodwork, shoemaking and basket making and girls studying cookery, laundry and needlework (Read and Walmsley 2006). Despite a report from the Departmental Committee on Defective and Epileptic Children (DCDEP 1898) which stated that 'in may cases these children were capable of answering and reasoning almost as well as carefully taught normal children' (para. 54), society's anxiety about their need for segregation meant that pupils did not transfer into mainstream schools and progressed from school into residential training homes at 16 years of age.

Locking away disabled children and adults was seen in these times as an effective way of ensuring that they did not disrupt other pupils' learning or influence them with their supposedly potentially criminal and sexually promiscuous ways. As more children, particularly from the working classes, entered the education system during the nineteenth century, schools encountered problems with increased numbers not achieving the required standards. This pressure on schools' capacity led to more children being educated outside the mainstream system (Armstrong 2003).

During the Second World War, children returned from residential special schools to be with their families. This led to a decrease in residential provision as children attended their local schools and found work, replacing those away at war (Armstrong and Barton 1999). As the war came to a close, the 1944 Education Act had a significant impact on increasing special education provision. The aim of the Act was to provide free education for *all* pupils, but as this involved testing and categorizing groups of learners, some were still deemed 'ineducable' and placed in non-educational settings such as Junior Training Centres or Subnormality Hospitals. The following Handicapped Pupils and School Health Regulations of 1945 identified 11 categories of handicapped pupil, which was later amended to ten. When identified with a particular 'handicap', all pupils regarded as educable were then provided for in a special school. These schools had their own special curriculum so transfers back into mainstream schools rarely occurred.

The comprehensive schooling system of the 1960s and 1970s started to challenge the ideas of separate special schools. The 1970 Education (Handicapped Children) Act gave the last group of pupils, those with severe learning difficulties (previously identified as ineducable), the right to education. In practice this was often in the same Junior Training Centres which were renamed 'Subnormal Schools' and had the same staff which were not qualified teachers, but was a great step forward in recognizing that all children could and should be educated.

Around this time it was noted that there were many more boys than girls in special schools, raising issues around gender bias, and also that children of Caribbean heritage were significantly over-represented, raising questions of racism (Coard 1972). Further criticisms of the quality of teaching and curriculum in special schools led to increasing questions about their role. Reflecting on this time, Thomas and Vaughan (2004: 31) suggested that special schools existed for the 'convenience of mainstream rather than the purpose of improving the lives of those in them'. This supported the views of earlier commentators, for example, Goffman (1968) who thought that segregated institutions were often presented 'as the rational and humane solution to people's difficulties, (whereas) they in fact operate merely as society's "storage dumps"' (p. 31).

The Warnock Report (DES 1978), followed by the 1981 Education Act, replaced the ten categories of handicap with a new label, special educational needs (SEN), and introduced the concept of statementing, identifying how and where children's specific educational needs should be met. Both the Report and the Act have a reputation for supporting the right for pupils identified as having special educational needs to be integrated into mainstream schools. However, they allowed for exceptions, which stated that education must meet children's needs, be financially efficient and not affect other children's education, so in effect, still provided the basis for mainstream schools to avoid taking on children seen as a 'problem' while maintaining a continuing role for special schools.

Although special schools were still to be required for a particular group of pupils whose needs could not be met in mainstream, the Warnock Report suggested that the educational goals should be the same for all pupils. This was later supported by the newly devised 'National Curriculum', which despite an opportunity for 'disapplication' for pupils with special educational needs, provided a defined curriculum for all children whatever school they attended. The effects of this form of integration within mainstream school practice caused a significant decline in special schools during the 1980s and 1990s.

Developing co-operative ways of working

The developments of integration during the 1980s started to affect the stability of special schools and it was the 1988 Education Act that increased their financial support and provided them with an opportunity for working with mainstream schools. The Act delegated powers and resources from the local education authorities to schools. Special schools were funded by a formula method that was applied on the basis of the number of places available rather than the number of pupils actually attending. This ensured that special schools were not affected by fluctuating rolls or placed under pressure to recruit or lose pupils (Lee 1992). Mainstream schools were encouraged to manage support for their children with special educational needs, but this led to concerns about efficient use of finances available. As a result, special schools were viewed in some situations to be a more efficient use of resources and so led to increased placements of pupils who would otherwise have been in mainstream schools. In contrast, some special and mainstream schools used this opportunity to work together co-operatively and develop joint provision in localized areas.

The 1997 Green Paper, *Excellence for All Children: Meeting Special Educational Needs*, set out the government's vision for raising standards of achievement for all children with special needs. The Green Paper, supported by a later programme of action (1998), identified a new role for special schools that focused on meeting the challenge of more complex needs and supporting mainstream schools and their teachers. This all took place in the context of an increasingly political agenda about inclusion of children identified as having special educational needs, supported by the Salamanca Statement (1994) which called on governments to adopt a policy of educating all children together, unless there were compelling reasons not to do so. At this time national directives continued to affect what teachers taught and school performance became increasingly monitored. Competition between schools was encouraged as their pupils' results were compared, leading to pressure for exclusion of children who provided too great a challenge for some mainstream schools. As a result, the new role for special schools also included taking on more children identified as having social and emotional behavioural difficulties who were becoming increasing casualties of the pressurized mainstream system.

The Green Paper acknowledged that although teachers in special schools had the necessary expertise to support their mainstream colleagues, they came from a small staffing group, and so it recommended that local education authorities should consider new ways of organizing schools. Mainstream schools could be specially resourced or have special units attached. Special schools could be amalgamated and where possible linked with mainstream schools to provide them with support and training.

During the following years, schools and local education authorities developed provision to meet local needs in line with the Green Paper's plan and the following Special Educational Needs and Disability Act (SENDA) (2001). In some areas this resulted in effective support for children with special needs, but in others, there was criticism about teachers being deskilled and children's un-met needs. For example, some mainstream teachers began to lose confidence in their own ability to teach all children as they were persuaded by special school claims of the need for highly specialized skills and knowledge

(Thomas and Loxley 2001: 26). In other situations, teachers from mainstream schools argued that although their colleagues from special schools had some specific expertise, they were inexperienced in the ways of mainstream schools and so the training they offered was not appropriate for the context. Thomas and Loxley (2001: 107) also expressed concern about the financial incentives used to place children in special schools: 'While six-figure sums of money go to pay for children at some residential special schools, those sums do not accompany these children if they move back into mainstream. Nor are they available as a resource to a mainstream school in the first place.' So, once again it seemed that special schools were seen to be caught in a conflicting situation; they were the key to providing innovative ways of integrating with pupils with special educational needs, while at the same time their very existence was viewed to be obstructing progress.

In 2004, the government released its latest strategy for educating pupils with special educational needs, 'Removing Barriers to Achievement'. This restated previous intentions to see special schools as the providers of education for children with complex needs, while sharing their expertise with mainstream schools to support inclusion. It stressed that the future role for special schools was to focus on 'cutting edge' partnership work with mainstream colleagues through federations and cluster school arrangements.

These partnerships were expected to benefit from the strengths of each part of the sector (mainstream and special) and so make communities of schools more effective in meeting children's needs. The intention was to break down the divide between special and mainstream schools and encourage increased pupil movement across them, meeting needs with a joint sector approach. It was intended that these partnerships would reduce the need for high cost, residential special school placements and bring provision to a localized level. Although the implications were that special schools could be working themselves out of a job in the future, the strategy stated that it was 'critical to ensure that high quality provision was available locally before special school places were reduced' (DfES 2004: 38).

For the first time, a government strategy drew attention to the expertise in mainstream schools from which special schools could benefit. Special schools at this time were three times more likely than mainstream to require special measures because of poor leadership and management, inadequate curriculum, low attendance and poor teaching (p. 38). The Department for Education and Skills recommended (2004) that the mainstream sector should provide training and resources to support special schools in these circumstances, laying the basis for more equal partnership arrangements.

In recent years, public awareness of the quality of special school provision started to increase as national reports became available through the internet and the media. This led to increased debate about the role of these schools and their future existence. Disabled people's voices, often absent in the past from discussions about their own education, joined this debate in larger numbers, giving them a more powerful input at national level. Criticism of special schools was made strongly by some prominent disabled people, for example, Mike Oliver (1995: 112), who argued that education in special schools was a failure in terms of any criteria applied to it as it wasn't equable with mainstream, it didn't aid integration and it didn't meet the needs of the children involved. Mason (2000: 9) supported this view and argued that the problem about lack of resources to support learners was based in a frustrating, circular argument, where: 'special schools must be kept because mainstream schools cannot cope, because they do not have the resources that are in special schools'. This identifies one of the key problems about having a dual system of education provision (special *and* mainstream schools). If the resources available are limited and split between special and mainstream schools, the need will always be there for special schools, as they have resources that mainstream schools need.

Other professionals argued that special schools still had an important role to play as long as what they offered was 'special': 'Special schools, with their limited staffing, resources and restricted peer groups should not try to emulate what can better be delivered elsewhere' (Southgate 1992: 78). This conflicted to some extent with the earlier views expressed by Dessent (1987) who challenged the right of special schools to exist, however high their quality, if the same education could be provided in a mainstream school.

What about the future?

So what is the future for special schools? Should they continue to reinvent themselves and find new roles as different pupil groups experience difficulties in schools struggling to meet increasing numbers of national initiatives that are seemingly at odds with inclusion? When we look back at the first part of this chapter and reflect on some of the arguments for early special schools, are there really any new roles involved, or are they similar ones, repackaged?

Will some types of school disappear as their pupils are accommodated in mainstream, while others such as Pupil Referral Units (PRUs), increase? Will 'inclusion' units be viewed as an alternative to special schools or just another way of segregating pupils in what is effectively a special school within a mainstream school?

What about the views of those involved and how do they see the future role of special schools? What are the views of disabled people about the education provision so many attend as the result of decisions made by others? What about school staff, parents and importantly for our intended audience for this book, what are the implications for the roles of teaching assistants?

Clearly, the government expect special schools to develop their role to meet changing pupil needs. As medical advances enable the survival of children with increasingly complex needs, and pressures in mainstream schools create more casualties for a widening group of learners, special schools can be seen as a kind of benign service industry to the mainstream (Thomas and Loxley

2001), providing access to an education previously unavailable or deemed inappropriate. Mason (2003) disputes this role, arguing that it is these pupils who most need to be included within mainstream schools as they are the most isolated. When you consider groups of children put together, unable to move independently or use verbal communication, her point about isolation is clear. How can these children interact with each other? Often their main access to any action or communication is through staff rather than their peers, not the preference of many children, however wonderful we all might be!

Mason pursues her point further, arguing that the 'idea that there are some disabled children who will do "better" in segregated schools is incompatible with the idea that society needs to learn how to include all its citizens' (p. 13). She claims that such ideas are caused by the government's complete misunderstanding of the aims of inclusive education. This view differs significantly from that of Ofsted in its 2006 report, *Inclusion: Does It Matter Where Pupils Are Taught?* Here, Ofsted argued that the most important factor was not the type of provision a pupil attended, but the quality of that provision. Good and outstanding education was identified in both mainstream and special schools, although more was available in mainstream and less in PRUs. Mason and other advocates for inclusion take issue with this, arguing as they have in the past, that it does matter where pupils are educated, especially when the longer view is taken. For them, segregated education is associated with 'impoverished social experiences and reduced academic outcomes, poor preparation for re-integration into adult society' (CSIE 2003: 110). This strongly held opinion has led to a powerful lobby from the inclusion movement to close all special schools by 2020. The experiences of disabled young people on the 2020 campaign website provide stark accounts of the impact special schools have had on them. For example, Maresa shares her experience of 'being hidden away with the assumption that I was worthless (which) still haunts me with a terror that I cannot describe' (www.2020campaign). The priority for this group is to retrain special school staff and reallocate all resources into mainstream schools.

Although this 2020 campaign has many parent supporters, for example, Parents for Inclusion (Pi), other parents support the continued role for special schools just as strongly. Many are concerned about the lack of support and resources within mainstream schools and have distressing stories of un-met needs and children 'failed by the system'. This is despite the large increase of teaching assistants in schools to provide support to pupils with identified 'special' needs and their teachers. Some have settled for the 'best of both worlds' with their children on dual placements, spending time in both mainstream and special schools.

School staff also appear to have conflicting views. Some are convinced that special schools are an outdated way to meet children's needs and that disabled children do better in mainstream schools (Avramides 2000; Utton 2006) while others, for example teachers supported by their union NASUWT (2004), want more special schools to be built, believing that integration has gone too far.

Often, teaching assistants are seen as the major resource to enable learners' movement from special to mainstream settings (Anderson *et al.* 2004) and certainly some identify this as one of their key responsibilities (Richards *et al.* 2007).

A champion for increasing the role of special schools was Baroness Mary Warnock, who publicly stated at the Annual Wales Education Lecture (3/10/2006) that her earlier recommendations for integration and the subsequent movement of so many children out of special schools had proved to be a disastrous legacy. She called for a change in the purpose of special schools, arguing that they should not be limited to providing for children with complex needs but should be part of a wider system serving an increased range of needs. This apparent change of attitude in turn angered those with positive experiences of inclusive practice and heartened those with opposing views, creating an even wider rift between groups.

So, what is the evidence that special schools work? What criteria are applied to judge their success against? We do know that the actual percentage of children attending special schools has dropped from 1.5 per cent in 1983 to 0.82 per cent in 2004, although the number of pupils solely registered in PRUs has increased by 37 per cent between 2002 and 2004 (CSIE 2005). Equally clear is the fact that in 2004 such percentages differ across local authorities, with the highest percentage of pupils attending special schools in South Tynside (1.46 per cent) and the lowest in Newham (0.06 per cent). This indicates a very mixed response to meeting the educational needs of disabled children, reflecting what could only be described as the conflicting messages from the government. We have directions to increase inclusion with additional funds provided to increase numbers of, and training for, teaching assistants, which are countered by initiatives that promote exclusion such as finance for building new 'Centres of Excellence' special schools and grant aid worth millions of pounds to charities so that they can run specialist schools for very small numbers of children (Mason 2006).

The evidence as to whether pupils do better in special or mainstream schools is inconclusive (Thomas and Loxley 2004; Ofsted 2006). This is interesting, as directives about our education system usually require us to produce 'evidence based practice' and 'value for money'. Such a lack of evidence leads us to a more crucial question, if we cannot prove that special schools provide the best education for our 'vulnerable' learners, why do they continue to exist? Certainly the current dual system means that neither special nor mainstream schools have the resources they need. How long should this be allowed to continue and what about the children whose lives are affected by this?

Conclusions

The origins of special schools were about keeping disabled people away from the rest of society and ensuring that they did not affect others' education. When we hear discussions today we might think that little has changed. In reality there have been many developments, but society is still reliant on this form of education despite a lack of undisputed evidence of its success. Those in favour of a continuing role for special schools suggest that these should be multi-dimensional, responding to localized needs (Ofsted 2006). Others are campaigning for all special schools to close by 2020. Teaching assistants' roles have changed significantly from their early days of supporting teachers with basic classroom tasks. Now, they are educational professionals whose duties require them to demonstrate a wide range of skills from supporting learning to personal care.

It is likely that if more children move from special schools into the mainstream sector, teaching assistants will need to increase their expertise both in methods of learning support and responding to the complexities of mainstream schooling, to enable the pupils with whom they work to gain the most benefit from it. Many teaching assistants are working directly with other professionals, but as multi-agency developments increase to support pupils identified as having special educational needs, this is an area in which they may require further training to provide effective inclusion for all learners.

Whatever the future of special schools, and I would argue that this is not clear today, good practice in any education provision usually suggests that we learn best about what we should do when we ask those who are experiencing it. Such an approach is one that promotes the rights of all children to have their views valued and is the very basis of working inclusively. The Disability Equality Duty (2006) requires schools to actively engage with disabled people about their provision. I would suggest that this is a very appropriate place to start discussions about what our future schools should look like.

Reflection on values and practice

1   Reflect on your own experiences of special and mainstream schools. What barriers within these schools are experienced by young people identified as having special educational needs? How could these be resolved?
2   If we know what is not working effectively in mainstream schools for disabled children and young people, why is the solution to use special school placements rather than make the changes necessary in mainstream?
3   There is no conclusive research evidence that special schools work effectively, particularly in the long term. Why do you think this is so, and should we continue to rely on them without this?

Suggested further reading

Armstrong, D. (2003) *Experiences of Special Education. Re-evaluating Policy and Practice Through Life Stories*, London: RoutledgeFalmer.

Mason, M. (2003) 'Rebuilding the Walls of Exclusion'. *Inclusion Now*, Summer 2003.

Read, J. and Walmsley, J. (2006) 'Historical Perspectives on Special Education, 1890–1970', *Disability and Society* 21(5) (August).

Reference list

Anderson V., Farady, S., Prowse, S. Richards, G. and Swindells. D. (2003) *Count Me in FE*. London: Learning and Skills Development Agency.

Armstrong, D. (2003) *Experiences of Special Education. Re-evaluating Policy and Practice Through Life Stories*, London: RoutledgeFalmer.

Armstrong, F. and Barton, L. (eds) (1999) *Disability, Human Rights and Education. Cross-Cultural Perspectives*, Buckingham: Open University Press.

Avramides, E., Bayliss, P. and Burdon, R. (2000) 'A Survey into Mainstream Teachers' Attitudes Towards the Inclusion of Children with Special Educational Needs in the Ordinary School in one Local Education Authority', *Educational Psychology* 20(2): 191–211.

Coard, B. (1972) 'How the West Indian Child is Made Educationally Sub-Normal in the British School System' in Richardson, B. (ed.) (2005) *Tell it Like it is: How Our Schools Fail Black Children*, London: Bookmarks.

CSIE (2005) 'Are LEAs in England Abandoning Inclusive Education?' Press release 8/7/05.

Department for Education (1978) *Special Educational Needs*, report of the Committee of Enquiry into the Education of Handicapped Children and Young People, Cmnd 7212, London: HMSO.

Department for Education (1997) *Excellence for All Children*, London: The Stationery Office.

DfES (2004) *Removing Barriers to Achievement*, London: HMSO.

Dessent, T. (1987) in Armstrong, F. and Barton, L. (eds) (1999) *Disability, Human Rights and Education. Cross-Cultural Perspectives*, Buckingham: Open University Press.

Goffman, E. (1968) 'Asylums' in Thomas, G. and Vaughan, M. (eds) (2004) *Inclusive Education Readings and Reflections*, Maidenhead: Open University Press Press.

Kevles, D. (1985) *In the Name of Eugenics: Genetics and the Uses of Human Heredity*, New York: Alfred A. Knopf.

Lee, T. (1992) 'Local Management of Schools and Special Education' in Booth, T., Swann, W., Masterton, M. and Potts, P. (eds) *Policies for Diversity in Education*, London: Routledge.

Mason, M. (2000) 'There Are Only Winners', *TES Curriculum Special*, 14/7/2000.

Mason, M. (2003) 'Rebuilding the Walls of Exclusion', *Inclusion Now*, Summer 2003.

Mason, M. (2005) *Incurably Human*, Nottingham: Inclusive Solutions.

Mason, M. (2006) 'Inclusion: The Current Debate' in Robinson, G. and Maines, B. (eds) *Lucky Duck*, Position Paper 13/9/06.

NASUWT (2004) Annual Conference. 'Special Education Policy "a disaster"'. BBC News 24, 16/4/2004, bbc.co.uk/1/hi/education.

Ofsted (2006) *Inclusion: Does it Matter Where Pupils are Taught?* London: Crown Copyright.

Oliver, M. (1995) 'Does Special Education have a Role to Play in the 21st Century?' in Thomas, G. and Vaughan, M. (2004) *Inclusive Education Readings and Reflections*, Maidenhead: Open University Press.

Read, J. and Walmsley, J. (2006) 'Historical Perspectives on Special Education, 1890–1970', *Disability and Society* 21(5) (August).

Richards, G., Anderson, V. and Drury, P. (2007) *Responding to Learners' Views*, London: Learning and Skills Network.

Southgate, T. (1992) 'Finding a New Place. Changes in Role at Osmerod Special School', in Booth, T., Swann, W., Masterton, M. and Potts, P. (eds) *Policies for Diversity in Education*, London: Routledge.

Special Needs and Disability Act (2001), London: HMSO.

Swain, J. (2005) 'Inclusive Education: Readings and Reflections' in Read, J. and Walmsley, J. (2006) 'Historical Perspectives on Special Education, 1890–1970' *Disability and Society* 21(5) (August).

Thomas, G. and Loxley, A. (2001) *Deconstructing Special Education and Constructing Inclusion*. Buckingham: Open University Press.

Thomas, G. and Vaughan, M. (2004) *Inclusive Education Readings and Reflections*, Maidenhead: Open University Press.

Utton, N. (2006) 'Heading for Inclusion – Responding to Warnock', press release 6/7/2006.

Chapter 10

Inclusion, extension and enrichment

Personalized gifted and talented provision

Martyn Worrall and Joanne Steele

The purpose of this chapter is to offer guidance and advice to teaching assistants in their work of supporting children who have difficulty in accessing the school curriculum. While the prime focus is on those children who have been assessed as being gifted and/or talented, many of the issues discussed and the recommendations made, are relevant to the majority of children. The education of exceptionally able children and young people is a contentious subject. The concept of gifted and talented education, together with the theories, philosophies and vocabularies that encompass it, can present an uncomfortable challenge to adherents of the over-arching theories and practice of inclusive education. The idea of identifying, assessing and making provision for society's minority of 'most able' youngsters raises questions about elitism and ethical concerns about resources being allocated to a 'group' that many educationalists may consider to be already naturally advantaged. All children have a right of access to a school curriculum, which has been designed to meet their educational, social and emotional needs by people who understand how they learn. Although all children have an equal right of access, some find it more difficult to exercise this entitlement than others. These children are often given labels such as 'special needs', 'bullies', 'challenging', 'disabled' or 'exceptional'. In each of these cases, as with 'gifted and talented', the label can act as a barrier to the successful inclusion of children into the life of a school and can help to deny access to the curriculum which it offers. Having said that, it is still legitimate to discuss children for whom a curriculum, which aims to meet the needs of the majority of children, is potentially inaccessible to a range of minority 'groups'.

Children who are identified as gifted and talented show outstanding achievement or potential ability in a wide range of contexts. They may have specific academic aptitudes, may be particularly creative or sporting or may exhibit outstanding leadership qualities. These youngsters, as is the case with all children, regardless of difference, deserve to have their developmental and curricular needs met.

In identifying gifted and talented children we are not seeking to select an elite. We are not suggesting that they are more valued members of communities than any other child. In many ways our most able youngsters are as vulnerable as other minority 'groups' whose needs are different from the majority of young people. We feel, therefore, that teaching assistants have a vital role to play in helping to create a culture in schools and early years settings, where all levels of ability can be identified and nurtured, where social and emotional needs can be addressed and where exceptional achievement can be celebrated without the youngsters themselves feeling the need to hide their potential because of possible negative reactions from their peers and others. As teaching assistants are now being given opportunities to assume responsibility for areas of the work of a school or early years setting, they are in a good position to help senior leadership teams, managers and governing bodies to review the culture of the organization by helping them to address the following questions:

- Do we have an ethos which encourages and celebrates all forms of achievement and success?
- Do we have high expectations of ourselves and our children?
- Do we recognize our responsibility for gifted and talented children within our organization's policies?
- Are we committed to providing an enriched and challenging curriculum for all learners, including those who are most able?
- Do our support systems include provision for all learners, including those identified as exceptionally able?
- Are we working in partnership with parents/carers, other agencies and community groups to develop challenging extra-curricular and out-of-school setting activities for all learners, including those identified as gifted and talented?

Answering these questions should help an organization to address the fundamental issues which lie at the heart of this chapter, namely:

- How inclusive are we when considering the needs of all of our children and young people, including those who have exceptional ability in one or more areas of our curriculum?

Definitions, labels, assumptions and prejudice

Throughout the latter part of the twentieth century and the early part of the twenty-first there have been (often heated) debates in government, local authorities, schools, early years settings, university research departments, international and local communities about how to define children and young people who are either achieving highly or who have the potential to do so. Our conclusion, having listened to these debates, and having participated in many of them, is that they are divisive in nature and therefore likely to lead to exclusionary, non-inclusive provision in practice. Labels such as 'gifted and talented' or 'severe learning difficulties' are inherently divisive and emphasize exclusive differences in children, which may develop prejudice among the adults who work with them. We use them in this chapter for the sake of convenience, in the knowledge that their use is currently widespread. Key workers, such as teaching assistants who work in inclusive mainstream schools, settings and communities, should try to avoid emotive labels and match their work to the central philosophy of inclusive education, namely:

All children and young people, regardless of difference, deserve to have their educational, social, emotional and cultural needs met.

This is their entitlement and this encapsulates their human rights.

Identification

Although many gifted and talented children and young people are easily identified in early years settings and schools, it is essential that identification strategies are broad and flexible enough to ensure that hidden gifts and talents are not overlooked. It is also important to acknowledge that some youngsters from vulnerable, traditionally underachieving 'groups' (e.g. children who are 'looked after' by local authorities, some ethnic minorities, teenage mothers) may also be gifted and talented. Since January 2004 central government has advised schools to nominate the most able 10 per cent of every year group to be included on a national register. This refers mainly to those who are academically 'gifted' but it is important for organizations to also identify youngsters who may be 'talented' musicians, artists and sports players and those who excel in the performing arts. Teaching assistants have a vital role to play in the identification process as they often have a close working relationship with children, within which a detailed knowledge of an individual's strengths and areas for development emerges. Identifying percentages of children to benefit from additional support does not sit easily within a personalized, inclusive learning philosophy. Does not every child have a gift or talent that should be nurtured and developed? By suggesting that a nominal 10 per cent of each year group in every school should be identified, government policy makers were not recommending exclusive provision. Rather they were seeking to ensure that every school should make effective provision for its most able children within the context of that particular school, using methods of identification which have been agreed by the whole staff team, governors and parents.

A good starting point for the identification process is to start with those youngsters who are clearly neither stimulated nor challenged by a curriculum that meets the needs of their peers. No one method of identification is satisfactory, but a combination of some of the following strategies should be reliable:

- checklists
- detailed knowledge of backgrounds and interests

- use of an observer/external expert
- peer group nomination
- teacher/teaching assistant assessment
- examination results
- information from parents/carers
- pupil self-awareness.

Teaching assistants may find it useful to consider the following profile, which identifies some possible characteristics which may be exhibited by gifted pupils, when they are helping to develop identification strategies:

Profile – a gifted child or young person

A gifted child or young person:

- learns quickly, easily
- strong reasoning ability
- possesses an extensive general knowledge
- ability to deal with abstract concepts
- great intellectual curiosity
- asks many provocative, searching questions
- good concentration, persistence, determination
- thinks quickly
- good memory
- reads rapidly; extensive vocabulary
- keen alert observer; pays close attention to detail
- vivid imagination
- preference for individual work
- keen sense of humour
- perfectionist approach; dislikes failure
- divergent thinking processes; looks for the unusual
- interested in 'adult' issues and problems
- a wide range of interests and demanding hobbies
- untidy writing; has an unwillingness to record work.

(adapted from George 2002)

In addition, and to be truly inclusive when identifying children, it is important for teaching assistants to remember that gifted and talented youngsters are sometimes overlooked because of their individual personalities and learning styles. For instance, they may be working in an additional language or their language skills may be undeveloped, which prevents them from articulating arguments. Occasionally they may be untidy, badly behaved or lacking in concentration. Quite often these children will seek to hide their abilities because they would prefer not to be identified and, if assessment programmes test only attainment in culturally or gender biased ways, underlying abilities may never be identified.

'Vulnerability' and underachievement

Gifted and talented children and young people may be 'vulnerable' in many ways. Individuals may find it hard to cope emotionally with the implications of their ability and how this makes them different from the majority of their peers. Equally they may never have experienced failure in their formative years and will need effective guidance and support when this (inevitably) happens. Some of these youngsters may also, as we have seen earlier, be members of other vulnerable groups such as those who are 'looked after' by local authorities or those who are teenage mothers. Thus, it could be argued, they are 'doubly vulnerable', and the likelihood of their underachievement is compounded. In our county of Cumbria this potential underachievement by socially, culturally and educationally disadvantaged gifted and talented children has been recognized. The year 2006 saw the launch of a three-year project entitled 'Most Able: Least Likely', which will give us the opportunity to work with colleagues from social care and schools to raise the achievement levels of vulnerable youngsters with high ability. The philosophy of inclusive education underpins our work in this field as many of the youngsters involved may have been excluded, or may have excluded themselves, from mainstream society and schools. It is important to stress here that we are not seeking just to raise the educational levels of achievement of these youngsters. We plan to improve the quality of their life chances by working with them to raise their achievement in each of the five Every Child Matters (ECM) (DfES 2004) outcomes of *Be Healthy, Stay Safe, Enjoy and Achieve, Make a Positive Contribution and Achieve Economic Well-Being.* We are thus acknowledging that gifted and talented youngsters from disadvantaged 'groups' are unlikely to succeed unless all of their varied needs are addressed.

In a field related to the concept of 'double vulnerability' is the work on 'double exceptionality' undertaken by Diane Montgomery (2003). She highlights the importance of identifying and providing appropriate support for gifted and talented children who also have special educational needs. These may be related to a category of impairment (such as 'Asperger's Syndrome'), visual or hearing impairment, dyslexia, non-verbal learning difficulties, or difficulties related to communication, relationships and behaviour. For teaching assistants in schools and early years settings it is essential to have a thorough understanding of ECM, special educational needs and their interwoven links to effective provision for gifted and talented children and young people.

Differentiation, extension and enrichment: personalized learning

It is important to recognize the different learning styles of children and young people and understand possible implications for teaching assistants and teachers with regard to their approaches to teaching. Examples of differences in learning styles relate to ability, aptitude, motivation, ethnicity, culture, gender, personality and home background (to mention just a few possible factors). For gifted and talented children these differences can be particularly acute, and can result in them feeling the need to 'fit into' the expectations of their peers and others. This can affect their confidence and self-esteem which in turn, impacts on how they apply themselves and how much they achieve. These facts bring a need and an entitlement for access to a *differentiated* school and community curriculum. Such a curriculum acknowledges the differences in youngsters and it as an essential part of the work of teaching assistants to help plan and support its delivery. The following table outlines the main types of differentiation which may be relevant for all children but, in the context of this chapter, are particularly focused on those who regarded as 'most able':

Main types of differentiation

- by outcome   – marking, assessment, different amounts of work, higher expectations of the more able;
- by resource   – access to a bank of materials, varied texts with different levels of complexity;
- by task   – open-ended activities, support/core/extension, must/should/could, higher-level ideas, differentiated homework;
- by dialogue   – teacher presentation, level, speed, quality, sophistication of languages, other adults, debates, discussion, thinking skills, higher order questioning/thinking;
- by pupil expertise – hot seating, group composition of abilities, think-pair-share, reading or writing partners;
- by support   – other adults, mentors, additional time, use of teaching associates, fewer/more prompts, teacher intervention;
- by pace   – less time allowed, waiting time in response to questions, time for review/evaluation by pupils, menu to work through;
- by recording   – spoken, written, use of information and communication technology (ICT), graphical, presentations, variation of time, amount and styles;

- by organization   — location of resources, layout of classroom, independence, pair/group; friends/ability, learning styles;
- by interest   — brainstorming, pupils involved in planning, setting own challenges, research, selecting from menus.

(adapted from *Excellence in Cities* 1999)

For gifted and talented children and young people essential elements of a differentiated curriculum are *extension* and *enrichment*. The former encourages youngsters to use higher order thinking skills, working practices and response skills than would normally be expected from children of their age. The latter is used as a distinct teaching and learning strategy when there is planned intervention and additional challenge on behalf of children, to broaden their knowledge and understanding of a subject or topic beyond the normal parameters for their age groups. Helping children to develop higher order skills and managing planned intervention and additional challenge, seem to us to be appropriate roles for teaching assistants. Differentiation for these children should be 'open-ended' and the teaching assistant is ideally placed to help them build confidence in their ability to enable them to understand other points of view and to encourage them to develop independent learning skills. In short, and as new early years and school curriculum models develop in the future, we envisage teaching assistants helping to *personalize* the provision that is made for *all* children, including those identified as 'gifted and talented', within an education system which is fundamentally *inclusive* in structure and philosophy.

Before moving on to the final section of this chapter which takes a look at the future of gifted and talented provision in England, we want to mention another element of differentiation, which is used for highly able children in some educational settings, namely: *acceleration*. This is the planned move of children to work on more advanced tasks with older young people. While this approach has led to successful outcomes for some youngsters, we have seen too many instances when a lack of preparation on the part of adults and a lack of physical and emotional maturity on the part of children themselves, has led to their being unable to cope and to a subsequent loss of motivation and enthusiasm. Therefore, we generally advise against the use of acceleration and suggest that a personalized, differentiated curriculum can best be provided by the use of extension and enrichment.

Where do we go from here?

In the foreseeable future there are two aspects of provision in the field of gifted and talented education which will assume greater prominence and which should, we believe, lie at the heart of continuing professional development

(CPD) for teaching assistants. First, there will be an even greater emphasis placed on 'Personalized Learning' as envisaged in the *Better Schools for All* (2006). Second, the recently developed 'Institutional and Classroom National Quality Standards in Gifted and Talented Education' (Mouchel 2005) will become the tools used by schools, Ofsted, the Department for Children, Schools and Families (DfCSF) and School Improvement Partners (SIPs) to plan, monitor and evaluate provision for gifted and talented children and young people. These two initiatives are exemplified and explained in detail in the following two sections. It is essential for teaching assistants to have a secure grasp of both of them as they represent the basis on how effective schools are at meeting the needs of their most able pupils.

Personalized learning

The term 'personalized learning' as envisaged in *Better Schools for All* (2006) has been used at intervals in this chapter as, we believe, it is a key concept in relation to ensuring successful learning experiences and outcomes for all children, including those who have been identified as 'gifted and talented'. Its five key elements are summarized in the diagram below.

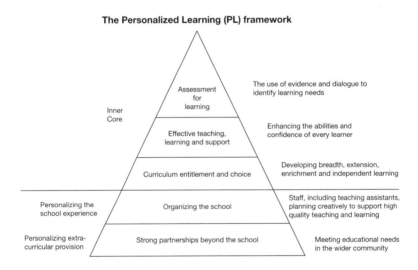

The Personalized Learning (PL) framework

Source: Adapted from *Better Schools for All*, DfES 2005

National institutional quality standards in gifted and talented education

The National Institutional Quality Standards (IQS) are closely linked to both the Personalized Learning (PL) and the ECM agendas. They have been designed to help schools and other organizations analyse and plan improvements for gifted and talented education. The standards are a supportive tool which can be used to audit practice and identify gaps in provision. Adoption of the quality standards will also provide an effective planning and evaluation tool for readers and managers in schools to use when evaluating teaching and learning across the whole school.

There are fourteen elements of the IQS with three levels of practice:

Level 1 – Entry: this indicates a baseline standard of practice, with scope for continuous improvement.

The level relates to a 'satisfactory' Ofsted inspection judgement.

Level 2 – Developing: this indicates that the school is effective in meeting the needs of children and young people and has scope for reinforcement, development and further improvement.

The level relates to a 'good' Ofsted inspection judgement.

Level 3 – Exemplary: this indicates exceptional and sustained practice with the scope for dissemination beyond the school/college and for continuous improvement as best practice evolves nationally.

The exemplary level relates to a 'very good/outstanding' Ofsted inspection judgement.

While the IQS are a self-evaluative tool to be used by schools, they will also be used by local authorities and by Ofsted to make judgements on school effectiveness. It is important, therefore, for teachers, and teaching assistants to consider the standards when developing personalized learning opportunities for individual children. The following small case study of a young girl called Rebecca is an example of how a school planned a personalized approach to learning. The effectiveness of this provision could be evaluated against the IQS.

Rebecca

Rebecca was a 6-year-old girl who attended a small rural school. Rebecca was identified as a talented artist with the ability of an 8-year-old. The school was already providing enriched provision, access to a range of resources and opportunities through which Rebecca could develop her artistic ability. Options were given to parents about how to further enrich and extend Rebecca's curriculum outside of the school, *if* they felt this was something they wished to pursue. The school suggested a number of community and voluntary groups, artists' workshops and Saturday clubs in the area, together with organizations that could support Rebecca's artistic ability. A mentoring system for the school and family to develop strong partnerships beyond the school for effective provision was arranged. The school had also recognized the need to further enhance teaching and learning in art through a professional development perspective.

A school that makes such effective in-house personalized provision, while brokering additional community-based enrichment and extension activities in partnership with parents and carers, would almost certainly be judged to be at Level 3 'exemplary' in terms of the IQS, provided that the outcomes for Rebecca were good. In fact, we know that the outcomes were excellent; Rebecca's art is the subject of a regional exhibition and she designs the sets for school productions. It is becoming increasingly expensive to purchase her work!

Values into practice

In this concluding section we raise five key issues and/or questions which teaching assistants and others may wish to consider in relation to their own values and working practice, about the education of children and young people who have been identified as being gifted and talented. In other words, we are attempting to give readers the opportunity to 'personalize' their response to the preceding sections and to consider related issues which have not been raised thus far.

First, it is important to consider the social, economic and geographical context of the workplace. Pupils in urban schools generally have better access to community resources and to pupils of similar ability than do those who live in rurally isolated communities and who often attend very small schools. In order to help address the issues of rural isolation and deprivation for children of high ability, Cumbria was invited by central government, in 2005, to take the national lead in developing and exemplifying effective provision for gifted and talented youngsters in rural areas of England. Support materials have been developed in partnership with colleagues from other predominantly rural counties.

Second, practitioners need to reflect on the links between inclusive education, personalized learning, the ECM curriculum and educational provision for all our children, including those identified as 'most able'. In Cumbria we have taken the five ECM 'outcomes' for children and young people of 'Be Healthy', 'Stay Safe', 'Enjoy and Achieve', 'Make a Positive Contribution' and 'Achieve Economic Well-Being' and linked them to five culminating outcomes for our children and young people with the intention that they become:

- inquiring and reflective thinkers
- effective communicators
- high achievers
- responsible citizens and
- self-directed ethical people.

(Steele, 2006)

These outcomes are underpinned by activities that are recommended to schools by the Local Authority.

Third, adults working in schools need to think creatively about provision for gifted and talented children outside the constraints of the national primary and secondary strategies for primary and secondary education. These strategies have tended to stifle creativity and inhibit personalized learning. A recent (December 2006) report of the Teaching and Learning in 2020 Review Group together with a report on nurturing creativity in young people (July 2006) by Paul Roberts, could form the basis of initial and continuing professional development for teaching assistants in the future.

Fourth, teaching assistants need time to reflect and consider their own personal values and principles in relation to inclusive education in general and to gifted and talented provision in particular. Teachers need thinking and planning time and this is now built into their contracts. In the spirit of professional partnership, this should also be the case for teaching assistants.

Finally, as an extension of our fourth issue for consideration and as a concluding thought for this chapter, teaching assistants need to consider their individual career development. There is now no longer a requirement for those who aspire to the Headship of a school to have a teaching qualification. There is, therefore, no reason why experienced teaching assistants who are committed to an inclusive, personalized learning approach to gifted and talented education should not aspire to become school leaders. Just go for it!

Reflections on values and practice

1   Which children and young people in your own work context might benefit from the kinds of policies outlined in this chapter?
2   What are the values underpinning the ideas and policies put forward in this chapter?
3   Do these ideas and policies support or conflict with the principles of inclusive education?

Suggested further reading

Gardner, G. (1993) *Frames of Mind: The Theory of Multiple Intelligences*, London: Fontana.
Sutherland, M. (2005) *Gifted and Talented in the Early Years: Practical Activities for Children Aged 3 to 5*, London: Sage.
Teare, B. (2004) *Parents' and Carers' Guide for Able and Talented Children*, Stafford: Network Educational Press.
Wallace, B. (2000) *Teaching the Very Able Child: Developing a Policy and Adopting Strategies for Provision*, London: NACE/Fulton.

References

Cumbria County Council (2004) *Gifted and Talented Pupils: County Policy and Guidance for Schools*, Carlisle: Cumbria County Council.

Cumbria County Council (2007) *Gifted and Talented in the Early Years: Guidance for Schools*, Carlisle: Cumbria County Council.

Department for Education and Skills (1999) *Excellence in Cities: Guidelines for Gifted and Talented Co-ordinators*, London: HM Government.

Department for Education and Skills, Gifted and Talented Education Unit (2005) *National Institutional Quality Standards for Gifted and Talented Pupils*, London: Mouchet-Parkman/HM Government.

Department for Education and Skills (2006) *Higher Standards, Better Schools for All*, London: HM Government.

George, D. (2002) *Gifted Education: Identification and Provision,* 2nd edn, London: David Fulton.

Gray-Fow, B. (2005) *Discovering and Developing Talent in Schools: An Inclusive Approach*, London: NACE/Fulton.

Montgomery, D. (2003) *Gifted and Talented Children with Special Educational Needs: Double Exceptionality*, London: NACE/Fulton.

Roberts, P. (2006) *Nurturing Creativity in Young People: A Report to Government to Inform Future Policy*, London: DCMS.

Steele, J. (2006) *Cumbria Gifted and Talented Education: Links to Every Child Matters Outcomes*, Barrow-In-Furness: Cumbria County Council.

Teaching and Learning in 2020 Review Group (2006) *2020 Vision Report*, Nottingham: DfES.

Chapter 11

How schools create challenging behaviours

Joe Whittaker and Navin Kikabhai

Introduction

This chapter focuses on the complex issues of behaviour seen by schools to be 'challenging', linking these to values and professional practice. It draws on the personal experiences of a teacher in a secondary school 30 years ago and the process of labelling two young people whose behaviour was seen as 'challenging' by the school, questioning whether values and attitudes have changed. As we explore issues of 'challenging behaviour' within the context of schooling, questions arise about where these behaviours are actually located, that is, how they are created, and by and onto whom the behaviours are attached. As we reflect critically on personal experiences and schooling contexts, it is hoped that we will generate a discussion about how teaching assistants can contribute to current understandings of 'challenging behaviour' and militate against some of the more negative consequences that arise for all members of the school community when such behaviours are created.

The shift towards a more inclusive educational system over the last few years has often led to the demand for teachers to have additional support in ordinary classrooms, providing for a greater diversity of learners and learning. Teaching assistants increasingly provide this additional support, with some arguing (Smith *et al.* 2004; Ofsted 2005) that their most significant contribution has been to provide support to learners who are described as having 'challenging behaviour'. This role has developed as government initiatives responded to schools' appeals for help with young people whose behaviour was seen as problematic, as they struggled to meet challenging demands of a nationalized curriculum (Bennett 2006) and externally set achievement targets.

Specialist settings such as boarding/residential schools, Pupil Referral Units, special schools (emotional and behavioural difficulties (EBD)), 'inclusion units' and nurture groups are increasingly used as solutions for dealing with young people that challenge schools. In addition, an 'alternative curriculum' may be provided (sometimes within further education colleges) and specialist support has become more commonplace within ordinary schools through the work of learning mentors and multi-agency teams that draw on specific skills of social workers, psychologists, health and youth workers. Specialist programmes such as the Behaviour Improvement Programme and Behaviour 4 Learning have been popular with many schools. Further 'support' may also involve administration of drugs such as Ritalin and operation of physical restraint techniques. Clearly, working in such a breadth of provision may offer teaching assistants significant scope for professional development (Visser 2003) and an opportunity to 'specialize' in their skills, however, it is important to consider that this may lead them to experience considerable stress as they 'learn on the job' or spend so much of their time with unhappy, angry or devalued young people.

In more recent years the number of learners with statements of special educational needs has slightly lessened and although many have been supported effectively in mainstream schools (approximately 60 per cent) there is a disturbing increase in learners identified as having 'challenging behaviour' and being excuded, particularly among boys and black minority groups (DfES 2005). Young people are now receiving a range of labels such as ADHD (attention deficit hyperactivity disorder), ODD (oppositional defiance disorder), school phobic, school refuser, pregnant schoolgirls (DfES 2003), all of which may be used to justify the need for their exclusion into separate 'specialist' places of learning (CSIE 2005). This has ensured that, despite increased inclusive education opportunities for some young people, the overall percentage of learners separated from the mainstream of the school has remained consistent.

This chapter aims to present learning and behaviour as a set of complex interactions between individuals and seeks to demonstrate how positive changes can emerge in relationships when the views of learners are valued and actively listened to. Teaching assistants have a crucial role to play in facilitating such good relationships, and enhancing greater inclusion for *all* learners (Visser 2003). They often spend considerable time working closely with young people labelled as 'challenging', so are uniquely placed to listen to their views and use these towards creating a more positive learning experience within the school setting.

Challenging behaviour

Defining behaviour described as 'challenging' is difficult, not least because what one member of staff views as challenging may be seen differently and tolerated by another. Studies such as Cooper (2001) and Cole *et al.* (1999) describe challenging behaviour as that which causes serious disquiet among staff. Early definitions such as those within the Education Acts of 1944 and 1981, concentrated on behaviours that were described as dangerous, aggressive, destructive, demanding of attention or withdrawn (Daniels *et al.* 1998; Garner and Hill 1995). More recent definitions suggest an increased awareness of the emotional aspect of behaviour, describing those identified as having challenging behaviour as being unhappy, with low self-esteem, easily hurt and significantly, as having 'feelings of helplessness' (Visser 2003). Increasingly there has been a move away by some educationalists from seeing challenging behaviour as a problem 'within' the learner, to recognizing the role of external factors such as the school environment on generating this behaviour (Emmerson 2001; Porter 2003).

As schools struggle with increasing demands on both staff and pupils, it is easy to understand how their environments can contribute towards alienation of young people. Teachers are expected to ensure that pupils' achievements rise, respond (often quickly) to new curriculum directives and deal with the wider social inequalities that affect their pupils. Meanwhile, some young people are coping with difficult circumstances within their home communities that affect their schooling, and others face an everyday experience of being educated in a setting where they feel 'rootless and unsupported, with many staff having little appreciation of their feelings or factors impinging on their lives' and so seek solace in 'challenging' behaviour (Visser 2003: 42). As pressures build up in schools, we cannot really be surprised when those feeling alienated respond in ways that appear to reject what schools offer. In such situations, teachers may also struggle when facing behaviour that they do not understand, or do not feel that they have the skills and time to deal with. This can lead to institutional responses that penalize young people, rather than reviewing fully why behaviours occur.

Accepting the importance of context can have an effect on schools both in the use of any formal diagnostic tools to 'identify' pupils with challenging behaviour and in the solutions adopted when responding to 'difficult' behaviour. Diagnostic tools often tend to focus on the child to identify set behaviours exhibited, so if the importance of context is recognized, this must be considered when reviewing when and why behaviours occur (Visser 2003). Similarly, if the role of the environment is seen to impact on learners' behaviour, then changing the environment must become part of the solution. This challenges actions such as removal to Pupil Referral Units and other segregated units where the emphasis is on changing pupil behaviour without dealing with the environment from which they came. As Visser and others argue (2003: 34), anyone working with pupils identified as having challenging behaviour and providing positive relationships, should recognize that becoming a 'significant other' can make a positive difference. This places a key responsibility on staff and schools to reflect on their own role in constructing and managing behaviour.

When discussing 'challenging behaviour' it is important to acknowledge the significant pain and distress it can cause individuals. However, the occasions when such behaviours occur in schools are still relatively few and tend to result primarily from 'low-levels of disruption of lessons' as reported by The Office for Standards in Education (Ofsted 2005: 4), who identified that: 'Most schools and other settings are successful at managing behaviour and creating an environment in which learners feel valued and safe.'

Background: current strategies and the role of teaching assistants

Let us begin by recognizing a contention in terminology, which is 'classroom assistant' or 'teaching assistant', terms that are often used interchangeably. The first, 'classroom assistant', implies an individual who assists in the classroom (possibly photocopying, organizing resources, etc.) and the second 'teaching assistant' implies an individual who assists in learning (possibly teaching small groups or one-to-one) but not necessarily in the classroom, and both being under the direction of the teacher. Such differences in terminology and interpretations can be subtle and create confusion, particularly when we consider the similarities in how teachers and teaching assistants may relate to the learners.

Thomas *et al.* (1998) and Wilson *et al.* (2001) argue that confusion exists because teaching/classroom assistants are not always explicitly told what is expected of them in the management of pupils' behaviour. Despite this, Groom and Rose (2005) report that learners labelled as having SEBD (social, emotional behavioural difficulties) were able to identify the positive role teaching assistants played in supporting them. Groom and Rose (2005: 25) developed this theme further, suggesting that, as teaching assistants supported teachers in the overall 'management of behaviour', it became implicit within their role to promote classroom rules, remind pupils of expectations, deal with conflict and keep individual pupils on task.

Woolfson and Truswell (2005) explored the question 'Do classroom assistants work?' by studying a local authority that placed five additional classroom assistants in three primary schools in 'disadvantaged areas'. They suggest that although a teaching assistant could make a strong contribution, it was difficult to evaluate whether this was successful. Moran and Abbot (2002) suggest that the construction of some challenges/difficulties lie in the boundaries between teaching assistants and teaching staff; the potential of uncertainty for the learner when different guidance is given from two adults in the same classroom can actually create the difficulties and tensions. Cremin *et al.* (2005: 415) support this, arguing that 'the presence of extra people in class does not automatically seem to improve the situation for children . . .', although adding that the result could be the 'host' teacher spending more of her or his time *without* pupils.

The importance of listening to learners is identified by Kikabhai, who actively sought the views of young people excluded from school for their 'challenging behaviour', about the way they were treated by teaching staff. One young person claimed that pupils were treated as statistics, just someone teachers were trying to teach who did not 'give a damn', rather than as learners who really did care about their future (Kikabhai 1999: 24). While this claim cannot be directed at all teachers, such concerns need to be 'heard' by school staff and reflected upon; recognizing that many young people do care, despite their presenting behaviours.

In earlier work by Whittaker *et al.* (1998) about learners' perspectives on school experiences, 2,527 responses were initially received, with a further 18,000 responses in a follow-up study. In the whole investigation there was not one spoilt paper, which suggests that if learners feel that you are genuinely interested in what they have to say, they will give you meaningful information. The study asked young people four questions: what made them happy and unhappy at school and what they thought made a good and bad teacher. In response to these questions, 63 per cent stated that 'friendships' made them happy at school, 33 per cent stated that 'bullying' made them unhappy at school, 54 per cent described 'good' teachers as those who were 'happy, kind and understanding' and 44 per cent described 'bad' teachers as those who 'shout and are bad tempered'. A key message taken from these learners' responses was the importance of friendship and relationships with peers and staff. This leads to reflection about the experiences of pupils labelled as challenging; what part might friendships and bullying play in their lives, and are their teachers 'happy, kind and understanding' or do they shout a lot?

Later, Kikabhai and Whittaker (2005) explored further the issue of relationships through the use of circles of support/friends, reporting that formalized social networks, such as those organized and controlled by schools, in the main resulted in participants having negative experiences. An example of this was 'Hilary's' experience, which highlighted the way teaching assistants became a barrier, seriously inhibiting inclusive practices. A family member described Hilary's situation as one where she was in a separate room all day with two teaching assistants, except lunchtimes. Here, it would appear that the teaching assistants were employed as 'body guards' keeping Hilary away from other learners. So while the rhetoric was that Hilary was included in mainstream school, the reality was that the teaching assistants were excluding Hilary from mainstream classes and preventing her developing meaningful relationships with her peers.

It appears then, that just as teachers without appropriate training can be a barrier to learning and create environments where challenging behaviours occur (Ofsted 2005: 10), teaching assistants can also be barriers to inclusion if they are employed as 'body guards'. The damaging consequences of such approaches to 'supporting' a learner can result in obstruction to meaningful inclusion. This can be further seen with the increase in use of 'segregated units' (often referred to as 'inclusion units or learning support units') in mainstream schools. As teaching assistants provide support within these, they may also become excluded from the mainstream of the school by their association with the units or the expectation that they have primary responsibility for monitoring the 'disruptive learners'. Taking on such a responsibility, may for some teaching assistants only compound the negative and, arguably the inevitable, consequences of 'segregated units'. If schools do not recognize teaching assistants' potential for facilitating relationships and promoting inclusion, there is a danger that they could end up in an educational 'cul-de-sac' with a group of learners estranged from the school community, where both teaching assistant and learner are equally devalued and disengaged from the ordinary life of the school.

Challenging behaviour: a personal view (Joe)

My early experience of challenging behaviour (has anything changed?)

My experience as a new teacher was on the whole a happy one, however this was not continuous. There were times, of course, when life in a secondary school was anything but happy. Tuesday afternoon and Friday morning with the 'non-exam group' were just such times. I can still recall the sensation of that 'sinking feeling' that would accompany me on the journey into school. On these particular days, a horrible dull ache permeated every cell in my body. I remember waiting for the class to arrive, hoping in those few moments some awful virus would attack my body and justify my speedy removal. Of course, this never did prevent the 'non-exam class' arriving. I always forced a smile while furtively checking the line to see if 'Jezz' and 'Finch' were among the group. Jezz and Finch invariably were, as unfortunately for me, they never missed one of my classes.

Despite the emotional pain and dejection I experienced with this group in general, and the two boys in particular, I too never missed a session. I suspected they turned up to make my life miserable and I turned up believing that if I took a day's sick leave I would never return to the school again – ever! My fear of Jezz and Finch influenced my behaviours towards the whole class. We had regular confrontations. I had come to expect trouble within the first 15 minutes of class and yes, trouble came! However, strangely, I found dealing with such confrontations more manageable than the anticipation of the confrontation itself.

After each session I retreated to the safety of the staff room. A detailed description of events was delivered and my then senior colleagues would give direction for the next session: 'don't let them get one over on you', 'be tough and they will eventually give in', 'give them dictation for the first hour' were all typical instructions. At that time I felt compelled to follow such instructions for fear of being seen as the 'weak' teacher or cast aside as being 'unable to handle' the 'difficult ones'.

Jezz and Finch were well known to the school before they joined my class. They had been given various labels, a number of which had been attached at primary school. Their journey through the school was unremarkable in relation to studies, but significant in the pain they caused teachers like myself. I remember not being able to rid myself of the horrible moments of fear and dislike I had of those boys. I remember saying and believing that if only I could remove them; my life as a teacher would be so much better.

It took me several years to realize that Jezz and Finch were not 'the problem', that 'their behaviours' were not particularly challenging, but rather that their behaviours, like mine, were a response to an environment that was dishonest, unfair and generally oppressive for many staff and young people alike. A dawning realization was that when these two 'non-exam kids' left the school they were quickly replaced by others who had been ascribed similar negative labels – their names had changed, but very little else – and so certain behaviours were repeated over and over again!

On one occasion, having been instructed to, I recall teaching maths (quadratic equations) to a group of 'disaffected kids'. I had no formal qualifications or teaching experience in maths, although, as I was to find out, neither of which were expected – simply having a pulse was sufficient to be put in charge of this class! I was physically sick with fear at having to teach these sessions.

Years later I remember meeting some young people from this group who were in the local pub. It was lovely to see them again and be with them in such a convivial setting. We stood huddled together in a group exchanging anecdotes about our time in school together. I was, however, aching to tell them about the 'quadratic equations' sessions that filled me with dread. I waited for an appropriate lull in our conversation before I ventured forth with my question: 'Do you remember those quadratic equations I taught you?' There was a silence from the whole group. One with a little hesitation said after the uncomfortable pause, 'Did you teach maths?' They had no memory of the sessions let alone the particular equations. One person did say, 'But you did work hard with Billy and you never took the piss out of him, did you?' Another went on to say, 'I remember you did wear a blue velvet jacket and brown flairs with that ridiculous tie.' At that moment I felt I was hit by a thunderbolt of lightening – a realization that I had no way of knowing what young people took away from the lessons I painstakingly planned, no matter what the detailed aims and objectives may have been. Indeed, this group commented on being in a place where they felt safe where there was a sense of justice and fairness.

Reflective discussion

It is now 30 years since that experience; and so what have I learnt? I did not listen to Jezz and Finch – I listened to the staffroom assumptions and gossip. It took years for me to recognize that Jezz and Finch did not own the 'challenging behaviour'. Staff passed comment on Jezz and Finch with phrases such as: 'they had missed the boat', 'they were time wasters', 'non-academic lads', 'not amount to much', and 'were only good with their hands' – euphemisms that amounted to labels of rejection. I never did have a meaningful relationship with Jezz or Finch – they never did know anything about me and I never did know anything about them other than the pain they caused me. I colluded with other adults within the school without listening to Jezz and Finch. My preoccupation was controlling them – my conversations were with other staff about them and nurturing comments that would reinforce my justification of them as being the source of the 'challenging behaviour', they were the 'problem'. However, such conversations never did help me understand what was happening to all of us in that school. Herb Lovett (1996: 5) wrote:

> our most pressing problem is that we have not listened carefully to those we would serve . . . no one can be wiser for a group than the group itself; no one can be better informed about individual wishes and needs than individuals themselves.

While *'listening to those we would serve'* may seem to be a challenging concept for schools, there is the question of how teaching assistants can assist in hearing pupils like Jezz and Finch. I did not know Jezz or Finch, I only responded to their action with similar actions, which I came to understand as being expected of me. I was further removed from them, bigger and had more power and status ascribed to me than they did. However, it is important to understand the context where the behaviours were created. I have, since this period in my life talked with many young people who I found difficult to manage. They again were typically in groups that were described as 'the non-exam group', 'the difficult to manage group' and 'the disaffected'. These individuals recognized that within the schools as a whole their status was 'very low', where general comments from many teachers echoed around the school, suggesting that it would be 'in their best interest' and better for everyone, if they were not there. The groups as a whole were not welcome – and they knew it! Interestingly, this theme was later taken up by Visser (2003: 37) when he argued that improvement in behaviour was more likely to occur in an environment where learners felt welcomed and valued by staff.

So, what can schools do to make learners feel wanted and valued?

Several writers argue that it is schools, colleges and universities that create 'challenging behaviours' since they continually fail to learn from those that present as a 'problem' or are reluctant to include (Ross-Epp 1996; Whittaker and Kenworthy 1997; Majors 2003). Lovett's (1996: 6) experience has been that 'extreme behaviour often comes from not feeling listened to' and he suggests that 'we might just as honestly describe a person's "learning disability" as our own "teaching disability"'. Good relationships are central to good learning and impact clearly on individual's behaviour (Whittaker and Kikabhai 2004). This view is supported by Ofsted (2005 and 2006), who also suggested that schools that focus upon good teaching skills and whole school approaches are more likely to manage behaviour effectively than those who concentrate on 'specialized strategies'.

Understanding 'challenging behaviour' or however else it is labelled, is anything but simple! As we discussed earlier, the whole area of definition and description is problematic, so there can be no simple solutions and no simple strategies. The whole situation demands that we give serious consideration to the learning environment we have created and how such environments can create 'challenging behaviour'! Indeed, the focus on the naming and removal of individuals described as having challenging behaviours, while not making any attempt to understand where such behaviours originate, is often the start of an unhealthy learning environment for everyone in it. For example, try asking a teacher which young people they would remove to make learning more effective. Then try asking the head teacher which teachers s/he would remove to make the school more effective. Then try asking the local education authority which head teacher they would remove to make the authority more effective. The chances are these respective individuals will always find people to remove, but the trouble with such an approach, in the case of learners, is that schools would soon be empty because once you have removed one 'offender' to whom you have attached the 'ills' of the whole organization, you are preparing the ground for the next to take their place.

Schools should instead seek to learn as much as they can about their pupils as individuals, discovering how they view their world and why they do the things they do. Learning about experiences that are important to young people can help staff support them both in the development of relationships and in becoming included within their school community.

Conclusion

At the heart of the debate about the effectiveness of teaching assistants in working with learners identified as challenging is whether they are there in the school for controlling/monitoring behaviour or are they there to offer meaningful support? The danger remains when schools locate 'challenging behaviour' as problems within individuals and expect teaching assistants to simply reinforce such a label rather than question its attachment to the individual and listen to learners about their experiences. Kikabhai and Whittaker (2005) highlight that effective and meaningful support is much more than just introducing more adults into the classroom, particularly if these adults do not listen to, and engage positively with, learners. Indeed, effective support engenders feelings of friendship, trust, honesty and openness, emotions that currently seem to be far removed from educational rhetoric about 'zero tolerance' and where 'raising standards' and 'testing' has become an obsession. There is no short cut to getting to know young people and it may be hard work. It may also result in a teaching assistant who understands an individual's behaviour far better than other school staff, which can lead to situations of conflict over 'management strategies'.

Facing these challenges could lead, as Majors (2003: 6) argues, to radical changes in our education practice:

The fact is, we are obsessed with controlling, monitoring, disciplining, punishment, excluding and labelling rather than focusing on relationships, communication and social justice. If our goal is to motivate, raise attainment and reduce behavioural problems among our children, it is critical we give greater status to social justice and human rights of young people in our schools.

This link to social justice and human rights can create the potential for the more meaningful inclusion of learners labelled as 'challenging' in our schools. Commitment to this moves us past the rhetoric of 'Education, Education, Education' on to a more meaningful 'Relationships, Relationships, Relationships' between learners and those who are there to serve!

Reflecting on values and practice

1   Which learners are identified as 'challenging' within your setting? What is challenging about their behaviour and how do context and relationships affect this behaviour?
2   How do you know when someone is actively listening to you? How do others know when you are actively listening to them? What opportunities do you take to listen to learners labelled as 'challenging'?
3   When do you feel included and/or excluded at your work place? How does this affect your behaviour?
4   Which learners will remember you? Why?

Suggested further reading

Lovett, H. (1996) *Learning to Listen: Positive Approaches and People with Difficult Behaviour*, London: Paul H. Brookes.
Mukhopadhyay, T.R. (2000) *Beyond the Silence: My Life, the World and Autism*, London: National Autistic Society.
Rieser, R (2000) Special Educational Needs or Inclusive Education. In Cole, M. (ed.) *Education, Equality and Human Rights*, London: RoutledgeFalmer.

References

Bennett, P.L. (2006) 'Helpful and Unhelpful Practices in Meeting the Needs of Pupils with Emotional and Behavioural Difficulties: A Pilot Survey of Staff Views in One Local Authority', *British Journal of Special Education*, 33(4): pp. 188–195.
Cole, T., Visser, J. and Daniels, H. (1999) 'A Model Explaining Effective EBD Practice in Mainstream Schools', *Emotional and Behavioural Difficulties*, 4(1): pp. 12–18.
Cooper, P. (2001) *We Can Work It Out: What Works in Educating Pupils with Social, Emotional and Behavioural Difficulties Outside Mainstream Classrooms?*, Barkingside: Barnardo's.
Cremin, H., Thomas, G. and Vincett, K. (2005) 'Working with Teaching Assistants: Three Models Evaluated', *Research Papers in Education* 20(4): 413–32.

CSIE (2005) 'The Centre for Studies on Inclusive Education', press release (8/7/05).

Daniels, H., Visser, J., Cole, T., de Reybekill, N. (1998) *Emotional and Behavioural Difficulties in Mainstream Schools*, Research Report RR90. London: DfEE.

DfES (2005) *Special Educational Needs in England* (National Statistics), London: DfES.

Emmerson, E. (2001) *Challenging Behaviour. Analysis and Interventions in People with Learning Difficulties* Cambridge: Cambridge University Press.

Garner, P. and Hill, N. (1995) *What Teachers Do: Developments in Special Education* London: Paul Chapman.

Groom, B. and Rose, R. (2005) 'Supporting the Inclusion of Pupils with Social, Emotional and Behavioural Difficulties in the Primary School: the Role of Teaching Assistants', *Journal of Research in Special Educational Needs* 5(1): 20–30.

Kikabhai, N. (1999) *Bolton Youth Challenge Project: Evaluating the Effectiveness of a 'Suitable' Education for Excluded Pupils*. Online: available at www.inclusion-bolton data.org.uk (accessed 19 January 2007).

Kikabhai, N. and Whittaker, J. (2005) *'Circles of Support/Friends' Exploring the Notion of Relationships, Intimacy, Friendship and Support*. Online: available at www. inclusion-boltondata.org.uk (accessed 19 January 2007).

Lovett, H. (1996) *Learning to Listen: Positive Approaches and People with Difficult Behaviour*, London: Paul H. Brookes.

Majors, R. (2003) (ed.) *Educating our Black Children: New Directions and Radical Approaches*, London: Routledge Falmer.

Moran, A. and Abbott, L. (2002) 'Developing Inclusive Schools: the Pivotal Role of Teaching Assistants in Promoting Inclusion in Special and Mainstream Schools in Northern Ireland', *European Journal of Special Needs Education* 17(2): 161–72.

Ofsted (2005) *Managing Challenging Behaviour*, HMI 2365, London: Ofsted.

Ofsted (2006) *Does it Matter Where Pupils are Taught?*, London: Crown Copyright.

Porter, J. (2003) *Challenging Behaviour and Learning Difficulties: A Context for Understanding Challenging Behaviour*, Birmingham: The University of Birmingham.

Ross-Epp, J. and Watkinson, A. (eds) (1996) *Systemic Violence: How Schools Hurt Children*, London: Falmer Press.

Smith, P., Whitby, K. and Sharpe, C. (2004) *The Employment and Deployment of Teaching Assistants* (LGA Research Report 5/04), Slough: NFER.

Thomas, G., Walker, D. and Webb, J. (1998) *The Making of the Inclusive School*, London: Routledge.

Visser, J. (2003) *A Study of Children and Young People who Present Challenging Behaviour*, London: Ofsted.

Willson, V., Schlapp, U., Davidson. J. and Mongiello, A. (2001) *Classroom Assistants: Lessons from the Pilot Project Preliminary Report* (SCRE Research Report 102), Scotland: SCRE.

Whittaker, J. and Kikabhai, N. (2004) *The Illusion of Inclusion: Exploring the Gulf Between Educational Rhetoric and Practice*. Online: available at www.inclusion-boltondata.org.uk (accessed 19 January 2007).

Whittaker, J., Kenworthy, J. and Crabtree, C. (1998) *What Children Say About School*, Online: available at www.inclusion-boltondata.org.uk (accessed 19 January 2007).

Whittaker, J. and Kenworthy, J. (1997) *Does Your College of Further Education have Learning Difficulties?* Online: available at www.inclusion-boltondata.org.uk (accessed 19 January 2007).

Woolfson, R. C. and Truswell, E. (2005) Do Classroom Assistants Work?, *Educational Research* 47(1): 63–75.

Chapter 12

Bullying in schools – or bullying schools?

Neil Duncan

What is bullying?

Most writing about bullying sees the problem as bullying children having a stronger tendency to be nasty than other children, or that victims of bullying somehow present a more inviting target, perhaps through irritating or unusual behaviour, or some obvious weakness or difference. Difference between children is natural and to be expected. Whether the difference is behavioural, physical or in ability, the human diversity in any group of pupils cannot explain the high levels of bullying in schools compared to other institutions, otherwise we'd have reduced bullying levels much more effectively than we have done. Understanding the complexities of bullying within schools is essential for teaching assistants to support pupils and personally contribute to a non-oppressive environment.

We know that bullying existed long before researchers started looking into the problem. *Tom Brown's Schooldays* (Hughes 1994) and other early literature about the English public school system featured bullies as typical characters.

There is a variety of definitions of bullying but no single definition has it perfect in every case. One popular example comes from the original Scandinavian research of Dan Olweus who pioneered anti-bullying initiatives in Sweden. Olweus (1993) states that bullying is an aggressive act with an imbalance of power (the victim finds it difficult to defend himself or herself), some element of repetition (these things happen frequently), can be physical (hit, kicked), or verbal (threatened, nasty and unpleasant things said) or indirect (sent nasty notes, no one ever talks to them).

Elements that appear in other formulations of bullying include *intent* and *outcome*. Intent refers to the purpose of the aggressor's behaviour: does he or she actually mean to hurt or upset the target? If a big boy barges through a group of smaller children in a rush to get to the toilet – even if this happens more than once, is that really bullying? Perhaps the bigger boy doesn't intend to hurt or alarm, but when his behaviour is pointed out to him and he doesn't understand or seem to care, is that then bullying? If the big boy has learning difficulties, does that change anything?

All this is very complicated and depends more on social relationships and feelings rather than simple acts and behaviours. The problem of defining bullying is important, but not easy.

One element often missed from formulations of bullying is the sense of intimate entrapment. There is something special about bullying that includes that element of being stuck in a relationship with your aggressor or tormentor. This idea is very hard to include in a short definition, but one working definition of bullying might be 'an interpersonal abuse of power'.

What is known about bullying?

From surveys carried out in the early 1990s by Boulton and Underwood (1992), Whitney and Smith (1993) and others, the number of pupils in secondary schools reporting being bullied was running at around 20–25 per cent. Figures for children reporting that they bully others are significantly lower than this but even so, some surveys note around 10 per cent of children will admit to sometimes bullying others. Importantly, some children fall into both categories: they are bullied by some children, and they themselves also bully others. Some researchers, for example Besag (1989), refer to these children as bully-victims.

More recently, Bullying Online carried out a national survey they claim to be the biggest ever in the UK. They surveyed teachers, parents, adults and pupils and returned a figure of 69 per cent of children claiming to have been bullied (Bullying Online 2006). While the exact details of how the survey was carried out can't confirm the validity of its claims, there is little doubt that the findings indicate that bullying is widespread, takes many forms and continues to be dealt with ineffectively.

Characteristics of bullies

I dislike the term 'bully' because it is a label and suggests that the person bullying is just a bully, never anything other than a bully from birth and will never be anything else. Olweus (1997) believes that bullies have higher levels of impulsivity – they act without thinking too much about the consequences, and typically resort to violence as a means of achieving their goals. They are usually physically strong and powerful and have low empathy, in other words they don't care about other people's feelings. There is little here that most lay persons would be surprised at, indeed the surprise is that researchers have bothered to announce this as findings when most teachers, teaching assistants, parents and pupils would have been able to give the same information from their own observations and experiences.

More interestingly, it has been shown that bullies who engage in non-physical aggression have unusually high social intelligence (Sutton et al. 1999). They can cause great pain and hurt in subtle ways, manipulating and entrapping their targets without adults being aware of what is happening.

Bullying appears to increase with age, and people who bully regularly tend to increase the verbal attacks and decrease their physical attacks as they get older. The targets of their abuse tend to be the same age or younger. Long-term bullies justify their behaviour through the development of beliefs that they are really doing nothing bad (Rigby 1997).

Characteristics of victims

As with the term 'bullies', the label of 'victim' makes me uneasy because it can suggest a fixed, unalterable state – 'we can do nothing for him, he's one of life's victims'. Often research will categorize these children as either *passive* or *provocative*. Passive victims display vulnerability that 'encourages' bullies to attack them. They put up no effective resistance and therefore bullies repeatedly abuse them without being punished. The other common category of victim is the provocative type. This child will not initiate aggression against others, but their behaviour is confrontational and teasing. Everyone finds them irritating, but bullies respond to them with violence – 'he asked for it'.

If these categories were so simple, then it strikes me as curious that so many children report being bullied in so many surveys. Take the recent National Bullying survey by Bullying Online (2006) where 69 per cent were victims. That's a lot of provocative or passive kids out there! This discrepancy suggests that there is much more to learn about bullying than most researchers think.

Effects of bullying

Whatever is the true reason for bullying in schools, one thing can be certain, its effects can be long term and in some cases fatal. The modern interest in bullying originated in Scandinavia after three pupils committed suicide in quick succession following bullying by their peers. Since then, many more tragic cases have come to light, but these often are bypassed as news stories unless they are particularly awful such as the suicide of five Japanese pupils in the autumn of 2006 (BBC 2006). For every suicide caused by bullying, there must be a hundred children who come close to taking such drastic action to free themselves from their torment.

Apart from suicide, self-harm and of course the direct pain from being beaten up, there are many lasting problems suffered by targets of bullying. These include loneliness, depression, panic attacks, anxiety, guilt, shame and low self-esteem (Schafer *et al.* 2004). When I teach university students about bullying, many of them become tearful or embarrassed recalling, and indeed reliving, their experiences from their childhood.

Another important effect of bullying is on school attendance. It is impossible to know exactly how many school days are lost each year by pupils who are too frightened to come into school because their life has been made intolerable. The true figures of this effect are masked by children's excuses, sometimes backed up by parents knowingly or not, telling the school that they are sick or otherwise unable to attend.

Besides these effects, the way that bullying creates a general atmosphere in schools should not be underestimated.

How is bullying dealt with by schools?

Management of bullying can be broadly split into *preventions* before, and *responses* after, bullying has taken place. Preventions include directly discussing bullying in the classroom, thereby promoting a 'telling school' to combat a culture of 'not grassing'. Some schools use 'buddying' systems to pair up vulnerable pupils with older mentors. These older pupils monitor the safety of their buddies and support them if there is a problem.

Some schools use a technique called *circle time* where all the children in a class are involved in activities that raise empathy, improve pro-social behaviour and increase peer support (Smith 2004).

Responses to bullying incidents after they have happened depend to some extent on the school's anti-bullying policy, and how rigorously the school staff follows its guidance. When a bullying incident is punished, it can range from school exclusion or even criminal charges brought by the police, through to a private apology and an undertaking not to repeat the offence.

Usually, school approaches are based on processes found in the courts of law. They don't always work very well as there is a natural tendency for people to lie over things they feel guilty about. The other unwanted outcome is the increased likelihood of retaliation by the accused or his/her friends against the complainant – a very real worry of many targets of bullying.

Some schools reduce these problems by operating a *no-blame* anti-bullying policy (Maines and Robinson 1992). In this seven-step programme, the facilitator/teacher concerns themselves with making the target feel better about things, and getting the perpetrators to stop their attacks and even getting them to befriend or support the target. Anti-bullying initiatives across the world testify to the effectiveness of the strategy, and particularly appreciate the way it attempts to break the cycle of aggression and hurt that abides in bullying.

Despite these successes, the no-blame approach has been heavily criticized by lots of campaigners and press commentators who think that it is being 'soft on the bullies'. As the no-blame approach takes more time and skill to apply than simple punishment, it can also be unpopular because of resource costs as well as its non-punitive values.

Back to basics

Consideration of our own values brings us back to an earlier idea – that of *why* people bully others. A view linked with the punitive approach to dealing with bullies (such as 'kick them out of school') is that some people bully others because they are just horrible people. If that was really the case, or even if that was the main reason, one might expect that once the bullies had been kicked out of school then bullying in that school would cease.

A review of the effectiveness of anti-bullying strategies and interventions carried out by Peter K. Smith, one of the UK's leading experts on bullying, revealed that despite years of expensive research and intervention, bullying wasn't reduced much at all (Smith 2005). Perhaps researchers have been too busily looking for faults in children and not spending enough time looking at faults in the schooling systems. After all, the term 'bullying' is powerfully linked with the term 'school' even though there are bullying incidents in other institutions, such as the armed forces, prisons, hospitals and all sorts of other workplace environments.

Furthermore, if bullying was entirely the fault of a few nasty kids, then why is it that schools of similar sizes and intakes have very different rates of bullying reported within them? Are there simply more nasty kids in some schools or is it something else? One clue to solving this puzzle comes from two Japanese researchers who spent some time in Australia's education system. Yoneyama and Naito (2003) were struck by the powerful differences within the two schooling cultures – the West (Australia, Europe, UK, and USA) and their native Japan.

In the West, they noted bullying tended to be one or two aggressive and violent pupils causing fear and harm to a larger group of pupils. In the Japanese school system, the situation was almost reversed with the whole class picking on one child as a scapegoat and making their life unbearable.

Their analysis is too complex to repeat here, but suffice to say that their theory is that if bullying was a fundamental part of a person's character, then it certainly expressed itself differently in different cultures. Indeed, the signs are evident that the culture itself is a producer of bullying, and that bullying is not just a part of a nasty character. Their message is clear: if you want to stop bullying, begin with how schools operate as institutions and take it from there.

Institutions, organizations and the bullying ethos

An institution is an identifiable community where its members spend considerable time together for a shared purpose. Institutions have their own way of doing things distinctive from how any one person in the institution might do them, and different from the ways other institutions do them. This way of doing things is perhaps hard to see or describe, but more usually it is felt by the members, and we call this *ethos*, or spirit.

The most famous study on the school ethos (Rutter 1979), found that it had a huge part to play in school effectiveness, overriding many other factors such as size and intake, staff qualifications and curricula. So if it is that important, how can we deal with it, shape it and make it as positive as possible?

Schools have a formal organization that aims to do two main things – educate and *socialize*. In this case, to socialize does not mean to have a party or just enjoy others' company. Socialization in this sense means to train people socially, so that they can get along with each other and enjoy what society has to offer as well as make a contribution to it. Usually we only hear about the first purpose of schooling – to educate. However, if you have any doubts about the importance of socialization, just imagine the outcry if schools were to provide no guidance on pupils' behaviour. Indeed, schools are often criticized for not shaping pupils' behaviour effectively enough.

As well as these formal and official rules, there are rules that are *modelled* rather than stated overtly. By modelled, I mean that the institution's members behave according to them, but they may not be written down. In virtually every school, these modelled behaviours indicate a power structure based on a *hierarchy*, a layered structure of the staff. At the top of the hierarchy is the head teacher, then the senior management team. These are followed by middle management staff such as special educational needs coordinators (SENCO), subject coordinators or, in high schools, heads of year or heads of house. Beneath this rank are the basic teaching staff followed by the teaching assistants, mid-day supervisors, ancillary workers and cleaning staff. At the bottom of this pyramid are the pupils.

Even between pupils, there is what is sometimes known as a pecking-order: some children will have more power than others, and we can see how pupils model their relations on the adult examples all around them. If we look carefully, there will be signs to show us what the ethos is of this structure.

In some organizations, the hierarchy is not so prominent as others: the boundaries are a bit blurred, or some people straddle more than one role so they are in charge of some things, but under someone else's charge on others. In some institutions the layers are fewer and the difference between them is less important. In other cases the power is much more visible and jealously guarded by those who have it. In order to display their importance over other people in the organization, they may demand that they are addressed in a different way, or they may have a specially designated parking space, a big office with a closed door, and a manner that says 'you'd better watch out around me, I'm powerful and can hurt you'.

In schools where the ethos is one of deference to superior rank rather than warm human relationships, bullying among pupils is more likely to thrive. The way that staff bosses and their subordinates talk and behave towards each other shows the pupils how *they* should relate to each other.

How schools can bully children

Imagine being made by law to attend an institution six hours a day, five days a week where you were controlled in everything you do, for no pay nor worthwhile outcomes for you personally. Imagine you were so controlled in this environment that you were punished for speaking without permission, for not sitting in a particular position, for laughing out loud, for whispering. Imagine being told to do things you had no interest in, and then being harassed for not doing it as well as that person thinks you can. Imagine your ability or performance being constantly measured and compared against those of your peers.

Imagine being told what to wear down to the tiniest detail, being forbidden expressions of personality such as jewellery or make-up. Imagine being forced to cut or to grow your hair until it met with someone else's approval. Imagine being so controlled in every way that even your bodily functions are at someone else's discretion and you need permission to eat, drink or go to the toilet. Put like that, it's a wonder we don't have a riot in schools across the land, but in fact, most young people cope pretty well in schools, many like it and plenty actually thrive. However, in schools where conditions such as those above exist in an *oppressive* ethos, bullying can become a real problem among the pupils.

Looking at things from this perspective can reveal reasons why some schools have a worse bullying problem than others (Xin Ma *et al.* 2001). There are a number of factors that reinforce one another to make schools into high-bullying schools. The obvious one, and the most commonly held, is that those schools have a higher number of nasty, aggressive children. The problem would be solved, we are told, if the school got tougher with those pupils and adopted a zero-tolerance policy against bullying to change those bad pupils' behaviour (Ball and Hartley 2003). But if this action was such an easy and effective one for schools to take, then it's hard to understand why so much bullying persists.

The mass scale of schooling requires schools to adopt regimented approaches to discipline and organization, and all schools have some form of hierarchy in order to run smoothly (Ross-Epp 1996). In some cases, however, that hierarchy can become self-serving and lose sight of the real purpose of schooling: the education and socialization of children.

Children quickly pick up on the importance of hierarchies. A simple understanding of age-hierarchies can be checked in any primary school. The importance of who fears whom on the staff is also quickly acquired. Think about the messages hidden in very common statements: 'Any more of that attitude young man and I'll send you to Mr Hassan.'

Most children are happy within a hierarchy as long as it is safe and fair. When they are abused, ridiculed in public, shouted at, punished as a group, or treated with sarcasm and disdain, they resent it. In the 11-year-long competition that is compulsory schooling, there are winners and losers. We all know which children rarely succeed in that competition, and for them, bossing someone else about can be the release from failure that they crave. Their predicament is described in studies of oppressed groups in other situations as *horizontal violence* (Freire 1972; Leymann 1996). This is where people are bossed around in a situation they can't change, and begin to take out their frustration and anger on the only targets available – their weaker peers. We might as well call it bullying.

Most teachers and teaching assistants are caring and intelligent people doing a difficult and demanding job. Sometimes they are less than perfect, and that can only be expected. When those lapses in their high professional standards prove effective, i.e. they achieve the right results in the wrong way, and others emulate the same undesirable tactics, essentially, they use bullying techniques to enforce discipline. I confess to such lapses myself, and indeed used them to great effect over a period of years where I was praised for getting good behavioural results from very difficult students. It was only when I witnessed one of my younger staff copying my approach that I realized I might be doing more harm than good.

I tried to come up with advice that would be helpful to young or new staff in managing discipline in schools. The best I came up with was to imagine in every exchange with students that their parents were present while you were dealing with them. If you could justify not only your words, but also your tone and body language, then you were pretty sure not to be bullying them. If we preach fairness and decency to them as values that we hold dear, we should not then be caught out being sarcastic and mean. We must retain a professional level of dignifying children equivalent to that which we would use in dealing with their parents or other adults. In my own (unpublished) research with high-school pupils, the issue of double standards of staff often arises:

> We have to be there on time or we get told off, but Sir always arrives late and he's only been chatting to Miss in the corridor.'

> I got shouted at and told to wash my make up off, but Miss wears far more than me.

> We were left with no teacher in Maths all morning, but no one even realized, but one day when I missed first lesson because of the bus, I was sent home for an absence note and missed the second lesson too.

> Sir knew only one kid had broken the projector but he kept us all in during break-time.

These instances of injustice may seem petty, but to some pupils they signal a strong message of 'might is right'. In other words, if you are powerful enough, you can get away with anything. Transpose this attitude to the world of the pupils, and you get a bullying culture where staff behaviour is seen as a hypocritical model for children to bully others.

Summary

No one deserves to be bullied, but all schools are organizations where bullying takes place. This is due to certain factors that are virtually inseparable from schooling and that most of us don't have the power to change, for example:

its compulsory nature, the vast numbers of people that need to be regulated in a small space, and the constraints on what we are allowed to do with children during the school day (which many pupils find irrelevant, difficult and boring).

Once the school staff have reflected on their own contribution to the ethos, the decision has to be made as to whether their common approach will be based upon punishment and retribution, or prevention and restoration. In other words, is the aim to hurt the perpetrators of bullying, or to make people feel better about occasions where someone got hurt or upset?

Most bullying is seen as the fault of particular children who are labelled as 'bullies'. Labelling in this way is not really helpful, as it prevents us from looking at things we as adults *could* change and *should* change (our personal relationships with children, our professional standards, our unnecessary or punitive rules), by focusing on things we are *unlikely* to change (individual children's personalities where bullying is a response to their situation). Interventions to reduce bullying, therefore, should be preceded by some discussion on what the school can do to improve its ethos and culture as an institution. It may well be more comfortable and acceptable to imagine bullying in school as purely a pupil problem, but until adults engage with their own role in creating and maintaining a pro-social and non-oppressive institution, the problem will resist our attempts to make a lasting impact on bullying.

Reflection on values and practice

1   Defining bullying. Instead of using the ready-made definitions of bullying so common in books and questionnaires on bullying, listen to the range of things that kids do to other kids that they say they don't like. That way, you'll hear what really bothers them, without getting tangled up in 'scientific' definitions.

2   Developing a sense of fairness. Young people have a strong sense of justice, though it doesn't always seem like it. If you have a pupil who is involved in bullying others, try to discuss occasions when s/he was treated unfairly. Consider how you can develop a sense of empathy by encouraging him or her to rethink the experience and see that s/he is emulating the unfair person in the incident.

3   The acid test. You are a model to the children, so you need to reflect on your own interpersonal exchanges with pupils. Think back to an incident when you were dominating a pupil (we all need to do this at some point!). Would you feel comfortable if someone said they'd videoed you and the child's parent was going to see it? If the answer is no, then always try to conduct yourself as though a parent was observing. Pupils will eventually pick up on the fact that you are dignified and professional and their behaviour will change accordingly.

Suggested further reading

Most of the books on bullying concentrate on seeing the individual child as the problem, whether bully or victim. If you have read this chapter carefully, you'll know that I don't think that is very helpful. The best advice is to be found on websites, particularly at www.antibullying.net/, which is a Scottish anti-bullying site, and at www.dfes.gov.uk/bullying/, which is the UK government advice. If you are interested in gender issues of bullying, try Duncan, N. (1999) *Sexual Bullying: Gender Conflict and Peer Culture in Secondary Schools*, London: Routledge. If you wish to develop your understanding of how organizations can oppress people and create a bullying environment, then a visit to Robert Fuller's site and purchase of his book at www.breaking ranks.net/ might just change your view on life!

References

Ball, C. and Hartley, M. (2003) *Zero Tolerance to Bullying*, Alberta: Chalk Face Project, Mentone Education Centre.

BBC (2006) *Suicide of Bullied Japanese Pupils*. Online: available at http://news.bbc.co.uk/2/hi/asia-pacific/6142816.stm (accessed 12 December 2006).

Besag, V.E. (1989) *Bullies and Victims in Schools*, Milton Keynes: Open University Press.

Boulton, M.J. and Underwood, K. (1992) 'Bully/Victim Problems Among Middle School Children', *British Journal of Educational Psychology* 62(1): 73–87.

Bullying Online (2006) *National Survey Report*. Online: available at www.bullying.co.uk/nationalsurvey/thenationalbullyingsurvey_results.pdf (accessed 12 December 2006).

Freire, P. (1972) *Pedagogy of the Oppressed*, London: Penguin Education.

Hughes, T. (1994) *Tom Brown's Schooldays*, London: Penguin Popular Classics.

Leymann, H. (1996) 'Psychological Terrorization – the Problem of the Terminology', in *The Mobbing Encyclopaedia* Online: available at www.leymann.se/English/11130E.HTM_1996 (accessed 18 December 2006).

Maines, B. and Robinson, G. (1992) *Michael's story*, video cassette recording, Bristol: Lucky Duck.

Naylor, P., Cowie, H., Cossin, F., de Bettencourt, R. and Lemme, F. (2006) 'Teachers' and Pupils' Definitions of Bullying', *British Journal of Educational Psychology* 76(3): 553–76.

Olweus, D. (1993) *Bullying at School. What We Know and What We Can Do?*, Oxford: Blackwell.

Olweus, D. (1997) 'Bully/Victim Problems in School: Facts and Intervention', *European Journal of Psychology of Education* 12: 495–510.

Rigby, K. (1997) 'Attitudes and Beliefs About Bullying Among Australian School Children', *Irish Journal of Psychology* 18: 202–20.

Ross-Epp, J. (1996) 'Schools, Complicity and Sources of Violence' in: Ross-Epp, J. and Watkinson, A. (eds) *Systemic Violence: How Schools Hurt Children*, London: Falmer Press.

Rutter, M., Maughan, B., Mortimore, P. and Ouston, J. (1979) *15000 Hours: Secondary Schools and Their Effects on Children*, London: Open Books.

Schafer, M., Korn, S., Smith, P. K., Hunter, S. C., Mora-Merchán, J. A., Singer, M. M. and Van der Meulen, K. (2004) 'Lonely in the Crowd: Recollections of Bullying', *British Journal of Developmental Psychology* 22(3): 379–94.

Smith, C. (2004) *Circle Time for Adolescents: a Seven Session Programme for 14 to 16 Year Olds*, London: Paul Chapman Sage Publications.

Smith, P.K. (2005) *BPS Seminar Series on Bullying*, London: Goldsmiths College.

Sutton, J., Smith, P.K. and Swettenham, J. (1999) 'Social Cognition and Bullying: Social Inadequacy or Skilled Manipulation?', *British Journal of Developmental Pscyhology* 17: 435–50.

Whitney, I. and Smith, P.K. (1993) 'A Survey of the Nature and Extent of Bullying in Junior/Middle and Secondary Schools', *Educational Research* 35: 3–25.

Xin Ma, Len L. Stewin and Deveda L. Mah, (2001) Bullying in School: Nature, Effects and Remedies, *Research Papers in Education* 16(3): 247–70.

Yoneyama, S., and Naito, A. (2003) 'Problems with the Paradigm: the School as a Factor in Understanding Bullying (with Special Reference to Japan)', *British Journal of Sociology* 24(3): 315–30.

Chapter 13

Disabled children, inclusion and the law in England and Wales

David Ruebain

Teaching assistants and the law

Teaching assistants have a key role to play for all children, but particularly for children identified as having special educational needs (SEN) and for disabled children. Most legal duties will rest on local authorities (LAs) and school governing bodies but staff, including teaching assistants, will be instrumental in ensuring effective provision. Sometimes, the legal obligations will provide for teaching assistants to assist in the classroom generally and sometimes to assist a specific child (for example, if the child's statement requires individual, one-to-one support). Either way, the obligations that are set out in this chapter will invariably depend on the involvement and expertise of teaching assistants.

Disabled children and children with special educational needs

Background

The provision of education for disabled children, and those identified as having special educational needs, has been transformed over the last 25 years. Prior to the 1981 Education Act, education for children who were not deemed normal was essentially based on their medical or quasi-medical diagnosis and educational provision, including what school they went to, was often almost automatically determined in accordance with that diagnosis. So, for example, children with 'physical handicaps' (as it was known) were usually placed in schools for such children, those with a visual impairment were placed in schools for blind children, those with a hearing impairment were placed in schools for deaf children, and so on. There were some categories in which children were placed which were somewhat obscure and some were positively offensive. For example, there were schools for 'backward' children, 'delicate' children and 'educationally sub-normal' children!

Then, on 1 April 1983, the Education Act 1981 came into force. This transformed educational arrangements for disabled children in two significant ways. First, instead of placing children in categories (e.g. blind, physically handicapped, etc.) what has become known as a 'child centred approach' was introduced, whereby each disabled child who has additional or different needs arising from a disability or learning difficulty, would have those needs assessed and should have provision tailored to meet them. Accordingly, a child with Downs Syndrome would have his/her needs individually considered and would not be assumed to have exactly the same needs as another child with Downs Syndrome. Second, the Act introduced, for the first time, a general presumption in favour of educating such children in mainstream (ordinary) schools where parents wanted it, providing that such a school could meet the child's needs, other children would not be adversely affected and that placement at such a school did not constitute an inefficient use of the LA's resources (The Special Educational Needs and Disability Act 2001 amended this requirement so that, now, LAs may only refuse a child with special educational needs a place at a mainstream school if other children would be adversely affected and there are no reasonable steps that the school or LA can take to overcome the difficulty – Sections 316 and 316A of the Education Act 1996). The Education Act 1981 has since been replaced by Part III of the Education Act 1993, but the frame work which it introduced largely remains in place, albeit in a strengthened form. Now, the law is primarily contained within Part IV of the Education Act 1996 (as amended by the Special Educational Needs and Disability Act 2001) and key guidance is given in the government's Code of Practice on Special Educational Needs.

Who has special educational needs?

Section 312 of the Education Act 1996 states that a child has special educational needs if they have a 'learning difficulty' (which includes children with a physical or sensory disability and those with challenging behaviour (but does not include exceptional ability, see *S v SENDIST and Oxfordshire CC* (2005) ELR 443.) which calls for special educational provision (SEP)). SEP is then defined as educational provision which is additional to, or different from, that available to children of that age in ordinary schools in the area. In other words, a child will have special educational needs if, as a result of their learning difficulty, they need additional or different educational provision. However, a child is not taken to have special educational needs solely because of having English as a second language. LAs have responsibility under the SEN framework for children and young people at least up to the age of 16 but up to the age of 19 if they remain at school (Section 321 of Education Act 1996).

The different stages of identifying special educational needs

Many people working in education are familiar with the concept of statements of special educational needs ('statements'). However, most children with special educational needs will not in fact have statements. Instead, they will be placed on a school's register of SEN at two 'pre-statement' stages – School Action and School Action Plus (or, for those in early years – Early Years Action and Early Years Action Plus). These stages are explained in detail in the SEN Code of Practice. The first stage, School Action, applies to those children with special educational needs whose needs can be met simply by the school deploying their own, existing resources. Then, School Action Plus arises for those children with SEN whose needs also require some outside help; perhaps from the LA's educational psychology service. For children registered with a school at School Action or School Action Plus, educational provision to meet their special educational needs is left largely to the discretion of the school, so that the detailed legal requirements of statements (described below), do not generally apply.

However, for those children with more severe or complex difficulties who may require ongoing, significant additional support, a statement, made and maintained by their LA is required. This is for children needing, for example, a specific amount of dedicated teaching assistant time, a specific amount of dedicated specialist teacher time, specific therapeutic provision (for example from a speech and language therapist, occupational therapist or physiotherapist) which the LA (rather than the school) will have to arrange, or, indeed, a placement in a specialist unit or school. Statements are legally enforceable documents, prepared and maintained by LAs in accordance with the detailed legal framework of Part IV of the Education Act 1996 (as amended by the Special Educational Needs and Disability Act 2001).

Statutory assessments of special educational needs

If it is considered that a child may require a statement, a statutory assessment of the child's special educational needs will be commenced. A request for a statutory assessment can be made by a parent or school (Sections 329 and 329A of the Education Act 1996) or, indeed, through another agency (such as a health authority or children's department of a local authority) who refers a child to the attention of the LA. LAs may also decide to conduct a statutory assessment of their own volition.

In considering whether to conduct a statutory assessment, the LA will determine whether the child's special educational needs call for the LA to arrange any SEP required by the child. If the LA agrees to undertake an assessment, they will then seek reports and evidence from a number of people (as set out in Schedule 26 to the Education Act 1996 and in the Education (Special Educational Needs) (England) (Consolidation) Regulations 2001, SI2001/3455 and the Education (Special Educational Needs (Wales) Regulations 2002, SI2002/152 ('the SEN Regulations'), including the child's parent(s), the child him or herself (if possible), the school or early years provision that the child attends, one of the LA's educational psychologists, a medical doctor and other professionals as necessary (including, for example, a speech and language therapist, an occupational therapist, a physiotherapist, a specialist teacher of blind children, a specialist teacher of deaf children, etc.) However, in the case of a child under the age of 2 years, the nature of the statutory assessment is left largely to the LA's discretion, pursuant to section 331 of the Education Act 1996.

Once all of this evidence has been gathered, the LA will consider it and decide whether, in fact, a statement is required (i.e. whether the child's special educational needs do require the LA to arrange the SEP). If they decide that a statement is not in fact necessary (perhaps because they consider that any needs that the child may have can be met at School Action or School Action Plus) then the LA will not produce a statement but, instead, produce a document known as a note in lieu. A note in lieu will summarize the advice obtained through the statutory assessment but is not a statement and therefore does not come with the legal obligations required of statements (as set out below).

However, if the LA decides that the statutory assessment does show that the child's special educational needs require the LA to arrange any SEP, they will produce a draft statement which the parents will then have an opportunity to comment on. That draft will then be finalized.

Statements of special educational needs

The format of a statement prescribed by law (in section 324 of the Education Act 1996 and the SEN Regulations) with six sections:

Part 1. This contains basic information about the child and his/her family, including the name, date of birth, address, religion, gender, home language and telephone number of the child and the names and contact details of his/her parents. This part will also list the advice and evidence considered in drafting the statement.

Part 2. This part then goes on to detail all of the child's special educational needs. Once an LA has determined that a child has some special educational needs requiring SEP, then all of the needs, even where some may not require any SEP arranged by the LA (for example, because some can be met by the school without the need for extra help) should be set out in Part 2 of the statement. Sometimes, LAs draft Part 2 of a statement in the form of a general discussion about the child but sometimes, they set out the child's special educational needs under different headings (such as 'Communication', 'Cognition', 'Physical Needs' etc.).

Part 3. Then, this part is itself sub-divided into three sections: Objectives, Educational provision to meet needs and objectives, and Monitoring arrangements.

The second section, the Educational Provision section, should detail exactly what SEP is required to meet the SEN described in Part 2. For example, if it is determined that a child requires some extra teaching assistant support, this should be set out in terms of numbers of hours of support and, where necessary, level of expertise (see decisions of the courts in a number of cases, including *L v Clarke and Somerset CC* (1998) ELR 129 and *Bromley v SENT* (1999) ELR 260.). The requirement to provide detailed support is less strict when a child attends a special school but generally, LAs should quantify and specify provision wherever possible.

Part 4. Then, Part 4 should name the school or other placement that the child will attend (see below).

Parts 5 and 6. Finally, Parts 5 and 6 mirror Parts 2 and 3 except that they deal with non-educational needs and provision (rather than educational needs and provision in Parts 2 and 3).

In addition, the statement will also consist of all of the evidence which has been gathered as part of the statutory assessment, which will be included as appendices.

What is the difference between special educational needs and provision and non-educational needs and provision?

The legal framework recognizes a key legal difference between educational needs and provision and non-educational needs and provision. As stated, special educational needs and SEP should be set out in Parts 2 and 3 (respectively) of a statement whereas non-educational needs and non-educational provision should be set out in Parts 5 and 6 (respectively) of a statement. The importance of the distinction is that LAs must arrange the special educational provision in Part 3, regardless of the cost or difficulty in doing so (see decision in *R v LB Harrow* ex parte M (1997) ELR 62). However, they do not have to arrange any provision which is set out in Part 6 (although may do so if they wish).

Accordingly, there have been a number of cases which have sought to test the boundary between educational and non-educational provision (most notably, *Bromley v SENT* (1999) ELR 260 and *B v Isle of Wight* (1997) ELR 390). Broadly, anything directly to do with a school, including the provision of teaching and teaching assistance, will be considered educational provision. In addition, speech and language therapy is virtually always educational provision while physiotherapy and occupational therapy may be, depending on the circumstances. However, the need for nursing support is very unlikely to be educational provision (even though a child may require a nurse on certain occasions) and it is also unlikely that other provision – such as clothing, warmth, housing, etc. – will be educational provision. Again, the importance of this is that if it is educational provision, it should be set out, usually in detail, in Part 3 of a statement and the LA then has an obligation to arrange it. (Note that that does not mean that the LA must necessarily pay for it. If they can persuade another agency or body – such as the school or health authority – to provide it then they are discharging their duty but, ultimately, if no one else does, they must secure and, if necessary, pay for it.)

Choice of school

For a child without a statement, there are separate provisions which determine which school they attend (contained within the Schools Standards and Framework Act 1998, as amended by the Education Act 2006). Broadly, the law gives parents a right to 'express a preference' for a state school and for that preference to be acceded to unless it would prejudice the provision of efficient education or the efficient use of resources (which often means that the school is full), or it is a selective school and the child does not meet the admissions criteria. However, for a child with a statement, the law is more different.

First, if a parent of child with a statement wants a maintained (state) school, Schedule 27 to the Education Act 1996 provides that the LA must agree that the particular school is named in Part 4 of the statement unless the school is unsuitable having regards to the child's age, ability, aptitude and special educational needs; or attendance of the child at that school would be incompatible with the provision of efficient education for other children there or the efficient use of the LA's resources. If a maintained school is named in Part 4 of a statement, the school must admit the child (section 324(5)(b) of the Education Act 1996). Separately, a child undergoing a statutory assessment may only be placed in a special school in limited, prescribed circumstances, with everyone's agreement (Section 316A(2) of the Education Act 1996).

However, quite apart from that, there are separate provisions which apply if a parent wants a mainstream (ordinary, not special) school (sections 316 and 316A of the Education Act 1996). In effect, LAs must agree to name a mainstream school in Part 4 of the child's statement unless the placement at such a school would be incompatible with the provision of efficient education for other children, and also that there is nothing that the school or LA can reasonably do to overcome any difficulty. The relationship between these two separate provisions is complex (see the decisions in *H v SENDIST and Hounslow LBC* (2004) LGR 844 and *Slough BC v C and SENDIST* (2004) EWHC 1759 (Admin)).

Sometimes, parents seek an independent or non-maintained special school (i.e. not a state school). Here, LAs need only agree to name (and pay for) such a school in Part 4 of a statement if it is not incompatible 'with the provision of instruction and training and the avoidance of unreasonable public expenditure' (section 9 of the Education Act 2006). Generally, independent and non-maintained special schools are more expensive than maintained (state) schools so that, in effect, LAs will only agree such a placement if a local, state school is unsuitable.

Occasionally, parents seek residential schools. The SEN Code of Practice (paragraph 8: 74) sets out limited circumstances where such a placement should be agreed. These are where the child: has severe or multiple special educational needs that cannot be met in day provision; has severe or multiple special educational needs that require an 'extended day' curriculum; is looked after by the local authority and has complex, social and learning needs (where the placement is joint-funded with the social services authority); or has complex medical needs as well as learning needs that cannot be managed in local day provision (where the placement is joint-funded with the health authority).

Finally, very occasionally, parents will seek educational provision other than at a school. For example, some families of children who have autism seek funding through statements of special educational needs for home based ABA (applied behavioural analysis) or LOVAAS type programmes. Currently, the law only allows LAs to fund such provision if placement at a school is 'inappropriate', which means, in practice, not possible (section 319 of the Education Act 1996 and *T v SENDIST and Wiltshire CC* (2002) ELR 704).

Time limits

The SEN Regulations set out detailed time limits for statutory assessments and the preparation and maintenance of statements. Broadly, the total period between the commencement of a statutory assessment and the production of a final statement should take no more than 26 weeks, but that period is itself broken down into stages, so that LAs have 6 weeks to decide whether or not to conduct an assessment, 10 weeks to do the assessment, 2 weeks to produce a draft statement and 8 weeks to consult over the draft statement before producing a final statement. There are also certain exceptions whereby LAs may take longer.

Disputes over assessments and statements

Sometimes, parents will dispute decisions by LAs over provision for children with special educational needs. In the following cases, those disputes can be determined by bringing an appeal to the Special Educational Needs and Disability Tribunal ('SENDIST') or, in Wales, the Special Educational Needs Tribunal for Wales ('SENTW'):

1   Decisions of LAs to refuse to conduct a statutory assessment or reassessment.
2   Decisions of LAs to refuse to produce a statement following an assessment or reassessment (i.e., where a note in lieu is produced).
3   Over the contents of Parts 2, 3 and/or 4 of a statement.
4   Decisions of LAs to cease to maintain a statement.
5   Refusals of LAs to amend Part 4 of a statement to name a different maintained school.

There is a detailed procedure for appealing to a tribunal (contained in the Special Educational Needs Tribunal Regulations 2001, SI2001/600) and ultimately, a Tribunal will have a hearing and give a decision. If they allow the appeal, they will order the LA to take the relevant step, within certain time limits.

Sometimes, however, there are disputes which a Tribunal cannot deal with. For example, there may be disputes about:

1   The contents of Parts 1, 5 or 6 of a statement.
2   A failure of the LA to arrange the SEP set out in a statement.
3   The refusal of a maintained school named in a statement to admit the child.
4   The failure of the LA to have regard to its general obligations towards children with special educational needs.
5   The general failure of schools with regards to children with special educational needs.
6   The failure of an LA to comply with statutory time limits.

In that case, there are number of potential alternative 'remedies' available to parents. These include: complaint to the LA itself, complaint to the Local Government Ombudsman, complaint to the Secretary of State for Education and Skills and, occasionally, court proceedings.

Miscellaneous issues for children with special educational needs

Aside from this, LAs may, occasionally, determine to reassess a child who already has a statement. This might be because it is considered that the statement, and the evidence upon which it was made, is out of date.

In addition, in any event, LAs must conduct an annual review of a statement at least once a year (Section 328 of the Education Act 1996). The purpose of such a review is to consider how things are going and although an annual review may lead to an amendment to the statement, equally, it may not.

Finally, if families of children with statements of special educational needs move into the area of a different LA, that 'new' LA takes over the responsibility for the statement and, having reviewed it, may maintain it as it is or amend it.

The Disability Discrimination Act and children at school

Quite apart from the SEN framework described above, since September 2002, schools and LAs have had obligations towards disabled children not to discriminate against them (as set out in Chapter 1 of Part IV of the Disability Discrimination Act 1995, as amended by the Special Educational Needs and

Disability Act 2001). The legal framework is complex and the first thing to note is that the definition of 'disability' set out in the DDA is not the same as the definition of children with special educational needs (described above).

In particular, a child is disabled if he or she: has a physical or mental impairment which has a substantial and long term adverse affect on his/her ability to carry out normal day to day activities. In addition, a child is disabled if they have a symptomatic, progressive condition; a severe disfigurement; an history of disability; cancer, multiple sclerosis or HIV; or if they have a condition that is corrected or controlled by the use of medication, prostheses or other equipment, where there would be a substantial impact if they did not have that medication or equipment (see Part I of the DDA).

For such children, schools (including independent schools) and LAs must not discriminate against them: by treating them less favourably without justification and by failing to make a reasonable adjustment to overcome any substantial disadvantage that they may face. In particular, in a case called *Buniak v The Governing Body of the Jenny Hammond Primary School*, a Tribunal determined that a school had discriminated against a disabled pupil in not ensuring that the necessary teaching assistant support, which was set out in his statement of special educational needs, was provided for him. Also, in *Unoajumhi v Mill Hill County High School*, a Tribunal confirmed that a school's refusal to permit a disabled pupil attending a half-term skiing tip could constitute discrimination.

Complaints of discrimination can be brought to the same Tribunal as for SEN appeals (see p. 143)[9] but in the case of alleged discrimination concerning refusals to admit non-statemented children to a maintained (state) school and also concerning permanent exclusions from a maintained (state) school, those complaints are brought to Independent Appeal Panels.

The Disability Equality Duty

Separately, in December 2006 (and for some schools, April 2007 and December 2007), maintained (state) schools and LAs (and, indeed, other 'public authorities') have had an obligation to make and maintain a Disability Equality Scheme (part 5A of the DDA). The purpose of such schemes are to show how the school or LA will seek to reduce disadvantage of disabled children generally and the scheme must be maintained and revised periodically.

In making and maintaining a scheme, a public authority, including a school must consult with disabled people. This ground breaking requirement means that disabled people (with all kinds of impairments) must be involved in thinking about what public authorities, including schools, must do to ensure that they operate in a non-discriminatory, broader equalities-sensitive way. There are parallel obligations under the Race Equality Duty (Section 71(1) of the Race Relations Act 1976, as amended by the Race Relations (Amendment) Act 2000 and attendant regulations) and under the Gender Equality Obligations (Sections 76A and 76B Sex Discrimination Act 1975, as inserted by the Equality Act 2006).

Schools and other discrimination provisions

The Sex Discrimination Act 1975 and the Sex Discrimination (Gender Reassignment) Regulations 1999 also make it unlawful for a school to discriminate on grounds of gender or gender reassignment, in the terms on which it offers to admit a person to the school, by refusing or deliberately omitting to accept an application for admission to a school, and in the way it affords access to any benefits, facilities, services or by refusing or deliberately omitting to afford the person access to them or by excluding that person from the establishment or subjecting him/her to any other detriment.

In the meantime, the Race Relations Act 1976 and the Race Relations Amendment Act 2000 gives similar obligations to schools in respect of preventing race discrimination. It requires them also to promote equality of opportunity and good relations between persons of different racial groups.

There have, however, been very few cases under this legislation thus far.

Reflecting on values and practice

1   Consider your own work setting. Reflect on the extent the law requires disabled children to be included; how effectively does your workplace achieve this? How may children be discriminated against and how can staff ensure that this doesn't happen?

2   Reflect on your own role. How can you make sure that you meet legal obligations of including learners with special educational needs?

Suggested further reading

Mason, M. (2005) *Incurably Human*, Nottingham: Inclusive Solutions.
Clements, L., Ruebain, D. and Read, J. (2006) *Disabled Children and the Law*, London: Jessica Kingsley.

Chapter 14

Social justice, human rights and inclusive education

Len Barton

Introduction

The chapters in this book have covered many important issues and raised some serious conceptual, theoretical, empirical concerns and questions. In this chapter, I will briefly seek to encourage further reflection and interest in the assumptions and implications for our personal and professional lives, of an informed understanding of inclusive education.

Exclusion and the need for change

One of the key hallmarks of a democratic society is the encouragement that is given to the generation of questions. This emphasis is a reflection of a belief in the importance of an examination and re-examination of the assumptions and values underpinning policy, provision and practice in all the major institutions and services. The intention is to challenge exclusionary factors and to identify and celebrate those qualities and conditions that are empowering and socially bonding. A questioning, reflective approach is a necessary and integral factor of an inclusive attitude to life.

This approach to life generally and education in particular is both demanding and disturbing. Two key features of education need to be recognized. First, educational issues are *complex* and not amenable to quick, slick answers or responses. For example, the relationship between society, the economy and educational policy and practice is real and influential. However, understanding the relationship between these factors requires grappling, struggling with conceptual, economic, political factors and ideas. School and educational provision must not be viewed in a vacuum or insulated from wider socio-economic concerns and interests. The second issue is that educational issues are *contentious* and involve the struggles between different interest groups over meanings and interpretations. Thus, the question of the nature of the curriculum, forms of assessment, the position of support staff and the relationship between the teachers and other professionals and home and the school, are all examples of contentious issues. I want to propose therefore, that the question of inclusive education is both complex and contentious, and the changes it will require will be fundamental and difficult to achieve.

When discussing the role education plays in the struggle for change, Hargreaves (1982) maintained that teachers, and I would argue in this instance, teaching assistants, need to be concerned with the political functions of education and ask such questions as: 'What kind of society do we want?' How is education to help us realize that society?' (p. 92). The urgency and seriousness of such demands for change are based on an informed conviction that there is something fundamentally unacceptable about many aspects of current policy and practice in education. These barriers to inclusion involve deeply rooted patterns of inequality and disadvantage in terms of access, experience and outcomes of education that need to be challenged and changed. These inequalities are not a natural, inevitable or unchangeable fact of life. No single factor can effectively remove these inequalities and exclusionary barriers and education, although important, cannot achieve the changes required alone. Exclusion is a complex process, involving assaults on a person's identity and dignity. It restricts the possibility of an individual being able to exercise the privileges and responsibilities of citizenship. It is a gravely serious issue, not only for those who are excluded and discriminated against, whether this be for example, on class, race, gender or disability grounds, or a combination of them, but also for the society generally.

Teaching, teachers and assistant teachers

In the modern classroom, teaching and learning is not merely about working with pupils. It is also about establishing and maintaining constructive working relationships with other adults, including teaching assistants. Nor is this easily achieved and it does raise the question of what 'working with others' means and to what extent do such relationships involve conflict and counter-productive processes and outcomes. While it can be claimed that the role of teaching assistants has changed over time, research has demonstrated that there are important differences between schools over the nature of job descriptions and actual practices. Several reasons for these have been identified including: confused aims, no clear career structure, lack of planned training and poor channels of communication (Vincett *et al.* 2005).

Thus the position and role of teaching assistants raises some complex and contentious issues. For example, to what extent are teaching assistants concerned with specially categorized pupils in comparison to pupils generally? Mansaray (2006) argues, that where the TA concentrates their attention on 'less-able' children, there is a danger of reinforcing possible peer group negative labels (such as 'thick'). This has an impact on some children's perceptions of adult support as stigmatizing. In order to counteract this possibility, some teaching assistants are also used to support pupils generally and to take more responsibility for teaching tasks under the supervision of a teacher

(HMI 2002). However, this is not without some difficulties in terms of tensions over the low pay of teaching assistants in comparison to teachers, the lack of training for specific tasks and the overall danger of exploitation (Vincett *et al.* 2005).

Part of the task of engaging with such serious issues is to understand how decisions are made in classroom interactions between teaching assistants and teachers, over the distinctive and complementary nature of their roles. This involves developing clear job specifications, which will then be the subject of careful monitoring and evaluation. Making each feel valued members of staff, enabling them and teachers together to undertake staff development that will contribute to their relationship being constructively developed, are all urgent factors needing serious and continual attention.

The question of collegial relationships within schools is of crucial significance and involves teachers and other support workers learning the value of the challenges of talking to one another over issues of professional significance. Talking is important. The form of talking being advocated is increasingly focused, developmental, a means of clarifying issues, raising questions, sharing ideas, insights, concerns and recognizing points of difference. Difference from this approach is real but also based on respect for each other. This is a demanding process and it is not easily achieved, nor is there a blue-print of how to undertake this task. Talking with one another and not *at* each other, is thus crucially important. It must not be viewed as an optional extra or a task for a select few. It is an imperative for *all* of us in that it ultimately concerns the welfare of all people. It is a learning experience in which there is no room for arrogance in that we are *all* learners and given the seriousness of the issues, there is no room for complacency. In this process, the re-examination of the meaning and use of such language as 'ability', 'achievement', 'success', 'learning', 'assessment' and 'special needs' will be a serious task. It will demand time, commitment and a resilience that is not easily undermined. The issues and questions we have outlined so far become even more serious when set within the context of inclusive values, relationships and practices.

Inclusive education and human rights

The question of 'inclusive education' is both complex and contentious and is shaped by historical, cultural, global and contextual factors. In an important EPPI Centre Review (2002) the question of definition is discussed. While recognizing the limitations of their position, inclusion for the author of this review is about three key perspectives. First, it is about responding 'simultaneously to students who all differ from each other in important ways some of which pose particular challenges to the school'. Second, 'it is not just about maintaining the presence of students in school but also about maximizing their participation'. Finally, 'inclusion is a process which can be shaped by school-level action' (p. 7).

Significant ambiguities in the concept of inclusion have encouraged Dyson (1999) to maintain that it would be more appropriate to talk about different inclusions. He argues that these differences arise from alternative discourses at work in the field through which different theoretical definitions of inclusion are contested. A crucial reason for proposing such a position is that Dyson is concerned that particular conceptions may have an impact in terms of stifling debate and ossifying values and beliefs.

While I do recognize the importance of the above approaches and concerns, I would want to argue that inclusive education is not an end in itself but a means to an end. It is about contributing to the realization of an inclusive society with the demand for a rights approach as a central component of policy-making. This perspective raises some important issues with regard to the question of inclusive education. First, it encourages the issue of change to be foregrounded. Unlike integration, the change process is not about assimilation but transformation of those deep structural barriers to change including the social base of dominant definitions of 'success', 'failure', and 'ability' within education as well as schools (Whitty 2002; Gillborn and Youdell 2000). Nor should we underestimate the difficulties of the task. Second, inclusive education is a 'distinctly political, "in your face", activity' (Corbett and Slee 2000: 136) and it involves a political critique of social values, priorities and the structures and institutions which they support. This is both a disturbing and challenging activity, which is an essential feature of the struggle for change. Lastly, inclusive education is fundamentally about how we understand and engage with difference in constructive and valued ways. It is a public process of naming and celebrating differences and engaging with the identification of what it is we value about one another. To do justice to the difference between pupils, to utilize these differences and to approach such factors as a resource, an opportunity for learning and not a problem to be fixed or excluded, thus becomes a crucial dimension of an approach that is working towards inclusive education (Ainscow 1999).

When trying to understand what constitutes inclusive values, thinking and practice, it is necessary that the focus of attention should be directed at the nature of the varied barriers to inclusion, both within education and society generally. The interest in inclusion is not solely about the position and experience of particular categorized individuals. It is about the participation of all pupils. This approach involves a perennial struggle for change and we must not underestimate the extent of the changes that are required. It is about much more than attitudinal change. The critique involved and the efforts for change need to be informed by a human rights approach. Human rights as Armstrong and Barton (1999: 211) note, involves: 'a set of principles based on social justice, a statement by which the conditions and opportunities of human life can be evaluated'.

Education from a rights approach is not a privilege for a select few, nor a matter of charity. No child is viewed as ineducable. All children are entitled to education of a high quality. A human rights approach to education entails issues of access, fair treatment with regard to learning, and fair access to the positive outcomes of education (Unterhalter 2006). The question of rights is derived from the qualification of being human. However, recognizing the formal equality of citizenship rights does not necessarily lead to equity in terms of respect, opportunities and resources. Too often there is a gulf between laudable rhetoric and practice. A commitment to human rights in education demands the highest form of expectations with regard to the learning and well-being of all pupils.

Outstanding issues for reflection

One of the starkest exclusionary issues needing serious and urgent attention concerns the position and involvement of pupils in decision-making in schools. Pupils have extensive knowledge of change within schools, both in terms of the organization, teaching and curriculum, but they are never seriously consulted over new policy initiatives, their implementation, nor are their views sought with regard to the purposes of education. An inclusive approach to education will give priority to the voices of pupils and the possible and essential contributions they can make to the struggle for change. A former Secretary of State for Education David Blunkett, called pupils 'co-partners' in the pursuit of inclusive relations and practice (DFEE 1997). Pupils from this perspective need to be viewed as a rich resource that future developments in schools must engage with in serious and respectful ways. How far is this a significant feature of relationships and practices within your school? What does it mean to listen to the voices of pupils?

Another key feature of working towards inclusion is a recognition of the absolute necessity of developing good and effective legislation, which supports the removal of all forms of exclusion and discrimination within education and society generally. Both the specific nature of the legislation and the degree to which it is enforceable are of paramount significance. Understanding children's entitlements under law and our responsibilities to meet those requirements within our institutions is an urgent task, which needs to be part of a carefully supported, monitored and evaluated staff development policy and approach. The extent to which we have an informed knowledge and understanding of the latest legislation and its effective impact on our daily practice is thus an issue of perennial importance.

Conclusion

In this brief chapter I have highlighted some contentious issues concerning the question of inclusive education and the position and practice of the teaching assistant in schools. This is an extremely important topic involving particular values, relations, practices, conditions and desired outcomes.

Inclusive education is about the maximization and continual participation of all members of the school community, staff and pupils. It is a learning process in which developing mutual respect, identifying, understanding and overcoming all forms of exclusionary values, relationships and practices as well as the generation of positive views of difference, are all essential features of this engagement.

Reflections on values and practice

If we are to contribute to this process of change, then we need to continually ask ourselves critical questions about our own perspectives, experiences and work contexts. These could include, for example:

1   What do we understand by inclusive education?
2   How inclusive is our own practice and what do we think we need in order for it to become more inclusive?
3   How far do we think pupils can contribute to the development of a more inclusive culture within schools?
4   To what extent and in what ways, do we value our working relationships with teachers and how far do we feel valued by them?

Suggested further reading

Barton, L. and Armstrong, F. (eds) (2007) *Policy, Experience and Change: Cross-Cultural Reflections on Inclusive Education*, Dordrecht: Springer Books.
Armstrong, F. and Moore, M. (eds) (2004) *Action Research For Inclusive Education: Changing Places, Changing Practice, Changing Minds*, London: RoutledgeFalmer.
Crozier, G. (2000) *Parents and Schools: parents or protagonists*, Stoke-on-Trent: Trentham Books.

References

Ainscow, M. (1999) *Understanding the Development of Inclusive Education*, London: Falmer Press.
Armstrong, F. and Barton, L. (1999) ' "Is There Anyone There Concerned with Human Rights?" Cross-Cultural Connections, Disability and the Struggle for Change', in Armstrong, F. and Barton, L. (eds) *Disability, Human Rights and Education. Cross-cultural Perspectives*, Buckingham: Open University Press.
Barnes, C. (1991) *Disabled People in Britain and Discrimination*, London: Hurst & Co.
Corbett, J. and Slee, R. (2000) 'An International Conversation on Inclusive Education', in Armstrong, F., Armstrong, D. and Barton, L. (eds) *Inclusive Education. Policy, Contexts and Comparative Education*, London: David Fulton.
DFEE (1997) 'Excellence for all Children: Meeting Special Educational Needs'. *Government Green Paper*, London: DFEE (Foreword by David Blunkett).

Dyson, A. (1999) '"Inclusion and Inclusions": Theories and Discourses in Inclusive Education', in Daniels, H. and Garner, P. (eds) *Inclusive Education*, London: Kogan Page.

EPPI (2002) *A Systematic Review of the Effectiveness of School-Level Actions for Promotion, Participation by all Students*, London: Institute of Education, University of London.

Gillborn, D. and Youdell, D. (2000) *Rationing Education Policy, Practice, Reform and Equity*, Buckingham: Open University Press.

HMI (2002) *Teaching Assistants in Primary Schools: An Evaluation of the Quality and Impact of Their Work. A Report by HMI*, HMI, 434, London: Ofsted.

Hargreaves, D.H. (1982), *The Challenge for Comprehensive School. Culture. Curriculum and Community*, London: Routledge & Kegan Paul.

Mansaray, A. (2006) 'Liminality and In/Exclusion: Exploring the Work of Teaching Assistants', *Pedagogy, Culture and Society* 14(2): 171–87.

Unterhalter, E. (2006) *Gender, Schooling and Global Social Justice*, London: Routledge.

Vincett, K., Cremin, H. and Thomas, G. (2005) *Teachers and Assistants Working Together*, Maidenhead: Open University Press.

Whitty, C. (2002) *Making Sense of Education Policy*, London: Paul Chapman.

Index

Page references in *italics* indicate illustrations.

abuse 68–9; *see also* bullying
acceleration of gifted and talented 114
accessibility 16, 21, 93, 108
adapting work for disabled learners 70
Ainscow, M. 12, 15
Allan, J. 90
Alliance for Inclusive Education (AIE) 65–6, 68–9
allies 70, 91; *see also* friends and allies
Anderson, Vikki 4, 73–83; partnerships between teachers and teaching assistants 78–81; roles and responsibilities of teaching assistants 73–7; training in inclusive practice 81, 82
anti-bullying policy 134
Applied Behavioural Analysis (ABA) 148
appreciation for teaching assistants 13–14, 71, 77–8, 82, 85, 86, 154; *see also* recognition of teaching assistants' role
Armstrong, D. 96
Armstrong, Felicity 1–6, 7–18; meanings and interpretations of inclusive education 10–13; origins of inclusive education 8–10; research on inclusive education 13–16; social justice 156
assessments *see* statutory assessments of special educational needs; testing
attendance, school 133–4
autism 148

Ball, S. 87
Bartlett, Steve 4, 51–61; gender and achievement 55–9; gender relations in recent British history 53–4; gender stereotypes 53, 55, 59; meaning and creation of gender 51–3
Barton, Len 6, 10, 87, 152–8

behaviour *see* challenging behaviour
Better Schools for All (DfES) *115*, 115–16
black minority ethnic (BME) groups 4, 47, 121; *see also* ethnic diversity; ethnicity; race
Blunkett, David 156
body guards, teaching assistants employed as 124
Booth, Tony 7
boys 53, 54, 56–9, 98, 99, 121; *see also* gender
British Empire 43
British history, gender relations in recent 53–4
bullying 5, 124, 131–41; characteristics of bullies and victims 132–3; definitions of 131–2; effects of 133–4; ethos 135–6; how schools can bully children 136–8; traveller communities and 33, 34
Bullying Online 132, 133
Buniak v The Governing Body of the Jenny Hammond Primary School 150
Burton, Diana 4, 14, 51–61; gender and achievement 55–9; gender relations in recent British history 53–4; gender stereotypes 53, 55, 59; meaning and creation of gender 51–3

Cantle, T. 41
caregivers, communication with *see* role of teaching assistants in reaching parents and caregivers
challenging behaviour 5, 120–30; definitions and descriptions 121–2; personal view of 125–6; role of teaching assistants and 120–1, 123–5, 127, 128
change in education, need for 152–3, 155

choice of school 147–8
circle time 134
class 40, 46, 51, 54, 58, 59, 98
classroom assistants (CAs) 74, 123; *see also* inclusion assistants; teaching assistants (TAs)
Clifton, Mary 15
Commission for Racial Equality (CRE) 33
communication between teachers and teaching assistants 78–9, 154
communication skills: of disabled learners 21, 69–70, 79; of teaching staff 24
communication with families *see* role of teaching assistants in reaching parents and caregivers
communities, defined 7; *see also* traveller communities
community participation in education 9, 16, 116–17
complexity of inclusive education 152–3
comprehensive schools 54, 99
conflicts about 'voice' 22–5
consultation with parents and caregivers *see* role of teaching assistants in reaching parents and caregivers
contentious nature of inclusive education 152–3
Convention on the Rights of Persons with Disabilities, UN 62
Corbett, J. 155
Cremin, H. 123
Cullingford, C. 20
cultural values of traveller communities 28, 30–2
Cumbria 112, 117
curriculum: differentiated 113–14; gender and 55–6, 59; *see also* National Curriculum

decision-making in schools, involving pupils in 156
democracy 6, 152
democratic practices in inclusive schools 16, 17
Departmental Committee on Defective and Epileptic Children (DEEDC) 98
Department for Education and Skills (DfES) 35–6, 37, 41, 45, 73, 78; *Better Schools for All* 115, 115–16; differentiated curriculum 113–14; Removing Barriers to Achievement 96, 101
differences 155
differentiated curriculum 113–14

disability, defined 150
discrimination 149–50, 150–1, 153
Disability Discrimination Act (DDA) 1995 149–50
Disability Equality Duty 21, 105, 150–1
Disability Equality Scheme 150
disabled children and the law in England and Wales 142–51; choice of school 147–8; Disability Discrimination Act (DDA) 149–50; Disability Equality Duty 150–1; statements of special educational needs 143–6, 147, 148–9; *see also* legislation
disabled people: communication skills of 21, 69–70, 79; historical perspectives on 97–9; listening to 21–2, 70–1, 101, 103, 105, 150; medical and social models of disability 63, 90, 91; rights of 62; support for 64–7; *see also* inclusion assistants
distance learning support 30, 35
diversity, meanings of 42; *see also* ethnic diversity
Duncan, Neil 5, 131–41; characteristics of bullies and victims 132–3; definitions of bullying 131–2; effects of bullying 133–4; how schools can bully children 136–8; school ethos 135–6
Dyson, A. 155

economic change, gender and 58
Education Act 1944 98, 121
Education Act 1981 99, 121, 142–3
Education Act 1988 11, 99–100
Education Act 1996 143, 147
educational provision *see* special educational provision (SEP)
Education (Handicapped Children) Act 1970 99
e-learning 30, 35
English as an Additional Language (EAL) 46; *see also* languages spoken by pupils
equity 10, 12, 156
ethnic diversity 40–50; in Britain 43–4; minority ethnic attainment characteristics 45–6; pupils 44–5; staff 41, 47–8
ethnicity: black minority ethnic (BME) groups 4, 47, 121; gender and 58, 59; meanings of 42–3
ethos, school 135–6
Eugenics movement 97
Every Child Matters (ECM) 45, 49, 78–9, 112, 117

Excellence for All Children: Meeting Special Educational Needs 96, 100
exclusion, challenging 152–3

fairground families 29, 33; *see also* Traveller communities
fairness 12, 126, 138, 139
feedback from learners *see* listening to learners
feeling valued 67–8, 77–8, 82, 85, 86, 127–8, 154; *see also* appreciation for teaching assistants
femininities 53, 58
feminist researchers 55
Finney, Maggie 4, 73–83; partnerships between teachers and teaching assistants 78–81; roles and responsibilities of teaching assistants 73–7; training in inclusive practice 81, 82
Florian, L. 12
Framework for Action 8–10
friends and allies 66, 68–9, 70, 91, 124

GCSE 56, 57
gender 4, 46, 51–61; achievement and 55–9; bullying and 140; challenging behaviour and 121; laws regarding 54, 150–1; meaning and creation of 51–3; in recent British history 53–4; stereotypes 53, 55, 59; special schools and 98, 99
Genderwatch 56
General Teaching Council (GTC) 40, 41, 46
George, D. 111
Gerschel, L. 80
gifted and talented 5, 12, 108–19; case study 116–17; differentiated curriculum 113–14; identification 110–11; personalized learning *115*, 115–17; profile 111–12; underachievement and 112
girls 53, 54, 55–7, 58–9, 98, 99; *see also* gender
Girls into Science and Technology Project (GIST) 55–6
Goffman, E. 99
government policy and initiatives 2, 5, 73; disabled people and 65, 98; Every Child Matters 45, 49, 78–9, 112, 117; on gender 54, 56, 150–1; on gifted and talented students 12, 110; on immigration 44; listening to learners and 19, 21–2, 23; National Curriculum 11, 56, 99; Removing Barriers to Achievement 96, 101; special education

needs (SEN) 81, 100–1, 103; *see also* Department for Education and Skills (DfES); legislation
grammar schools 56
Green Paper 1997 96, 100
Groom, B. 123
Gwynn, J. 22
Gypsy families 30, 32, 33, 46; *see also* Traveller communities

Hammett, N. 14
Handicapped Pupils and School Health Regulations 98
Hargreaves, D.H. 153
high achieving pupils 45
Higher Education Statistics Agency (HESA) 47
Higher Level Teaching Assistant (HLTA) status 2
historical development of teaching assistants 4
history of special schools 96–9
Holmes, P. 31
home education 34
home visits 90
horizontal violence 137
House of Commons Education and Skills Select Committee 81
Howard, Gary 48
human rights *see* rights
Hutton, Nigel 63

immigrants 44
Inclusion: Does it matter where pupils are taught? (Ofsted) 103
inclusion assistants 66–71
inclusion of teaching assistants 84–5, 93
inclusion units 102, 120, 124
inclusive education: advocates for 103; background to 62–4; barriers to 124; characteristics of 16, 93; complex and contentious nature of 152–3; human rights and 154–6; meanings and interpretations of 3, 7, 10–13, 110, 154–5; origins of 8–10, 99–102; partnerships between special schools and mainstream schools 100–2; Pittlesden School 84–5, 90, 93, 94; role of inclusion assistants 66–71; role of Learning Support Assistants (LSAs) 14, 64–5; training teachers and teaching assistants in 81, 82
inclusive schools, characteristics of 16, 93
inclusive society 155

independent living movement 65
individual support 14–15, 80
integration, difference between inclusion and
    11
integration of pupils with special needs
    99–104
international children, listening to 15
Irish Traveller families 30, 32, 33, 46; *see
    also* Traveller communities

Japan, bullying in 133, 135
job descriptions for teaching assistants 77,
    153, 154; *see also* roles and responsibilities
    of teaching assistants

Kaplin, I. 20
Kikabhai, Navin 5, 120–30; definitions and
    descriptions of 'challenging behaviour'
    121–2; personal view of 'challenging
    behaviour' 125–6; role of teaching
    assistants and 'challenging behaviour'
    120–1, 123–5, 127, 128

labels 12, 53, 59, 80; bullying 132, 133,
    139; challenging behaviour 120, 121,
    123, 124, 125–6, 128, 129; disabled
    children 64; gifted and talented 108,
    109–10; parents 85; special educational
    needs 99
Lacey, P. 14
laddishness 57, 59
Landsman, Julie 48
languages spoken by pupils 32, 40, 46, 143
learner voice *see* listening to learners
learning, personalized 5, *115*, 115–17
learning difficulties 143
learning styles 113
Learning Support Assistants (LSAs) 14,
    64–5, 66, 68, 74; *see also* inclusion
    assistants; teaching assistants (TAs)
legislation 5, 6, 142–51, 156; 1944
    Education Act 98, 121; 1970 Education
    (Handicapped Children) Act 99; 1981
    Education Act 99, 121, 142–3; 1988
    Education Reform Act 11, 99–100; 1996
    Education Act 143, 147; affecting
    Traveller families 30, 33; Disability
    Discrimination Act (DDA) 1995 149–50;
    Disability Equality Duty 21, 105, 150–1;
    regarding disabled people 21–2, 65, 67,
    98; regarding gender 54, 150–1;
    regarding race and ethnicity 42, 150, 151;
    Special Educational Needs and Disability

Act (SENDA) 21–2, 100, 143; statements
    of special educational needs 143–6, 147,
    148–9
listening to learners 3, 4, 15, 16, 19–25,
    156; conflicts about 'voice' 22–5; disabled
    people 21–2, 70–1, 101, 103, 105, 150;
    learners with 'challenging behaviour'
    123–4, 126–7
literacy skills 31, 32, 74
local authorities (LAs) 2, 34, 142–50
Lovett, Herb 127
Loxley, A. 101

mainstream schools 23, 64, 73; challenging
    behaviour and 121, 124; law and 143,
    147; special schools and 98, 99, 100–2,
    103–4
maintained schools: ethnicity in 40, 41, 44,
    45; law and 147, 148, 149, 150
Majors, R. 128–9
Mansaray, A. 153
marginalization of teaching assistants' work
    13
Marks, Ken 4, 28–39; cultural values of
    Traveller communities 28, 30–2; mobile
    lifestyle of Traveller communities 29–30;
    prejudice against Traveller communities
    33–4; teaching assistants and Traveller
    communities 36–7; Traveller Education
    Services 29, 30, 34–6, 37
masculinities 53, 58
Mason, Lucy 66
Mason, Micheline 4, 62–72, 102, 103;
    background to inclusive education 62–4;
    inclusion assistants 66–71; independent
    living movement 65
medical model of disability 63
men 54; *see also* gender
middle class 59
Midlands study of teaching assistants 76, 77,
    78, 79, 80–1
minority ethnic, use of term 43; *see also* black
    minority ethnic (BME) groups; ethnic
    diversity; ethnicity; race
minority ethnic attainment characteristics
    45–6
minority ethnic staff 41, 47
Moore, Michele 4, 84–95; assumptions
    around the role of teaching assistants at
    Pittlesden School 85–7; enhancing the
    role of teaching assistants at Pittlesden
    School 88–92
Morrow, V. 20

Mosslands School 77
Moyles, J. 74

Naito, A. 135
National Curriculum 11, 56, 99
National Institutional Quality Standards
    (IQS) *115*, 115–16, 117
no-blame anti-bullying policy 134
non-educational needs and provision 146
non-exam kids 125–6
notes in lieu 145

Office for Standards in Education (Ofsted)
    28, 103, 115–16, 122
Oliver, Mike 102
Olweus, Dan 131
origins of inclusive education 8–10, 99–102

parents 9; of disabled children 62, 66;
    special educational needs and 148; in
    Traveller communities 31, 32, 34, 35, 36;
    see also role of teaching assistants in
    reaching parents and caregivers
Parents for Inclusion (Pi) 103
pay, teaching assistants' 74, 75, 77, 82, 154
personal assistants 65; *see also* inclusion
    assistants
personalized learning 5, *115*, 115–17
Phillips, Gary 47
Phillips, Trevor 41
Pittlesden School, research at 84–94;
    assumptions around role of teaching
    assistants 85–7; enhancing the role of
    teaching assistants 88–92
policy *see* government policy and initiatives;
    legislation
political nature of inclusive education 155
power 24, 131, 132, 136
prejudice 29, 33–4, 110
primary education 9, 31, 32, 54, 77
principles of The World Conference on
    Education for All 9
principles underpinning inclusive schools 16
professional development 81, 114–15, 121
professionals, views of teaching 22–3
Pupil Level Annual School Census (PLASC)
    44
Pupil Referral Units 102, 103, 120, 122
pupils' role in inclusive education 156

race 42, 121, 150, 151; black minority
    ethnic (BME) groups 4, 47, 121; *see also*
    ethnic diversity; racism

racism 33, 99
Race Relations Act 1976 150, 151
Race Relations (Amendment) Act 2000 150,
    151
raising standards 11–13, 21, 84–5, 100,
    128; *see also* school improvement
Read, J. 98
Reay, D. 53, 87
Rebecca, case study on 116–17
recognition of teaching assistants' role
    13–14, 71, 77, 78, 85, 89, 91; *see also*
    appreciation for teaching assistants
relationships within schools, collegial 154
relationships, teaching assistants' role in
    school 4–5, 14, 66, 67, 85, 124–5, 128;
    see also role of teaching assistants in
    reaching parents and caregivers; roles
    and responsibilities of teaching
    assistants
Removing Barriers to Achievement 96,
    101
research on inclusive education 13–16; *see
    also* Pittlesden School, research at
research on teaching assistants *see* Midlands
    study of teaching assistants; Pittlesden
    School, research at; surveys of teaching
    assistants
residential schools 147–8
resource assistants 77
Richards, Gill 1–6, 19–27, 96–107;
    conflicts about 'voice' 22–5; future for
    special schools 102–4; historical
    perspective on special schools 96–9;
    listening to learners' views 19–22;
    partnerships between special schools and
    mainstream schools 100–2
Richards, Raphael 4, 40–50; ethnic diversity
    in Britain 43–4; minority ethnic
    attainment characteristics 45–6; pupils'
    ethnicity 44–5; White staff 47–8
rights 8–10, 11, 67–71, 110, 129, 154–6;
    listening to learners and 105; special
    educational needs (SEN) and 99; to refuse
    involvement 24; UN Convention on the
    Rights of Persons with Disabilities 62
role of teaching assistants in reaching parents
    and caregivers 84–94; assumptions around
    85–7; enhancing 88–92
roles and responsibilities of teaching
    assistants 73–7, 85–7, 104, 105, 114,
    118; relationships 4–5, 14, 66, 67, 85,
    124–5, 153; supporting learners with
    'challenging behaviour' 120–1, 123–5,

127, 128; *see also* role of teaching
assistants in reaching parents and
caregivers
Rose, C. 22
Rose, R. 80, 123
Rouse, M. 12
Ruebain, David 6, 142–51; choice of school
and the law 147–8; Disability
Discrimination Act (DDA) 149–50;
Disability Equality Duty 150–1;
statements of special educational needs
143–6, 147, 148–9
rural schools 117

Salamanca Statement 9, 10, 100
Salmestone Primary School 77
Salmon, M. 20
School Action 144
School Action Plus 144
school attendance 133–4
school culture, gender and 58–9
school ethos 135–6
school improvement 11–12, 84–5, 87, 93,
94; *see also* raising standards
School Improvement Partners (SIPs) 115
Schools Census 44
Scottish Traveller families 30, 32, 33; *see also*
Traveller communities
secondary education 31, 32, 54, 77; bullying
in 132
segregated education 97, 98, 99, 103, 122,
124
self-esteem of teaching assistants 85
sex, difference between gender and 51–2;
see also gender
Sex Discrimination Act of 1975 54, 151
Sex Discrimination (Gender Reassignment)
Regulations 1999 151
Shaw, L. 75, 80
Slee, R. 155
Smith, P. 75, 76
Smith, P.K. 135
social change 58, 153, 155
social class *see* class
Social, Emotional Behavioural Difficulties
(SEBD) 123
socializing aim of schools 136
social justice 6, 10, 129, 156
social model of disability 63, 90, 91
Sorsby, Cath 15–16
Southgate, T. 102
special educational needs (SEN) 81, 99–101;
statements of 143–6, 147, 148–9; time

limits and 148; teaching assistants and
105; *see also* special schools
Special Educational Needs and Disability
Act (SENDA) 21–2, 100, 143
Special Educational Needs and Disability
Tribunal (SENDIST) 148–9
Special Educational Needs Tribunal for
Wales (SENTW) 148–9
special educational provision (SEP) 143,
144, 145
Special Education Needs (SEN) Code of
Practice 81, 143, 147–8
specialist support 120–1
special schools 5, 23, 64, 96–105, 142, 147;
challenging behaviour and 120; future for
102–4; historical perspective on 96–9;
partnerships between mainstream schools
and 100–2; percentages of children
attending 104; *see also* Pittlesden School
statements of special educational needs 80,
99, 121, 143–6, 147, 148–9
statutory assessments of special educational
needs 144–5, 148–9
Steele, Joanne 5, 108–19; differentiated
curriculum for gifted and talented
113–14; gifted and talented case study
116–17; identification of gifted and
talented 110–11; personalized learning
115, 115–17; profile of gifted and
talented 111–12
suicide 133
support: distance learning 30, 35; individual
14–15, 80; learning support assistants
(LSAs) 14, 64–5, 66, 68, 74; nature of 14;
specialist 34, 120–1, 144, 145; *see also*
inclusion assistants; teaching assistants
(TAs)
surveys of teaching assistants 74–6; *see also*
Midlands study of teaching assistants
Suschitzky, W. 74
Swain, J. 53, 96

talents 110; *see also* gifted and talented
talking among school staff, significance of
78–9, 154
teachers, consultation between parents and
87–8
teachers and teaching assistants: distinction
between roles of 74, 75, 154; partnerships
between 78–81, 86, 94, 123; training in
inclusive practice 81, 82
teaching assistants (TAs) 73–82; difference
between classroom assistants and 123;

legal obligations 142; partnerships
between teachers and 78–81, 86, 94;
training in inclusive practice 82; *see also*
inclusion assistants; role of teaching
assistants in reaching parents and
caregivers; roles and responsibilities of
teaching assistants
teaching staff, ethnic diversity of 47–8
testing 56–7
thinking and planning time 118
Thomas, G. 99, 101
training programmes, teacher and teacher
assistant 23, 67, 81, 82
Traveller communities 4, 28–39, 46;
cultural values 28, 30–2; mobile lifestyle
29–30; prejudice against 33–4; teaching
assistants and 36–7; Traveller Education
Services 29, 30, 34–6, 37

under-achievement 45–6, 55, 57–9, 112
UNESCO World Conference on Special
Needs Education 9–10
United Nations 8, 9, 62
Unoajumhi v Mill Hill County High School 150

values 1–2; democratic 6, 16, 17, 152;
equity 10, 12, 156; fairness 12, 126, 138,
139; inclusive 154, 155; social justice 6,
10, 129, 156; of Traveller communities
28, 30–2
valuing children with high-level support
needs 67–8, 105
valuing learners with 'challenging behaviour'
127–8
valuing teaching assistants 77–8, 82, 85, 86,
154; *see also* recognition of teaching
assistants' role
Vaughan, M. 99
victims of bullying 133
Visser, J. 122
vocational education 10, 32, 36

'voice', conflicts about 22–5
voices of learners, listening to *see* listening to
learners
voices of teaching assistants 24

Wales *see* disabled children and the law in
England and Wales
Walmsley, J. 98
Warnock, Baroness Mary 23, 104
Warnock Report 23, 99
West, bullying in the 135
White staff 47–8
Whittaker, Joe 5, 120–30; definitions and
descriptions of 'challenging behaviour'
121–2; personal view of 'challenging
behaviour' 125–6; role of teaching
assistants and 'challenging behaviour'
120–1, 123–5, 127, 128
women 54, 58; *see also* gender
Wood, Margaret 4, 28–39; cultural values of
Traveller communities 28, 30–2; mobile
lifestyle of Traveller communities 29–30;
prejudice against Traveller communities
33–4; teaching assistants and Traveller
communities 36–7; Traveller Education
Services 29, 30, 34–6, 37
workforce remodelling 77
working class 40, 46, 54, 58, 59, 98
World Conference on Special Needs
Education, UNESCO 9–10
World Declaration on Education for All,
The 8–9
Worrall, Martyn 5, 108–19; differentiated
curriculum for gifted and talented
113–14; gifted and talented case study
116–17; identification of gifted and
talented 110–11; personalized learning
115, 115–17; profile of gifted and
talented 111–12

Yoneyama, S. 135